Ethics

Fundamentals of Philosophy

Series editor: John Shand

This series presents an up-to-date set of engrossing, accurate, and lively introductions to all the core areas of philosophy. Each volume is written by an enthusiastic and knowledgeable teacher of the area in question. Care has been taken to produce works that while evenhanded are not mere bland expositions, and as such are original pieces of philosophy in their own right. The reader should not only be well informed by the series, but also experience the intellectual excitement of being engaged in philosophical debate itself. The volumes serve as an essential basis for the undergraduate courses to which they relate, as well as being accessible and absorbing for the general reader. Together they comprise an indispensable library of living philosophy.

Published:

Piers Benn
Ethics

Colin Lyas
Aesthetics

Alexander Miller
Philosophy of language

Forthcoming:

Alexander Bird
Philosophy of science

Stephen Burwood, Paul Gilbert, Kathleen Lennon
Philosophy of mind

Richard Francks
Modern philosophy

Dudley Knowles
Political philosophy

Harry Lesser
Ancient philosophy

Ethics

Piers Benn

McGill-Queen's University Press
Montreal & Kingston · London · Buffalo

© Piers Benn 1998

ISBN 0-7735-1700-6 (bound)
ISBN 0-7735-1701-4 (pbk)

Legal deposit first quarter 1998
Bibliothèque nationale du Québec

Published simultaneously in the European Union by UCL Press.
The name of University College London (UCL) is a registered
trade mark used by UCL Press with the consent of the owner.

Canadian Cataloguing in Publication Data
Benn, Piers, 1962–
Ethics

(Fundamentals of philosophy)
Includes bibliographical references and index.
ISBN 0-7735-1700-6 (bound)
ISBN 0-7735-1701-4 (pbk)

1. Ethics. I. Title. II. Series.

BJ1012.B45 1997   170   C97-900915-4

Typeset in Century Schoolbook and Futura.
Printed and bound by Arrowhead Books Ltd, Reading, UK.

To my father and mother, David and June Benn,
and my sister, Frances Benn

Contents

Preface

Both in the realm of academic philosophy and in that of public affairs, recent years have heralded considerable interest in ethics. Traditionally, there is a distinction between philosophical reflection on the nature of moral judgement (sometimes called *metaethics*) and the promulgation of moral views about such things as abortion or warfare. Only three decades ago, most philosophers considered that metaethics alone was of interest to them as philosophers. Although they might have held opinions about moral issues, this was only in their capacity as intelligent people rather than as professional philosophers. Nowadays, however, although the division between *metaethics* and *applied ethics* still remains, philosophy has widened its realm of concern to include many contemporary issues. Even though most philosophers do not claim that a training in philosophy in itself makes them good moral judges, they still hope that the intellectual discipline philosophy gives them enables them to argue well and to think clearly. More importantly, many contemporary moral debates – in the area of medical ethics for example – lead almost at once to issues that are properly philosophical, such as rights, the good, autonomy, paternalism and utility. Thus, in ethical debate about the rationing of health care, we soon notice that people make different assumptions about people's rights to treatment, or about the value of promoting the "overall good". The analysis and criticism of these assumptions is quite properly the job of moral philosophy, even if moral philosophers are not moral experts.

Philosophers *theorize* about such things as rights and utility. Although such activity rarely leads to total consensus, at least we can gain a clearer idea of what the real issues are if we look at them philosophically.

This work is an introduction to ethics, rather than to "practical ethics". It is predominantly concerned with central philosophical issues, such as relativism, objectivity and theories of right action. Nevertheless, I have tried to relate the themes of this book to some practical concerns. Some of these matters are found in the familiar areas of public policy investigated by applied philosophers. But I have deliberately used other sorts of example as well. It may be that I produce examples of moral choices that seem to be either trivial or not philosophical at all. But I believe that reading works of applied ethics can leave you with a misleading picture of what most people's moral choices are really like. Of course, professionals such as doctors and soldiers do have to make hard choices of the sort discussed in standard textbooks – for instance, about killing and letting die. But most of the time, our moral challenges are less dramatic even if no less important. They concern such things as gossip, friendship, fantasy, work, sexual relations, loyalty, self-realization, honesty, tolerance and self-sacrifice. In line with this, the sort of approach to ethics for which I offer a suitably qualified defence may be called *virtue theory*, which places importance on the question of the sort of people we should be, and not just on what we should do. For the virtues and vices find expression in the most ordinary choices of everyday life.

However, I am suspicious of the idea that any one theory, such as utilitarianism or Kantianism, provides the whole truth about morality, to the complete exclusion of other theories. For that reason, I have tried to bring out what is both distinctive and valuable in a range of approaches. In particular, I find good things to say both about the Kantian approach to practical reasoning – which insists on the existence of objective reasons for action – and the Aristotelian approach, which says that we have objective reason to cultivate certain motives and desires. These two theories are often set in opposition, but there is much to be said for both. Moreover, they both offer fruitful insights, in their different ways, to the perennial puzzle of how moral requirements can be *objective*.

Throughout the book I try to alert readers, *en passant*, to certain questions raised and lines of enquiry opened, and I try to anticipate some of the objections to particular claims that they are likely to think of. I also try to be suggestive rather than dogmatic, though for reasons of clarity it is often necessary to avoid a clutter of qualifying clauses when making a suggestion. But the philosophical interest of the problems discussed is as much in the enquiry as in the conclusion, and some issues, especially that of the objectivity of morality, are so hard to understand, let alone solve, that no solution so far suggested is entirely believable.

Nevertheless, there can be progress in moral philosophy, particularly when it comes to the exposure of falsehood and confusion. Such confusion is especially to be found in discussions of moral relativism, and I expound and criticize some of the more common relativistic arguments that occur to people (Chapter 1). I suggest that the most of these arguments do not support moral relativism, but rather support tolerance or open-mindedness. A widely shared misconception is that in order to be tolerant, and able to learn from others whose moral views and customs are very different from your own, you must believe that all moral opinions are equally true or valid. It is in criticizing ideas like this that philosophical argument is well employed. In my final chapter, on reasoning about ethics, I try to delineate the ways in which moral thinking might be a rational activity. I suggest there that while it is certainly not necessary to be clever or intellectual to be capable of sound moral judgement, nevertheless moral decency and common sense is a broadly rational accomplishment – and bad moral convictions are often a result of lazy and muddled thought.

As to my own tendencies to lazy and muddled thought, I am grateful to various people for helping clear this up as I prepared drafts of this book. Specifically, I wish to express my gratitude to my colleagues Matthew Kieran and Mark Nelson for their useful and painstaking comments on individual chapters. I also wish to thank three anonymous readers for UCL Press Ltd., who offered perceptive and helpful comments on my penultimate draft, and alerted me to various mistakes and confusions. Most of all I wish to thank the Fundamentals of Philosophy series editor, John

Shand, who commented promptly, extensively and most helpfully
on several chapters, and offered me great encouragement throughout.

October 1996

Chapter 1

Authority and relativism

Educators, it is frequently said, should firmly teach our children the "difference between right and wrong". Those of a suspicious turn of mind will ask exactly whose conceptions of right and wrong are to be planted in the minds of the young, suspecting that this piece of apparent common sense is really a slogan to justify indoctrinating the young with conservative or "traditional" values. Others, with a dryly philosophical bent, will be prompted to wonder what the "difference between right and wrong" really is, in any case. Yet more critics will want to know whether the slogan covertly assumes that there is only one set of true moral convictions, rather than many. If so, they will complain, education risks leaving the young with a false conception of morality – for in fact, *moral relativism* is true: there are no moral principles which are valid for everyone. Different cultures have different practices and moral priorities, and those which prevail in any one culture are right for that culture. Other critics of our seemingly innocent slogan will raise yet another worry. Perhaps, they will admit, there are moral principles which are valid for everyone, but how can we possibly know what they are? Would not the attempt to educate people morally be the ultimate *hubris*, arrogantly attributing moral expertise to people who are really as confused and fallible as the rest of us? Finally, certain cynics among us will breezily adopt a different line. Armed with various political works – or some commentary on them – they will declare that morality is nothing but a tool for advancing the interests of some dominant group (men, the ruling classes, the former colonial powers) and should therefore be regarded with profound suspicion.

The problem of whether morality can be taught is not a new one. Plato grappled with it in his dialogues *Meno* and *Protagoras*, and faced the difficulty of saying what virtue is, let alone whether it is possible to teach it. Yet it may well seem surprising that so many difficulties can be raised. Do not most of us hold some set of moral principles, even if not very reflectively? Is it not common to engage in moral debate, with the hope of getting closer to the truth? Furthermore, most people do not see moral awareness as an optional extra, a minor accomplishment alongside others. It is commonly believed that it is far more important to be good than to be clever or knowledgeable. If that is so, then ought not some kind of moral education be regarded as the most fundamental requirement for leading the good life?

Many of us would agree with this, when it is put in this way. Of course, it is essential to lead a morally decent life; to observe basic requirements not to harm the interests of others without good reason, to refrain from major acts of dishonesty. But we might still be disturbed by the suggestion that some individuals, traditions or institutions, are moral authorities. We might think that individuals should be left to make up their own minds about what is right and wrong, that they should not be indoctrinated and should certainly not be coerced. We might insist that nobody is entitled to tell others how to behave – or at least, not beyond reminding them of certain requirements that they regard as obvious anyway. The reason we would give for all this is that no one is a special authority on morality. Perhaps all of us have some ability to determine moral truths, if there are any. But to say that special sorts of people have a particular skill in this, and should be listened to by the rest of us, is to go far beyond this basic claim.

These reservations about moral authority are common ones, and they may contain important truths when spelled out clearly. But we must first confront some worrying questions, which are generated if we reject the notion of moral authority and expertise.

First of all, why should there be more doubt about moral authority than about authority in other spheres? We tend to accept the conclusions of recognized experts in the natural sciences and in areas supposed to be "factual". We also accept the practical authority of instructors in various skills, such as driving. In thinking of them as authorities we do not, of course, have to regard them as infallible – that is, literally incapable of error. It is enough that they be reliable. We know that physicists have fundamental disagreements among themselves and that in consequence some of them are mistaken on important issues. But it would be wild to infer from this that anybody's views on quarks, quasars or the nature of gravity are as worth listening to as anybody else's. An expert may be wrong on important matters within the field of his or her expertise, but he or she may still be a more reliable judge than laymen. Why, then, should ethics be any different? True: nobody's opinion about moral matters is infallible. But this does not show that some people's opinions are not more worthy of attention than those of others.

As our opening paragraph suggested, there are a variety of reasons why the idea of moral authority has been rejected. Some such reasons, as we shall see, invoke highly disputable theories about the nature of moral truth and moral knowledge. Some of these theories will be subjects of extended discussion later on. For example, a highly influential doctrine – *subjectivism* – maintains that moral judgements are, in some suitably refined sense, judgements of personal taste. As such, there is no arguing about them; what appeals to me may not appeal to you, and that is more or less the end of the matter. Judgements of taste are subjective: if, for example, I like the colour blue and you dislike it, it would be senseless to argue about whose taste more closely reflects the "objective degree of pleasantness" of blue, for the only facts are that blue is pleasant for me but not for you. Another, more radical theory which was once popular among philosophers,[1] maintains that there are no experts on morality – at least, in the sense of possessing superior moral knowledge – because there is literally speaking nothing to know about right and wrong conduct. Utterances like "Cheating in exams is wrong" do not strictly *state* anything about the activity of cheating, since there is no such property as "wrongness" and therefore no true statements ascribing such a property. Such utterances *express attitudes* rather than state facts. In this sense they are rather like polite expletives. The attitudes in question cannot be spelt out as moral propositions, because moral judgements are not genuine propositions.

We cannot pretend that these theories are not important. But there is equally no reason to assume that we must refute them before we can allow ourselves to construct an alternative. The burden of justification does not rest only with the defender of authority in morals. Perhaps what we should now do is argue for the *possibility* of moral authority; that is, provide an intelligible account of how there could be such authority and how it might be gained.

Most people, when they make moral judgements, probably see themselves as stating truths which can, however crudely, be based upon reasons. Moreover, when they make judgements about matters close to their heart, it is almost impossible to imagine that they regard what they say as "just an opinion" – and regard the opinions of others as just as valid, even though they are opposed to their own. It is true that there are some issues that we make judgements about, but without much personal feeling, perhaps because they do not affect our own lives. In such cases, we do sometimes *say* (whatever we may actually mean) that we are not claiming absolute truth for our own view. Moreover, in other cases we may be able to recognize that there are powerful moral reasons both for and against a certain course of action, with no ultimate arbitrating principle able to decide whether we should take such a course or not. Decisions about which of two needy people to assist, when it is impossible to help both, may be of this kind. There may be a moral reason for helping one of the two people, because she is my aunt, or the other, because he helped me in the past. Cases like this, however, are not typical, and it may take some philosophical sophistication to recognize their true moral structure. Most of the time when we entertain moral opinions, we do suppose that we have probably got the right answer to the relevant moral questions, and correspondingly we think that those who do not share our view are mistaken.

Another feature of moral judgement is also important here. Our convictions are typically based upon reasons, which we often hope will seem persuasive to others. "Because it causes suffering", "Because it is in breach of an agreement" or "Because you wouldn't like it if others did that to you" are typical grounds people offer to justify their moral commitments. This is not to say that we are always conscious of our reasons or that we always reason particularly well. But the fact that reasons are generally offered, at least when we are pressed, suggests an interesting difference between moral judgements and pure judgements of taste. It seems absurd to call upon me to justify my preference for the colour blue over green, or to argue that someone who prefers green is mistaken. But it appears unintelligible to have a moral conviction, whilst thinking that no reason whatsoever can be offered to back it up.

Nothing said so far entails that there *are* objective moral truths or binding principles, or that anyone has justified beliefs about such things. Perhaps, for all we have shown, we are all moral incompetents, unable to draw any sound moral conclusions. Maybe we are all pursuing a chimera when we attempt to determine moral issues. On the other hand, our practice of moral reflection must be based on the assumption that there is some point in it. Given the fundamental place of morality in our everyday deliberations, we need a weighty reason if we are to judge that we have been engaged with a fantasy all along. For the time being I shall assume that such a weighty reason has not been found, and ask what the implications of our normal practice are for the question of moral authority.

The process of deliberation, of weighing up reasons, involves a kind of competence if it is to achieve its aim. Non-human animals do not engage in this – at least in the relevant sense – because they cannot; they lack the necessary concepts. But if most humans do possess some competence in moral reasoning, does it follow that they all possess it equally? And if some are markedly more competent at moral reasoning than others, is there any objection to regarding them as moral authorities?

The idea of authority

We need to say something of a more general nature about authority, at this point. The term is used in at least two distinct, though related, senses. First, there is authority of a purely theoretical kind. If we want to know something about the Corn Laws in nineteenth century Britain, we are likely to consult a historian whom we think of as an authority in the field. Doubtless he or she will not have the last word – there may be other authorities with a different perspective on the matter. But at least we are more likely to find out reliable information by consulting an authority in the area, than by asking anyone else. In this sense, then, an authority is an expert, someone who is usually a reliable source of information. But there is a different meaning of the word, brought out well in the distinction between "being *an* authority" and "being *in* authority". The historian is an authority, but an army drill sergeant is in authority (however nonsensical the procedures that placed him in this position). To be in authority entails having the right to obedience, at least in certain specific circumstances. It is different from power, which is simply the ability to enforce your wishes regardless of your right to do so. At the same time, the position of being in authority does not necessarily bring with it wisdom, justice or any particular expertise. A foolish person may be in authority over others, through being placed in that position by some agreed procedure, for instance, by being put there ("authorized") by somebody already in authority. Whether the authority he claims is genuine usually depends more on the legitimacy of the procedures which put him in this role than on his own personal qualities.

One who is in authority, then, has a legitimate claim to the obedience of others in some particular context. It is perhaps this idea of having a claim to others' compliance that explains the revulsion some people feel to the idea of moral authority. In fact, though, it is better to construe the idea of moral authority in the first way mentioned rather than the second. To speak of moral authorities is really to speak of individuals whose moral guidance may reliably be sought. This does not mean your compliance is a duty owed to them. To see this point, it is useful to distinguish two ways in which the guidance of authority may be said to oblige you to act in a particular way.

When people demand reasons why they should act in some particular way, they may be met with the impatient riposte "Because x says so". But this conceals an important contrast between two ways in which the utterance of x is relevant to what should be done. In one, simple way, the obligation to perform some action is *created* by the utterance of the supposed authority. The reason for acting is just the fact that x has told you to do so; if he had not, that reason would not exist. But there is another, more subtle and acceptable way in which listening to an authority makes one aware of an obligation. Perhaps there is, quite independently of the fact that x issues such guidance, a reason why this course of action should be followed. Such a reason would exist whether or not x told you to act in that way. At the same time, perhaps you would not be aware of such a reason unless x had told you about it. To speak of x being an authority, in this case, is only to say that he is a reliable guide as to what you are morally obliged to do. It is not the fact that he urges the action that makes it obligatory; on the contrary, he urges it because it is already obligatory.

The authority in question, then, is *an* authority rather than someone *in* authority. This is not to deny that those who seek his guidance are morally obliged to do as he says. The point is that compliance is not a duty they owe *to him*. He has only pointed out an obligation which existed anyway. But we are still left with our earlier question, even after these distinctions have been made, namely: how can there be any authorities in morals? What kind of expertise is moral expertise?

Hypothetical and categorical reasons for action

The question would be easier to answer if we believed that moral reasons for action were similar to reasons of prudence, or to any reasons which take the form: *if* you want X, *then* do Y in order to get it. Suppose there is something that everyone desires, and which can be acquired only by leading a morally good life. In that case, everyone has a straightforward reason for leading such a life. The role of a moral expert would be that of telling us exactly what we need to do in order to accomplish that desire. Moral knowledge, on this view, is a kind of instrumental knowledge, an ability to judge how to achieve what we desire. Of course, anyone who does not desire the end in question has no reason to follow the advice of the expert. It is only on the assumption that we do want the end in question, that we have any reason to follow the authority.

There is, indeed, a view of moral obligation which says precisely this. According to this doctrine, moral requirements are *hypothetical imperatives*. That is to say, they consist in imperatives which are valid for you *on the assumption* that there are things that you want, or are aiming at, which you can attain only if you obey these imperatives. A very crude version of this theory – which is often parodied although it is not clear how many people really believe it – says that unless you obey moral requirements, you will be punished by God. Those who offer this as a reason for living a morally worthy life, assume that no one wants to suffer divine retribution. If you do not want to court punishment, and if you can be made to believe that you will be punished unless you comply with certain requirements, then you have a straightforward reason for living according to those requirements.

There are considerably more refined versions of the theory, and here is not the place to discuss all the complex details. But it shows us one way of making sense of the concept of moral authority. An authority (and this need not be a person; it may be a text, a tradition or an institution) is a reliable guide to how you should act if you want to achieve your most important aims, needs or desires.

Unfortunately, the above theory of moral obligation is highly controversial. By no means all philosophers accept that moral requirements are hypothetical imperatives. Immanuel Kant,[2] for instance, insists that on the contrary, moral obligations are not hypothetical but *categorical*. They are absolutely and inescapably binding upon all rational beings, regardless of what desires they happen to have. It is for this reason that Kant sternly rejected all moral arguments that relied upon inducements and threats, including the threat of divine punishment. Genuine moral motivation is corrupted by considerations like that. The true source of moral obligation is *reason*, not *desire*. Reason alone can determine my duty, and it is open to all rational beings to submit to what pure practical reason demands. If the ability to act morally depended upon having certain inclinations or desires, then not everyone would be equally able to act according to moral considerations. For we are not responsible for our inclinations – at least not directly. It may be beyond our control whether we instinctively feel sympathy for our fellow humans. Yet it is possible to act benevolently towards them, even if we feel little inner sympathy. Lacking such natural warmth is no excuse for not acting with their interests at heart.

If Kant is right to maintain that the demands of morality are categorical, is there any place for authority in morality? In one sense there isn't. Indeed, Kant's doctrine amounts to the claim that reason itself is the only authority. The mere fact that someone – even God – commands a certain deed, can never be the source of the obligation to perform it. God may be morally perfect, and it may always be wrong to disobey him. Still, an action is not right *because* God commands it; it is right because reason requires it. God's moral perfection comes from his being perfectly rational and unable to be swayed by errant inclinations. But if he didn't exist, the moral law would exist all the same.

Authority, autonomy and reason

But it seems clear that Kant need only reject one particular way of construing moral authority – the way already discussed above, which relies upon an over-simple interpretation of "Because I say so!", offered as a reason why you should obey. Could his theory, however, accept the other way? Again, in one sense it could not accept that either, since morality has nothing to do with instrumental (means–end) reasoning. But suppose that rather than tell us how to achieve our aims, a supposed expert were able to determine, through rational reflection, what reason requires of us. Could it not be that, through his evident competence to do this, he gained a justified reputation as an authority on moral requirement?

One immediate objection to this would say that obedience to such an authority would be blind. How can we know that something is right, unless we can see it for ourselves? And even if the person (or traditions or institutions) we followed were indeed authoritative, how can we gain any moral credit for following them, unless we could see for ourselves the true reasons for behaving as morality demands? For a Kantian, it is of the first importance that our actions should be autonomous – that they should issue from our own rational deliberations and that our reasons for them should be truly ours.

However, this objection can be met, while conceding the strength of its basic insight. For we may distinguish between appeals to authority, and appeals to *mere* authority. An appeal to mere authority is of the form already mentioned and dismissed: roughly, it takes the fact that X commands us to act in a certain way, as sufficient in itself to make that course obligatory. But there are informed, as well as blind, appeals to authority. To make an informed appeal to authority, one needs some reason for taking the person or institution in question as an authority in the first place. Clearly, one's choice of authority cannot depend upon the authority in question, for that would be viciously circular. (Compare with the evangelist who argues that Scripture is the Word of God, on the ground that it says so in Scripture. Of course, *if* Scripture is the Word of God, then what it says about itself is also divinely inspired. But one has to establish independently that it is what it claims to be). The grounds upon which one chooses whom to take as authoritative are various. But in the moral case, it may be that one has been impressed with a person's judgement in the past and has come to see the soundness of his or her principles after due reflection. Even if, as Kant maintains, moral principles are derived purely from reason, there may be good grounds for trusting that a particular person's moral reasoning powers are sound. There could thus be good grounds for trusting them, in conditions in which it is hard to work things out for oneself.

This reminds us once again that the fact that we actually engage in moral deliberations suggests that we regard ourselves as competent to do so. As we noted, this does not establish that we really are. But if we are, we must take seriously that such competence may not be distributed evenly among us. It is possible that not everyone's judgements of right and wrong are equally valid. As in other areas, such as science, it may be justifiable to seek an authority in our ethical lives.

The challenge of relativism

It is worth reminding ourselves of the kind of objection to authority in morals that we have been putting into question. It is usually expressed in any of the following statements: that everyone is entitled to his own point of view; that all moral convictions are only opinions; that what is right for me may be wrong for you; that no one has a right to lecture others on moral matters. As we shall see, each of these protests makes a distinct point that needs separate investigation. But although they are different, it is tempting to run them all together, since they all seem, broadly speaking, to express hostility to the idea of moral authority.

One influential doctrine, to which such protesters are likely to appeal, is moral relativism. Strictly speaking, there is more than one way of understanding this claim and the doctrine comes in varying degrees of refinement. It was articulated by the Greek sophist Protagoras, enjoyed a revival following the anthropological discoveries of the late nineteenth century and remains popular to this day. Its guiding thought is that *there is more than just one true morality*. Different systems of ethics, which appear to be in conflict, can all claim to be true. There is no one system of morality – say Christian or Islamic – which is binding at all times and in all places. Different cultures, at different times and places, have different ways of life and moral practices. It is possible that all such practices are correct. We see this once we realise that the very concept of moral truth (to use the word once again) is relative. A moral system is not true absolutely, but *true for* a particular culture, or a particular individual.[3]

Is moral relativism true? To answer this question, we had better be clear what sort of truths are meant to be relative, and what sort are not. For many people inclined towards moral relativism end up saying that *all* truth is relative – not just moral truth. According to them, there is no such thing as a detached, objective perspective on truth: all judgement (or "discourse") is made from within a particular standpoint, which is sometimes held to be "ideologically conditioned" – perhaps reflecting hidden power relations in society.[4] Here, it is enough to note that if there are *no* statements which are absolutely (i.e. non-relatively) true, we are faced with an embarrassing question about the status of the claim that moral relativism is true. Is that statement true absolutely, or only relatively? It cannot be absolutely true without contradicting the doctrine that all truth is relative. So it can only be relatively true. But if it is only relatively true, then someone who denies it is not uttering an absolute falsehood when he denies it. Perhaps, on this account, moral relativism is only true for late twentieth century, western secular liberals. In which case, it need not be true for anyone outside that particular culture – from which it follows that those outside it, for example, Muslims of the Indian sub-continent, need not feel troubled by its challenge.

However, it may be that *moral* relativism is true, even if some *non-moral* truths are absolute. There is no obvious contradiction in this. It may be that truth *per se* is not relative, but that morality has special features which make moral claims capable only of relative truth. Thus, there is nothing paradoxical about saying that moral relativism is absolutely true, and that anyone who denies it is simply wrong. For the statement that moral relativism is true, is not itself a moral claim. It is, rather, *a claim about morality*.

This is a very important distinction. Unfortunately, it is not made as often as it needs to be. Furthermore, the fact that moral relativism is really a claim about morality, rather than a moral claim, helps show up a certain popular misconception. In popular debate and in newspaper columns, the *moral relativist* is usually portrayed as having liberal or permissive opinions about moral issues (e.g. about sex), while the *moral absolutist* is usually represented as having conservative and strict moral opinions. People who want to hammer home the wickedness of adulterous politicians and bishops often do so by invoking the language of absolutes, while people who want to play down the importance of some virtue or principle frequently do so by using the language of relativism. This suggests that there is a strong psychological connection between holding moral convictions with fervour and confidence, and believing that they are guided by a realm of objective moral facts.

But the connection is, in fact, only psychological, not logical. Let us call ordinary moral opinions (e.g. that lying is wrong) *normative judgements*, and contrast them with judgements *about* moral judgements, which we shall refer to as *metaethical judgements*.

Let us also assume that moral relativism is a metaethical doctrine. That is, it does not, in itself, make any moral judgement about lying, adultery and so on – it just tells us what kind of judgement is made when we make judgements about lying and adultery. The immediate question to ask is: does moral relativism even make sense?

Does relativism make any sense?

Return to the idea that moral judgements are really judgements of personal taste, like one's preferences for certain colours. We saw that it makes perfect sense to say that the colour blue is pleasant for me, but not for you. It is nonsense to talk of how pleasant it "really" is. Now this analogy with colour can be extended still further, in a way that may be helpful to moral relativism.

Consider a familiar philosophical conundrum, which many of us entertain when we first start thinking philosophically. Some people are said to be colour blind, and this can be established by various tests. In one well known test, you are presented with a pattern of coloured dots within which you are asked to discern a number. The coloured dots that make up the number stand out from the other dots, at least for those with normal colour vision. For those who are colour blind, however, the "correct" number is indiscernible. Instead, colour blind people either see nothing at all, or they see a different number. This test detects our ability to make certain discriminations; it thus provides an objective measure of how normal our colour vision is.[5] However, it may be that normality here is only a matter of making the discriminations made by the majority. If the dot test revealed that, say, red–green blindness was rapidly increasing and that it would soon affect a substantial proportion of the population, we would be less willing to talk of those people as having abnormal colour vision. Instead, we would talk of their seeing things differently, but no less correctly than the others. If one half of the population thought that grass was the same colour as blood, and the other half thought it was the same colour as a clear sky, then perhaps we would conclude that people just saw things differently, and that there was no underlying "correct" way to see them.

Contrast this with a different scenario. Suppose that due to a brain defect, a large number of people started making unusual judgements about the shape and size of the objects around them. We would hardly need a sophisticated test to detect their condition. They would crash about, take wrong directions and become a danger to themselves and others. It would be absurd to say that apples were larger than grains of salt for some people, but not for others. In short, we would judge that their perception was just wrong.

An important question concerns whether moral judgements are more like judgements about the shape and size of objects, or judgements about their colour. One way of making moral relativism appealing is by pursuing an analogy between moral judgements and judgements of colour. If the picture painted above is conceivable, then we can make sense of objects being red for some people but green for others – without it making sense to ask who sees the colours correctly. In fact, being red and being green are *no longer incompatible*, once we realize that both ascriptions are relative to particular perceivers, rather than absolute. Is it possible, then, that the same is true of at least some moral judgements? Can the apparent conflicts over morality between different cultures be dispelled in this way? Consider: some cultures allow polygamy whereas others regard it as an abomination. But it may be that there is no real clash between these views. All we can say is that one view is right for some cultures, but another view is right for others.

This is an attractive way of making moral relativism intelligible – which is all we are trying to do at the moment. The example of colour is a useful starting point, since it shows how we can make sense of relativism about colours. But can the same sort of approach be taken with morality?

An important distinction

To begin with, people often argue for relativism by pointing out the vast diversity of moral views, of customs and traditions, that have held sway in different societies. The discoveries of anthropologists had an important role in making moral relativism popular, since they brought to light the diversity of moral codes in the world. They caused many people to doubt that the moral values of western Europe in the late nineteenth century reflected an eternal and universal morality. Surely it was possible that, like the practices of other cultures, western morality was not inspired by eternal and absolute values, but simply had contingent, natural origins? All the cultures under scrutiny seemed to take morality seriously, yet what was tolerated and forbidden varied widely. It seemed obvious, then, that no one system of morality was universally valid.

Is this a good argument for relativism? Let us scrutinize more carefully the statement that "no one system of morality is universally valid". It is clearly presented as the conclusion of an argument. But there are two distinct things it could mean. First, it could be an anthropological observation; an empirical judgement, to the effect that *what is believed* to be morally good and bad differs from culture to culture. In denying the universal validity of any system of morality, the statement really means that no such system is *taken* to be valid by everyone. It may be based, for example, on the observation that infanticide is regarded as acceptable in some societies but thought of as murder in others, or the observation that some societies have far stricter codes governing sexual activity before marriage, than others. On the other hand, the claim may really mean something quite different. Its real meaning could be that there is no one moral code which *applies* to everyone – in other words, that there is no one morality that everyone *ought* to follow. On the contrary, what people ought to do is culturally determined.

The difference between the two interpretations is that one is descriptive, while the other is normative. That is, one describes what people think they ought to do, while the other prescribes what people actually ought to do. Now, if moral relativism amounted only to a descriptive claim, a mere observation that different cultures believe in different moral values, it would not be a very interesting doctrine. For we already know that such cultural differences exist. But are the codes that people *ought* to follow, culturally determined? Are certain things "right" for some cultures, but not others – in the sense that the members of some cultures have certain obligations which members of other cultures do not have?

The argument from cultural diversity

It is fairly evident that moral relativism is making the second kind of claim. But how is that claim argued? As we noted, people are often swayed towards relativism by the fact that there are cultural differences concerning morality. Thus, we may call one popular argument for relativism the *Argument from cultural diversity*. In effect, it takes the truth of the statement "no one system of morality is universally valid", when interpreted in the first way, as a ground for the truth of the statement, when interpreted in the second way. Moral beliefs differ across cultures, therefore no one set of moral beliefs has a monopoly on the truth.

When this argument is spelled out starkly, it hardly looks convincing. Surely, we want to say, some beliefs are simply false? Why can't some people's moral beliefs be closer to the truth than others? Why can't people be wrong about morality, however sincerely and earnestly they cling to their convictions? As we noted earlier in this chapter, morality is not the only subject which admits of great diversity of opinion. Historians, natural scientists and economists differ among themselves, but fewer people say that there is therefore no objective truth that these disciplines can reach. To this, another remark is relevant. People deliberate morally, weighing up reasons and trying to become well informed about situations which call for moral decisions. If, however, the fact that an opinion prevails in some culture somehow makes it true, then why should individuals within that culture bother deliberating about morality at all? The answers would already be settled. Indeed, this form of cultural relativism seems to make individual dissent within a particular culture illegitimate.

These remarks do not, in fact, dispose of all versions of relativism. For the doctrine can be modified to deal with the most obvious objections, and has considerable resources to tackle some of the more basic accusations of fallacious reasoning. But before seeing how it can do this, we should briefly look at one of the obvious objections levelled against the simplest versions of the theory. This is not merely an attempt to answer arguments for relativism. It is attempt to show that relativism cannot be true. It has been referred to – in parody of the various Latin terms used in logic – the *Argumentum ad Nazium*.

The *Argumentum ad Nazium*

This challenge to relativism is simple, and essentially relies on most people's bedrock intuition. It serves to illustrate the thought spelled out above, which insists that some individuals and cultures may be radically mistaken about basic moral principles. Suppose somebody were to point to the culture of the Nazis, and comment that the ethical values (or lack of them) of that culture were "right for them", and that nobody should criticize them. To make the point more vivid: imagine that Germany had won World War II, established Nazi values in the whole of Europe, killed all remaining European Jews, and gained wide acceptance of its doctrine that the human good emerges from conflict and domination. It remains intuitively abhorrent to suggest that Nazi values would thereby become right, merely because they would be part of an established culture. Even if nobody challenged them, they would surely still be wicked.

Although the Nazi example is often used as a paradigm of evil, there are plenty of other examples that will also serve the purpose. Since such instances are used to back up basic convictions (or "intuitions" as they are sometimes misleadingly known), they are always vulnerable to the objector who decides to "bite the bullet" and accept the counterintuitive consequences of a particular position. However, the *Argumentum ad Nazium*, or some variant, is enough to suggest to most of us that there is something wrong with a crude and simple type of moral relativism. For the logical consequences of such a view do indeed appear unacceptable.

This is not to say, however, that there cannot be more refined versions of relativism which can overcome this objection. We shall presently see whether any such version has more chance of success. But first, it is important to examine some of the normative consequences that relativism is sometimes said to have. One central objection to relativism arises from the unacceptability of those normative consequences.

Relativism and the universal ethic of toleration

Think again of the historical roots of relativism. In both the ancient Greek case, and its late nineteenth century resurgence, it

17

arose from the observation that other societies survived perfectly well, in spite of having different moral codes from those the observers were brought up in. This in turn led to doubt that there was only one correct set of values. It was inevitable that this growing uncertainty led to increased tolerance and acceptance of other ways of life. In the twentieth century, and especially since the 1960s, relativism became even more popular, perhaps to the extent of generating a culture of its own. The prevailing virtue of that culture is a "non-judgemental attitude". Even when people do express a moral opinion, they sometimes qualify it with the remark that it is "just an opinion", as if trying to deny that it is any more correct than the opposing view. At the risk of over-simplification, we can say that according to many relativists, the truth of relativism entails that we should not morally judge others.

Is this acceptable? It seems strange to withhold judgement from cases of palpable and extreme evil. It looks somewhat like moral cowardice or confusion. But it is more interesting to find out whether there is a *logical*, rather than a *moral* problem, with this ethic of toleration.

Suppose we are faced with a culture which openly despises relativism and the ethic of toleration. Perhaps an authoritarian ideology or religion is at the heart of its existence, dictating certain moral values with firm conviction. For that reason, it regards toleration, freedom and human rights as nothing more than indifference towards evil, freedom to be wicked, and the right to do wrong. What stance should a relativist take towards such a culture?

It is perfectly in order for a relativist to disagree with this opposition to relativism. For, as we saw earlier, our moral relativist need not regard *all* truth as merely relative (if he does, he is in trouble). He need not regard moral relativism as only relatively true. The problems begin, however, when we ask what moral stance the relativist should take towards the prevailing attitudes of this culture. If intolerance, dogmatism and certain illiberal moral certainties are *an integral part of the culture in question*, is it possible to question them? It looks as though the relativist must accept that culture's prevailing attitudes. But if the relativist wants to avoid this option, he starts on a path towards advocating a universal ethic of toleration.

This brings us to a central problem with the sort of relativism under discussion. As we saw, although relativism is strictly speaking a metaethical doctrine, in practice it has usually been taken to justify certain normative conclusions: in particular, that toleration is morally virtuous. But for whom is toleration a virtue? If the answer is "for everyone", that is, that everyone ought to be tolerant, then we have at least one moral requirement which applies universally. The relativism has thus been compromised. The relativist is effectively saying: "Relativism is true, therefore, in the light of this, everyone ought to be tolerant towards other societies." We thus end up with a non-relative ethic of universal toleration. On the other hand, a relativist, wishing to avoid saying this, may try to accommodate the intolerance of other cultures. But if he does this, he will probably end up saying that tolerance is still a requirement for his *own* culture – even if not for others. Indeed, some wry critics of relativism are apt to remark that the doctrine is really a smoke screen for the abject abasement of one's own culture and the elevation of the virtues of others. There may be a connection between sympathy for relativism, and hostility towards the values of one's own society. One difficulty, however, for this combination of attitudes is that if other cultures and societies ought not be judged by outsiders, then outsiders should refrain from *approval* of other cultures, as well as disapproval. Another, more serious difficulty is this: that if no culture should be judged by another, then other cultures ought not to judge our culture, either. It is therefore inconsistent, if natural, to use relativism as the stick with which to beat the values dominant in your own society.

Why tolerance does not entail relativism

We suggested earlier that there may be ways of rescuing some of the insights of relativism, even if we cannot support simple versions of the doctrine. This is important, for there is surely something unsatisfying and arid about a purely negative appraisal. Some relativists may be on the side of the angels, even if – as if often true of such people – their arguments are confused. It would be good to concentrate on the idea of tolerance, to start with, as this is often thought to be inextricably bound up with moral relativism.

Many people rightly regard tolerance as a virtue. A tolerant person is usually not abrasive in the delivery of his judgements, is prepared to give others the benefit of the doubt, and is inclined to regard them as sincere and rational until shown otherwise. He pursues his disagreements by means of argument rather than force or abuse, and is open to the possibility that he may be wrong himself. But he does not thereby come to believe that his own views are no more true than the views of those who seem to disagree with him. It is possible to be tolerant while believing that others, to put it brutally, are simply in the wrong.

This point is well illustrated in non-moral contexts. We might speak of tolerating a bore at a social gathering, or putting up with a colleague's persistent demands for praise. Such tolerance is to be contrasted with being rude to the bore or deliberating putting down the person who fishes for compliments. In tolerating them, we do not believe they are anything other than they are. But we still owe them restraint in expressing our objections to them, and we should still be open to their good qualities. There are several good reasons for cultivating tolerance. One is that the consequences of intolerance have often been catastrophic, especially when deeply intolerant people have gained power and influence. Another is that extending tolerance to others sometimes helps them to be tolerant towards ourselves. Final agreement on important matters is often impossible; in the meantime, each individual has more to gain from a policy of mutual tolerance than from one of mutual, overt hostility.

But to tolerate something, or somebody, is to put up with what you do *not* like, or do *not* approve of. This is clearly illustrated in the debate about "legal moralism", that is, the view that the law should reflect morality as extensively as practicable.[6] Even among those who maintain certain traditional, conservative views on certain moral issues, it is common to accept that there are some matters of morality that should not be the law's business. To hold this opinion is to take a liberal view of the law, and it is consistent with maintaining anti-liberal views about the requirements of morality. Of course, many who hold a liberal view of the law are also liberals about morality: indeed, it is precisely because of their liberal moral views that they may, ironically, come closer to legal moralism than liberals of a more old fashioned variety. For example, they may think that the law should concern itself, roughly speaking, only with preventing people from harming (non-consenting) others, and they may think this because they believe that this is all that morality requires anyway. But there is still a position which says that there are genuine immoralities which the law should not prosecute. Such practices, in other words, should be tolerated but in no way condoned.

We have seen that relativism is generally associated with valuing toleration of what is, or seems to be, alien to what we are accustomed. But the important point is that we do not need to be relativists to value toleration. Some evils – though perhaps not all – should be tolerated. In fact, it is only by rejecting the most extreme kinds of relativism that we can consistently regard tolerance as a universal value.

Relativism and chauvinism

Another, related charge made against the opponent of moral relativism, is that of chauvinism. Even in view of all the cultural variations in humans' conceptions of the moral life, the anti-relativist is accused of clinging with zealous certainty to those with which he has been brought up, dismissing variations found in other societies as perversions and distortions which deserve forthright condemnation. Only his own way of doing things is right. He is unimpressed by the fact that other cultures take their own morality as seriously as he takes his; what matters is that they have false conceptions of the good life.

The above has an air of caricature, but it does capture an attitude found in some people. The moral relativist is anxious to avoid this sort of bigotry, and may think that it is only by embracing relativism that he can avoid it. But it is easy to see that this is not so. For one can be against relativism and still doubt that one's *own* society has a monopoly on moral insight. Indeed, this should be obvious: if it isn't, it is only because opposition to relativism tends – psychologically speaking – to be accompanied by chauvinism. Many people who are suspicious of relativism tend to think of their own way of doing things as being the best possible. But in fact, if there are absolute moral norms, there is no reason why other cultures should not be closer to appreciating them than our own culture. In other words, there is no logical connection between chauvinism and opposition to relativism. We could decide that other cultures, from an absolute standpoint, are morally superior to our own.

In sum, then: there are two vices, intolerance and chauvinism, which many relativists are anxious to avoid. They are right to want to eschew them. Where they go wrong is in thinking that if they are to do so, they must uphold relativism. Tolerance is the virtue of putting up with what you do not approve of, and it has nothing to do with a non-judgemental stance. Chauvinism is the vice of refusing to scrutinize your own cultural conceptions with the same rigour you apply to those of other cultures. But if you do scrutinize your own conceptions, you may find them deficient in the light of an absolute standard.

Relativism refined

In spite of all this, could some suitably refined version of moral relativism be true? One interesting possibility focuses on what it is to have a reason for action. What conditions must be fulfilled if I am to have a reason for doing something?

On one account, having a reason to do something is entirely dependent on your ability to acquire the relevant motivations. This idea is similar to what was said earlier about the distinction between hypothetical and categorical moral requirements. Those who maintain that moral requirements are hypothetical, say that they are valid for you only on condition that you have certain desires whose fulfilment depends on your doing what morality dictates.

There is a subtle kind of relativism which says something a bit similar to this. However, it does not specify whether moral obligations depend for their validity upon any *desires*. Instead, it says that the validity of moral requirements depends on whether you share the *relevant set of values*. If you do not, then no command depending on them can have any binding force upon you.

Consider, as an example, the claim that morality requires us to bring our standard of living down to the bread line, and to distribute all our surplus goods and money to the starving. Some philosophers, indeed, take this proposal seriously – even if they tend not to live accordingly. What could be said against this view? One counter-proposal is that nobody is able to acquire the motivation needed to live by this austere principle. This degree of altruistic devotion to the poor is simply beyond any of us. If that is so, then it is not only practically futile, but intellectually misguided, to maintain that morality requires this of us. It is rather like saying that although cats have a regrettable tendency to persecute creatures smaller than themselves, such as mice and voles, they really shouldn't. But, of course, cats are under no moral obligations at all, since they cannot represent to themselves any moral claims. They cannot acquire that sort of motivation.

Perhaps, then, there are types of motive that human beings can acquire only under certain specific cultural conditions. Perhaps, to take an example, certain hitherto unrealized circumstances could eliminate the almost universal tendency towards sexual jealousy. In such circumstances, sexual morality may become very different. On the other hand, if a disposition to jealousy cannot be destroyed (at least, for most of us), then this fact may shape the truth about sexual morality. Thus, if someone claimed that the only rational approach to sexual morality is one which makes no concessions to the jealousy and possessiveness that many of us experience, we could retort that such an approach would be credible only if we were able to abandon these feelings. If we are not, then we have no reason to do so.

This line of argument has been offered by Gilbert Harman,[7] in support of moral relativism. Harman asks what we should say about the moral obligations incumbent upon certain unusually evil or amoral individuals. Taking Hitler as a paradigm case, Harman thinks there is something odd about declaring that he acted *wrongly* in ordering mass exterminations. The point is that Hitler's values and aspirations had nothing in common with those of even minimally decent people – for example, he was entirely uninterested in the avoidance of innocent suffering. By contrast, we *can* say, of an "ordinarily" bad person, that his actions were wrong. For such actions may still be intelligible in the light of values he has that we can approve of. Perhaps a pro-life campaigner who kills doctors who are about to perform abortions, would merit this judgement. His deeds (we might maintain) are clearly wrong, but his desire to protect the unborn could still derive, in however distorted a fashion, from a praiseworthy respect for human life – even if he is mistaken in thinking that abortion is murder *per se*. In the case of truly evil individuals, a normal moral outlook has no influence whatsoever on their motivations. Since they lack even minimally commendable motivations, they lack a reason to behave as most decent people do.

Some criticisms

Perhaps Harman is right in a certain, limited way: there is a certain conception of "reasons", according to which evil people lack reasons to be good. At any rate, it is an empirical truth that some individuals are unamenable to reason; however sound our arguments, they will take no notice. But it is questionable that this account exhausts the concept of having a reason. Other accounts of having reasons stress that there are reasons to do certain things, even if they do not hook up with our existing values and motivations. A reason for me to do something is also a reason for you to do the same thing, in similar circumstances. If you cannot appreciate that reason, perhaps that shows something wrong with you. It does not take away from the universal character of the reason. In line with Harman, however, we should concede that in order to have reasons of a certain kind (say, moral reasons), we must have the *potential* to entertain them. Animals do not have moral reasons, precisely because they cannot (as far as we know) grasp moral concepts. So if Hitler was so far beyond the pale that he was literally incapable of moral motivation, then, in this sense, he had no reason to be moral.

Now although it is hard to resolve this matter decisively, the claim seems implausible. Hitler was a member of the human species, one of whose defining capabilities is moral consciousness. Unlike animals, he probably had some concept of morality – but either he was uninterested in shaping his life in accordance with it, or he held a corrupt set of moral values. Furthermore, the relativism that Harman advocates, with evil people in mind, is very limited. It does not deny that these men were evil; it only says they lack reasons that most of us possess. But the sort of moral relativism we are discussing makes a bolder claim than that.

Why relativism can seem plausible

Whatever the faults of standard versions of relativism, there is an interesting insight behind the argument we have just looked at. This is that morality must be somehow linked with motivations that we can actually acquire, even if it is hard for us to acquire them. The fact that we can, or cannot, acquire a certain motivation may be explained by general facts about human nature. So there is a sense in which the content of morality must be determined by the human condition, even if not by mere cultural convention. But what is the human condition? Are there activities and motivations which are, by nature, proper to our species, or are humans far more malleable than that? A comparison with the ethical theory of Aristotle is useful here. Aristotle[8] based his ethical philosophy on the idea that we have a "function" (*ergon*) which we must live by if we are to achieve the "good for man" (which is *eudaimonia* or well-being). Core facts about humans – that they are social animals, for instance – constrain what morality demands of us. A set of supposed moral requirements that required us to ignore such facts altogether – demanding that everybody live as hermits, for example – would be not just false, but unintelligible.

If this is correct, then we can understand why moral relativism can seem so attractive. For, like Aristotle's theory, it points to facts about human nature and motivation, and suggests that moral truth must, at least partially, be determined by those facts. Unfortunately, however, we cannot derive genuine moral relativism from these considerations. For relativism is really something much more specific than the very general doctrine that our shared nature and motivations have a role in determining the content of morality. Relativism insists, much more controversially, that the idea of absolute moral truth, independent of facts about specific cultures and societies, and not just human nature, is incoherent. It says that since cultures and societies differ, and since many such societies have little chance for interaction with other societies, the best moral insights available within each society fail to converge on only *one* moral code. Consequently, there is more than one true morality. Relativism frequently emphazises that the most refined moral thinkers in each society can draw only on their own form of life, and that this may exclude certain values familiar to other societies: a good example is the prominence of the idea of human rights in liberal democracies, a concept that some traditional cultures do not have use for at all. Nevertheless, although relativism has some plausible claims, it still faces important difficulties.

One such difficulty is that the fundamental values of different societies are not really in as much conflict as relativists tend to make out. For it is remarkable that the morality of most cultures gives prominence to the central virtues of justice and benevolence. These are moral concepts of special kind. They are not merely terms of approval: they also have a fairly specific descriptive meaning. Not just any actions or dispositions could count as just ones, or benevolent ones. So if most societies find a central place for the idea of justice, we should expect there to be some common agreement as to what kinds of actions count as just.

This is what we do find. Obligations of truthfulness, of respecting the property of others, and of not falsely accusing people of crimes, are given importance in all parts of the world. There is no doubt, of course, that many political systems encourage grossly unjust behaviour by individuals, but this does not show that at the level of custom, rather than politics, these moral principles are not given an important place. What does differ significantly between cultures is the range of beneficiaries of these virtues. Deceiving those outside one's immediate clan is thought permissible in some societies, and others do not encourage benevolence towards strangers. But no society could hold together without some rules of keeping trust and altruism. They seem to be basic prerequisites of leading harmonious lives and of flourishing as human beings.

Authority again

We have looked at a number of confused arguments for moral relativism, and have tried to show how duties of tolerance and moral open-mindedness do not, after all, depend upon the adoption of relativism. It is time now to remember how this debate began. The initial enquiry concerned the existence of moral authorities – people or institutions which are reliable sources of moral guidance. Relativism, in its most simple forms, presented a challenge to this idea. This challenge has a number of shortcomings. But are we really able to believe in the existence of authorities about morality?

Merely disposing of relativism will not establish that we can. Other problems still face the claim that there are moral authorities. For example, are there really any moral facts? Is there such a thing as moral knowledge? Are there really any ends which we all have, merely as human beings, which necessitate the adoption of certain principles in order to achieve them? These questions are not settled merely be rejecting moral relativism. However, once we see the problems for the view that all moral truth must be "merely relative", or that the practices in any one society must be as good as those of any other, we have at least removed significant obstacles in the way of belief in authority.

If there are moral authorities, though, in virtue of what are they authoritative? This is an important question, since one of the most common reasons for rejecting the whole idea of authority is that no answer to this question seems at all plausible. It is important, then, to understand the question. This is best done by means of a brief analogy with political legitimacy. To ask what makes a certain sort of government legitimate, with a moral right to our allegiance, is in some ways similar to asking what makes a moral authority authoritative.

Consider the idea of aristocracy. As an (almost defunct) political theory, it claims that the best people to run a country are those with a certain privileged social background. The possession of "blue blood" running through the veins is what fits a person to be a member of the ruling body. Or, as an alternative, consider the doctrine advanced by Plato in the *Republic*,[9] which argued that the state should be strictly divided along hierarchical lines, with the philosophers holding a monopoly of power. In both these cases, there is something *in virtue of which* the rulers have a right to hold power: i.e. being born an aristocrat, or being born in the "Guardian" class and reared as a "philosopher ruler". Now many people will find such ideas objectionable, for familiar reasons – for what has your social origin got to do with your political judgement and wisdom? Likewise, to return to the purely moral sphere, what attribute or fortune could possibly equip someone to be an authority on morals? It certainly has nothing to do with social class, IQ or religious affiliation. Nor is it easy to think of any other qualification necessary or sufficient for moral expertise.

There is an answer to this objection, however. If there is such a thing as moral expertise, there may well be no other quality which is a reliable criterion of it. It may indeed have nothing to do with any of the things mentioned. Moral expertise may be a *sui generis* property, no doubt loosely correlative with other qualities, such as general intelligence, but not definable in terms of them. Think again of the political analogy. The fact (if it is a fact) that social origins, education and so on, do not qualify people to rule, is sometimes adduced in favour of democracy – a system in which almost everyone has a say in the running of the country. But in fact, it is not a decisive argument for democracy, for it is still possible that some people really are better fit to rule than others, even if this does not arise from class, education, IQ or any similar qualities. So with moral authority: some people may be blessed with insight and moral wisdom, even if there is no other quality they all share.

But there are certainly mysteries, calling for urgent clarification. How are we to argue that there really are experts? How are we to identify them? What makes their moral beliefs cases of *knowledge* (if that is what is claimed)? There is no denying that these are important issues, which nothing said so far resolves. The purpose of this chapter has been to clear the ground for serious consideration of the idea of authority, not to argue that it actually exists. By surgically removing some of the most common arguments for a democratic approach to ethics, including bad arguments for relativism, we give to these relatively unpopular ideas the breathing space they deserve.

Further reading

Benedict, R. *Patterns of culture* (New York: Penguin, 1934). A classic defence of relativism from an anthropological perspective.

Harman, G. Moral relativism defended. *Philosophical Review* **84**, 1975. A seminal philosophical defence of a moderate relativism.

Williams, B. *Ethics and the limits of philosophy* (Cambridge, MA: Harvard University Press, 1985). See Chapter 9. Quite a difficult discussion, which distinguishes different kinds of relativism.

Wong, D. *Moral Relativity* (Berkeley CA: University of California Press, 1984). A comprehensive survey.

Chapter 2
The objectivity of morality

Our discussion of authority and expertise in the moral sphere encountered the ancient and familiar challenge of relativism. We rejected certain unconvincing arguments for this doctrine and some excessively simple versions of the doctrine itself. It is not correct to say, in the moral sphere, that anyone's view is as good as anyone else's – assuming that there is some point in making moral judgements at all. But it is lame to leave the matter there. In popular discussions, such as in newspaper columns on ethical matters, it is sometimes assumed that a triumphal dismissal of relativism is sufficient to establish the objective character of certain moral absolutes. This is unduly optimistic. To begin with, the falsity of relativism does not imply that any particular type of moral outlook – for example, a conservative or a progressive one – is correct. The content of morality is not determined by these metaethical issues. But more importantly for the ensuing discussion, even if relativism is false, there may still be no such thing as moral truth. This sounds surprising, perhaps, but there is no contradiction here. Relativism holds that there can be more than one true moral system: it is therefore opposed to the view that there are *no* true moral systems. What we must now consider is the challenge that morality may, for all we know, be a collective delusion – that nothing matters morally, after all.

This extreme view is known as *moral nihilism*. It holds that there are in fact no moral rights, no moral obligations, and that nothing is morally better or worse than anything else. Although this belief may seem sinister, we should note that a nihilist does not necessarily favour, or indulge in, behaviour conventionally regarded as immoral – such as lying, cheating and seeking to dominate others. It is important to distinguish between the *endorsement* of conduct that almost everyone else thinks of as wicked and a simple rejection of the claims of morality. Indeed, there is nothing paradoxical about a nihilist living a gentle and peaceful life, if he or she construes this as a mere personal preference rather than a moral obligation.

It is significant, on the other hand, that there are few, if any, contemporary philosophical defenders of nihilism. Hardly anyone can be found who thinks that nothing matters morally. When people seem to think this, it usually turns out that they reject only a particular set of moral conventions, such as those of their "bourgeois" parents, and want them replaced by a different set of moral values or priorities. In other words, they have not really rejected morality. At the same time, there are many people who take morality seriously but who nevertheless reject the view that moral requirements are objective, or that there are moral facts. Such people think that although we ought to concern ourselves with morality, our moral claims do not answer to any reality independent of them. There are no moral facts, or objectively binding moral principles.

This brings us to an important set of puzzles. Is it coherent to maintain the importance of morality, to be morally committed, yet deny that such commitments answer to an external moral reality? If there is a tension between these two elements, which should be preferred? A natural response is to resolve the issue in favour of objective moral facts. For certain moral convictions do seem undeniably well-founded, and if we can preserve our intuitions about them only if we accept their objective grounding, then that is what we must do. However, that seems to have certain costs. For what precisely does it mean to say that there are objective moral facts? What kind of evidence could possibly count for or against this doctrine? How can *value* possibly be objective?

Why is there a problem?

This is an area where technical distinctions abound, and where the very nature of the dispute is itself a matter of dispute. Before looking at some of these complex issues, it is a good idea to acquire a general impression of the basic problem underneath all this discussion.

When some people talk of their moral commitments, it transpires that they take them to be a kind of *belief*. When I form beliefs, I am guided, in some way, by how things are in the world. We speak of beliefs as justified or unjustified, true or false. Hence we contrast them with *desires*, which, although somehow referring to the world, cannot be true or false. We assess and evaluate our beliefs and our desires, for we think that there are better and worse beliefs, and better and worse desires. But different criteria for assessment apply to each. Our "better" beliefs, the ones we think are worth having, are judged so because in some sense they fit the world – or to put it more simply, they are true. Thus, to use jargon, they are *truth-assessable*: it is appropriate to assess them for their truth or falsity. But desires, however they are judged, are not judged for their truth or falsity.

If there are moral beliefs, then, these are moral beliefs about how things are, about how the world is, morally speaking. Moral beliefs worth having are those that somehow fit a moral reality external to them. But it is at this point that many begin to worry. The most fundamental doubt is whether it is even intelligible that moral commitments answer to states of the world. Does it make sense to imagine there is some state of the world that is *about* what we ought to do? Underlying this concern is also a difficulty of verification. How could we establish that there are or are not such moral states of the world (or, we may say, moral facts)? Two people might agree on all kinds of factual matters concerning some situation, yet disagree morally. If their moral disagreement is really a factual disagreement, it ought to be possible in theory for one disputant to bring the other round to his opinion by pointing out such a fact. But, notoriously, this is not only difficult to accomplish – it is obscure what would count as trying to point out a moral fact, once everything else has been agreed upon. We simply do not know how to verify the existence of moral facts, and thus the intelligibility of the whole concept is thrown into doubt. Put more loosely, the general problem concerns the nature of the states of the world which provide the proper basis for moral beliefs. The natural idea that moral judgement is authoritatively guided by something external to itself is problematic, because the nature of what does the guiding is hard to understand.

But this sceptical metaethical judgement sits ill with our commitment to certain moral claims. Suppose I find myself having to argue that it is morally wrong to enslave children and work them to death. I offer reasons for this view, based on considerations of cruelty, suffering and exploitation. But someone, to my astonishment, disputes my view. Can I really maintain that neither of us is objectively right? Is it not *essential* to holding a moral view that one regards that view as correct and opposing ones as wrong? It certainly seems that way. But this is, of course, the issue: are moral opinions capable of being true, correct, or objectively justified? (Note that these may not all amount to the same thing). Are some moral views closer to moral reality than others? Ordinary statements of empirical fact are thought of as being true or false. I believe that I am typing the present chapter, and this belief, in some (no doubt controversial) sense, corresponds with the fact that I am indeed typing the present chapter. To affirm this is correct; to deny it, incorrect. The question is whether moral judgements can be at all like that.

Facts and values

These puzzles about the objectivity of morals have often led to talk of the *fact–value distinction*. The term has gone out of favour, to a certain extent, but it finds an echo in some popular conceptions of morality. There is, on a robust version of this view, a realm of hard, verifiable fact, perhaps expressed in statements like "Beth's remark to Alice hurt her badly." Concerning facts like that, there seems no special problem about reaching agreement with reasonable people – even if we can't all agree on such facts, they exist nonetheless. However, once people start making moral judgements, saying for example that greed is a *vice* or that misery is *bad*, they have ventured into different territory altogether. They are stating things which are neither equivalent to, nor deducible from the above-mentioned facts. One cannot logically infer that Smith is vicious from the fact that Smith is unconcerned about suffering. One cannot logically infer that one ought to alleviate Jones' pain, from the mere knowledge that he is in pain. Of course, people do invoke such things as grounds for their moral judgements: people with a normal conscience are moved to action by the suffering of others. Undoubtedly we should, and do, give reasons for our moral judgements, and these reasons appeal to facts about the situation. The crucial point, however, for one who invokes the fact–value distinction, is that judgements about what we *ought* to do cannot be strictly *entailed* by facts about a particular case, and properties (or alleged properties) such as goodness cannot be *identical* to natural properties possessed by actions or states of the world, such as a tendency to produce happiness or misery, pain or pleasure.

The "naturalistic fallacy"

One way of understanding this point is through a simple and highly influential argument offered by G.E. Moore, in his *Principia Ethica*.[1] The argument seems dated nowadays, but it has the virtue of clearly showing why the fact–value distinction has seemed so persuasive. Moore believed that he had discovered an error in many traditional ethical theories, which he christened the *naturalistic fallacy*. This was the fallacy of identifying the property of goodness with a natural state of affairs, such as happiness, pleasure, or tendency to confer an evolutionary benefit. (In fact, although Moore called the mistake the naturalistic fallacy, his argument is really directed against any attempt to define goodness, whether in naturalistic terms or not. For this reason, some writers prefer to speak of the *definist fallacy*). The argument that this is indeed a fallacy is called the *open question argument*. Take anything which is allegedly identical with goodness, says Moore, and you will soon see that even if the said thing *is good*, it cannot literally be *the same thing as goodness*. Thus, to borrow from utilitarian thinking, even if things which promote happiness are good, the property of being good cannot be the same thing as the property of promoting happiness. For one can always sensibly ask: "Are things which promote happiness good?" In other words, it is an open question whether these things are good; even if they are, it is possible to deny this without contradicting oneself. If, on the other hand, "good" simply *means* "productive of happiness", then it is a tautology to claim that things that produce happiness are good. It is like saying merely that things which produce happiness produce happiness – something which, although undoubtedly true, cannot be presented as a great discovery.

It is important to note that although much of the inspiration for the fact–value distinction comes from Moore, he did not deny that goodness and badness were real properties and that true factual statements could be made about them. He did insist, however, that goodness was a simple and indefinable property, which could not be identified with any natural state like happiness.

However, although his "open question argument" was influential, it is not very convincing. For the apparent openness of questions about what things are good may be just the product of our own ignorance, or even corruption. Certain questions may seem open when really they are not. It is a fact, for example, that water is H_2O – i.e. the property of being water is the property of being H_2O. It is impossible that a fluid could be water but not H_2O. But for one ignorant of basic chemistry, this is surely not obvious. Similarly for all kinds of truths: even if they could not be otherwise, we may be under the illusion that they could be.

Nevertheless, one may still feel that the argument points to something important, even if it needs more careful formulation. The argument illustrates the appeal of the fact–value distinction: that evaluative statements, such as moral ones, somehow go beyond ordinary factual ones. To say that Smith is greedy and for that reason bad, seems to say more than merely note that he is greedy. Perhaps this is an illusion – perhaps that badness of his character just is his greediness. But is it not plausible that there is a distinction here?

One reason for thinking that there is a difference is that we typically give *reasons* for our moral judgements. It is because Smith is greedy that we condemn him, and because his poorer neighbour is envious that we condemn her. Moreover, we argue about morality even when certain facts are agreed upon. I say that Alice's resentment of Hilda's wealth is bad, while you say that it is commendable because the situation is unfair. Certain facts can be agreed upon – our disagreement concerns what evaluative judgement is justified. This brings us squarely back to our original enquiry. Can these evaluative judgements be true or false, warranted or unwarranted? Can one moral disputant be objectively right, and the other wrong?

Objectivity again

In principle, nothing suggested so far says otherwise. Even if natural properties of the world cannot be identified with moral properties, there is no obvious reason to deny the reality of moral properties. And indeed, much of our ordinary moral discourse suggests that most of us would not deny it. Those who morally condemn needless violence or indifference to the lot of the poor tend to think they are making claims to truth. They usually think that those who do not agree with them have failed to see moral reality for what it is. Maybe, if they thought about it, they would admit that moral claims state more than the basic factual claims upon which they are based. But why is this a problem? Isn't the moral badness of violence and indifference to the poor, a perfectly intelligible notion? Don't most of us have a more or less reliable sense which alerts us to such moral properties?

No doubt we think we do. But there has been considerable philosophical disquiet about the idea that moral judgements can strictly speaking claim truth or falsity, or that they can reflect an independent moral reality. There are a number of grounds for scepticism. Some philosophers claim not to understand the idea that there are moral *facts*, preferring to think of moral utterance as a perfectly legitimate but nevertheless non-fact-stating practice.[2] Others claim to grasp the idea that reality contains moral properties, but think it unlikely on metaphysical and

epistemological grounds. Still others complicate matters by holding morality to be a perfectly objective matter, not because there
are moral facts, but because moral discourse is about (non-factual)
principles which are objectively binding simply because they are
rational.

Perceptions and projections

In this quagmire of disagreement, it is useful to begin with a
distinction, recently given importance by Simon Blackburn,[3] between *perceiving* an aspect of reality, and *projecting* onto reality
some aspect of our subjective make-up. (Hume is the principal
originator of this idea, and many anti-realist ideas trace themselves back to him).[4] In a variety of areas of dispute, by no means
limited only to metaethical enquiry, philosophers align themselves
with "realism" or with "anti-realism". In spite of important disputes about how the very issue is to be framed, a realist, roughly
speaking, claims that statements in some area (for example, about
causation, the past, or moral value) refer to a mind-independent
reality. According to a realist, we can grasp the idea of such a
reality, even though some aspects of this reality may be perma-
nently beyond our knowledge. One implication of this is that
reality may be radically other than we take it to be, perhaps
containing kinds of thing whose nature we can never come to
grasp. What we *can* grasp, however, is the idea that there may be
some things we *cannot* grasp. By contrast, an anti-realist typically
denies that we can grasp this notion. In one formulation, an anti-
realist says that our concept of truth in some domain, for instance
about the past or causation, is really the concept of what would
warrant certain statements about past events or causal relations.

In ethics, anti-realism takes a somewhat different form, although the general idea is similar. Anti-realists are sometimes
drawn to a "projectivist" view of moral utterances. Rather than
say, as a realist will, that moral values are a genuine, mind-
independent aspect of reality which we may perhaps apprehend in
some way, the projectivist says that when we make moral judgements, we *project* onto the world our attitudes, preferences, needs
or desires. That is, the world does not really contain properties like

good and evil – or at least, not in the way we might naïvely suppose. Rather, we undergo certain reactions towards states of affairs, which are largely caused by our needs, desires and aspirations. In saying that something is good or bad, virtuous or vicious, we are really superimposing onto reality aspects of our subjective make-up. Nothing is commendable or vicious "in itself" (whatever that may mean); when we ascribe moral qualities to actions or people, certain naturalistic features of the world produce certain reactions in us, which we then project back onto the world, uttering judgements like "x is morally evil".

One important assumption underlying a projectivist approach is that moral judgement stands in an intimate relationship to attitudes and feelings. To judge something good involves, or at least tends to involve, a certain emotive reaction – perhaps a certain pleasure in its contemplation. The assumption is plausible enough, at least if loosely construed, even if it is not beyond question. If we make the assumption, it is not too hard to see what the projectivist has in mind. Contemplation of some act of heroic virtue – or just of basic human kindness – often fills us with a pleasant feeling of admiration, just as reflection on outrageous cruelty fills us with anger. These feelings are projected from the judge back onto the object, and as a result the object seems to be endowed with a particular moral quality, as part of its constitution. But according to the projectivist, this is an illusion. All that exists in reality is natural features of things, and our reactions to them.

Most projectivists are careful not to say that morality itself is an illusion, however. They think that even though there is no literal perception or cognizance of moral reality, this does not invalidate our practice of moral judgement. When we ask ourselves carefully what we mean when we say that a person's character or deed is morally good or bad, we see that all that *could* be meant by this is as the projectivist claims. An obvious parallel is with beauty. The adage "beauty is in the eye of the beholder" is familiar, and people are generally happy to accept this without feeling that their aesthetic judgements are somehow threatened by it. I may be able to accept that the extraordinary beauty of parts of the Old Town of Prague, with its golden facades, its narrow, intimate alleyways and yellow lanterns, is not part of its objective constitution. But this sober reflection does not stop me from finding it beautiful, and

I know from my experience what I mean by this, even if I need to be careful when I try to formulate this thought in philosophical terms.

But all of this leaves an important question unanswered. Even if we can make sense, at least initially, of a projectivist view of morality, we have not yet been told why we should believe it. For what, after all, is wrong with adopting a realist view of the matter? Doesn't it accord more with common sense, to think that moral properties are no less part of the constitution of reality than physical features such as shape and mass? This is one of the hardest questions of metaethics, not least because the exact interpretation of terms like *realist, objectivist* and *projectivist* is in crucial dispute. But some arguments have emerged to challenge the opinion that moral features of the world can enjoy the same kind of existence as its physical features.

Are moral properties "queer"?

One much-discussed argument is the "argument from queerness", advocated by J.L. Mackie.[5] According to this argument, the existence of objective moral features of the world would involve "entities of qualities or relations of a very strange sort, utterly different from anything else in the universe" (p. 38). In essence, the "queerness" is in the idea that features of the world, or ends that we might choose to pursue, somehow have a "magnetic" property of "to-be-doneness" built into them. Suppose we say that human happiness is good. Then, on one view of what this means, we are saying that we ought to promote happiness. If we believe that the goodness of happiness is an objective property of it, then we are saying that a property of happiness is that it should be pursued. And the mystery now is: how can this "should-be-pursuedness", this prescriptivity, be an intrinsic property of happiness? Put another way, how can features of the world generate reasons for action, independent of any motives and desires that people actually have?

We have already seen how people's decisions and moral reactions may be based upon factual considerations. Recall the distinction between hypothetical and categorical imperatives. The notion of having a reason for action, *given* the fact that we already have certain desires, seems quite straightforward. But part of the queerness of objective moral properties, according to Mackie, is that certain facts are supposed to generate reasons for action, in and of themselves. In other words, certain facts (in this case, alleged moral facts) are supposed to have a kind of magnetic quality – a quality of being both fully factual and yet also inescapably prescriptive. By contrast (thinks Mackie), it is much more intelligible, as well as more in accord with ordinary psychology, to explain people's moral reactions and moral decisions not in terms of the arcane apprehension of mysterious, hybrid prescriptive facts or properties, but simply in terms of the projection onto the world of attitudes, needs and desires.

Objectivist responses

Those who believe that moral judgements can lay a claim to truth or objectivity can reply in various ways. Most simply, they can point out that talk of queerness is rhetoric dressed up as rigour, and that no real argument has been offered for the intrinsic improbability of objective value. Some might add that, in view of the role played by moral reasoning in most of our lives, it would be very queer if there were in fact nothing in the world to which such thinking was a response. In any case, all kinds of things are queer, if this just means that they are difficult for us to understand: the implications of relativity theory are certainly odd, but we don't take this as a reason to disbelieve them. It is only *scientism* – the dogmatic conviction that science alone opens the secrets of reality – that explains why people accept all kinds of strange things if they appear scientific, but are sceptical of the utterances of people without scientific credentials, such as moral philosophers and theologians.

These replies are on the right lines, although I believe the advocate of the argument from queerness can say more things in support of his view. The best such counter-attack would stress the difficulty in claiming both that moral utterances *describe properties* in the world, and that they are inherently *action-guiding*. In view of this, a fruitful strategy for the moral objectivist is simply to deny that moral reality, or objectivity, should be conceived as Mackie thinks it should. For Mackie thinks that if you really take moral objectivity seriously, you are led to something like Plato's Theory of Forms[6] – and this is indeed metaphysically extravagant. However, the concept of moral objectivity may really be far more simple and intelligible that the argument from queerness makes it seem.

In essence, Mackie's problem is this: how can a thoroughly objective feature of reality be, at the same time, internally connected to reasons for action? Here is one possible reply. Mackie has adopted an unduly scientific account of objective reality, and is prepared to accept as features of ultimate reality only those entities that would feature in a physicist's account. But this may be a mere dogma. There are all kinds of things, such as sounds, colours, smells and tastes, that seem perfectly real yet not part of such an account. If we can construe moral reality as being somehow analogous to these things, we may have an interesting way of seeing how moral values can be real, even if not in the way that the ultimate entities of physics are. Thus, arguments such as Mackie's may be circumvented. But does this line of argument succeed?

Values and secondary qualities

To refute Mackie some philosophers – eager to defend the objectivity of value – have seized upon a supposed analogy between moral properties and *secondary qualities*, as named by John Locke. According to Locke, qualities of objects such as smell, colour and sound are not part of their intrinsic constitution, in the way that *primary qualities* such as shape and mass are. Secondary qualities like colours are powers to produce sensations in the perceiver, such as sensations of redness, sweet smells or bitter tastes. In Locke's view of perception, the primary qualities are perceived correctly whenever the perceiver experiences an idea representing these qualities, which faithfully resembles the quality in the object itself. However, there is nothing in red objects that is like our sensation of redness, if by this we mean that there is a resemblance between the redness of the object, and the sensation of redness which is experienced. All that really happens is that certain physical properties – microscopic primary qualities – of the objects cause light of a certain wavelength to be emitted, which then interacts with our sensory apparatus and causes us to experience the sensation of redness.

But it may now seem surprising that the analogy with secondary qualities is used to *defend* the objectivity of moral values. For the account of secondary qualities so far given appears to suggest that if there is an analogy at all, it pulls in quite the opposite direction. (This, in fact was Hume's view: he thought that secondary qualities and moral qualities were alike in being subjective). On Locke's account, attributions of colours and smells, etc. are best seen as a kind of error – what may be called a *projective error*. That is, we project our colour-experience back onto objects and mistakenly think colours to be really in physical objects. (These mental items have physical *causes* in the objects, but that is something altogether different). How then might we use the distinction between primary and secondary qualities to the advantage of the moral objectivist?

The answer is that while we can believe in a real distinction between primary and secondary qualities, we can nevertheless construe it differently from the way Locke did. Locke in effect regards it as the distinction between that which really belongs to physical objects *as they appear* and that which does not; but it is quite possible to understand it instead as a distinction between two different modes of existence – one which is somehow experience-dependent, and the other which is not. On this view, we can say two things about redness: that it is an *intrinsically phenomenal* quality, and that it is a genuine property of objects that look red. In calling it intrinsically phenomenal, we are saying that in order to know what redness is, we must have a subjective grasp of a certain experience – we need to know what redness is like. But in calling it real we are saying that red things can be just as they appear – namely, red. In saying that they are red, we are not saying that there is some *similarity* between the object's colour and the way the colour appears. Rather, in these cases we directly perceive the colour. Direct perception just means having a certain colour-experience.

This account of secondary qualities is of course disputable, as is the theory of perception that underpins it. But it does at least provide a clue as to how we might dissolve the tension between the action-guiding, or perhaps emotive, aspect of moral attributions, and their objectivity. For just as colours can be both genuine properties of objects, and at the same time essentially phenomenal (i.e. their appearance is their essence, roughly speaking), so moral values might also be both objective, and at the same time essentially related to emotions, attitudes and/or states of will. To be good is to be disposed to arouse approval among normal judges, yet this dispositional property is still part of the objective order of things. And some supporters of this view also urge that only naïve scientism can find anything fundamentally wrong with the idea.

Some difficulties for the analogy

The analogy between moral values and secondary qualities is an attractive one at first glance, but there are difficulties with it upon reflection. One problem is that it seems to imply a kind of moral relativism, and this is unacceptable to most of those who advance some form of moral objectivism.[7] We saw in the last chapter how colour ascriptions might be *true relative to perceivers*: for if some physical object looks to have one colour to one set of people, but another colour to another set, it is hard to see how we can declare that either set of perceivers is ultimately correct, in the sense of seeing the colour as it really is. For colours are just appearances, and talk of how they really are can only amount, in the end, to talk of how they really appear. But if the analogy with moral values holds, we should expect a form of moral relativism to be true: infanticide seems right (i.e. is right) for the ancient Spartans, but seems wrong (i.e. is wrong) for the British. It would, on the analogy, be difficult to see how a whole community could be morally mistaken, since the analogy would suggest that for something to *be* morally good is for it to *seem* morally good to some moral judges. We could, if we wanted to be more cautious, specify that such moral judgements have to be made by "normal" judges in "normal" conditions, but if an entire community of judges made some particular moral judgement, and did so consistently, then it would be difficult to argue that they, and the conditions, were not normal.

Furthermore, if the analogy with secondary qualities really holds, we face a mystery about how we can give *reasons* for our moral judgements. If values are analogous to secondary qualities, then we might expect our grasp of value to bear some analogy to our awareness of secondary qualities. This is, of course, sensory awareness – objects are simply presented to the senses as red or sweet smelling. But can moral awareness really be at all like sensory awareness? Even if we loosely speak of seeing that something is right or wrong, or having intuitions to this effect, moral judgements can usually be underpinned by reasons: we say that some action is wrong because it is cruel, or deceptive or mean. But it seems absurd to ask for reasons why an apple is red, or a rose has a certain smell. We can investigate the causes, of course, but an account of the causes would only *explain* rather than *justify* secondary quality appearances, whereas what we need in the moral case is justification.

Such are two reasons why there is probably little to be gained from pursuing analogies between values and secondary qualities. These criticisms, it may be noted, also apply to attempts to exploit the analogy in an anti-objectivist direction, which seems at first the most obvious thing to do. Hume takes his stance *against* the objectivity of morals, and defends the analogy between moral and secondary qualities. Just as colours are "phantoms of the senses", so moral sentiments are caused by natural, non-moral features of the world, which in turn "gild and stain" the world with their own emotive colouring. It may be that the projectivist picture toward which Hume feels his way can still be vindicated, but if it can, it is unlikely to be on the basis of any analogy with secondary qualities.

Interlude: theism and neo-Aristotelianism

Let us briefly mention two other ways in which the objectivity of morality is said to be grounded. One way derives from what is known as the divine command theory of moral obligation. The other is based on supposed features of human nature. We shall see the various strengths and weaknesses of these approaches, and why, despite points in their favour, they are unlikely to provide the case for moral objectivity that their proponents seek.

In a predominantly secular society, the belief that the content of morality is exhaustively determined by the commands of God seems, to many people, something of an anachronism. One criticism often made is that if it were true, then people who do not believe in God could not be offered any reason for being moral that they would accept. This, however, is beside the point: the fact that appeal to divine revelation would not in fact persuade non-believers to act well, does not show that they have not been offered a sound reason to do so. For they might just be mistaken in not believing in God. In any case, even if religious commitment is waning in the western world – a supposition surely open to question, especially considering the religiosity of many Americans – the influence of the divine command theory, which holds that there is a strong, logical connection between moral requirements and the commands of God, is still in evidence. This is, paradoxically, because it is logically possible to accept the divine command theory without actually believing in God. If one adopts this position, one will, if consistent, take the non-existence of God as a proof that there are no moral requirements. There seem, in fact, to be many people who reject the objective reality of moral requirements precisely because they do not find the existence of God credible.

Such an opinion has affinities with that of Fyeodor Dostoevsky, the nineteenth century Russian writer and Christian, who pronounced that if God does not exist, then everything is permitted. He did not think that everything was permitted, but he accepted that morality does depend upon theism. A significant variant on the view was also upheld by Friedrich Nietzsche, the nineteenth-century German philosopher. But whereas Dostoevsky thought that if there were not a God, there would be no moral requirements, Nietzsche thought that the falsity of Christianity meant there was no reason to assume that the specific content of Judaeo–Christian morality was all true. He did not reject morality wholesale – indeed, he tried to reinvent it – but he was entertainingly contemptuous of those non-believers who retained the moral outlook of puritanical Protestants while no longer believing in God. If the theological foundations for traditional Christian morality were built on sand, was it not irrational to continue to hold distinctively Judaeo–Christian moral values? (Their emphasis on humility and self-denial was among the main things to annoy him).

The Euthyphro dilemma

A simple version of the divine command theory can be put thus: moral obligations are logically equivalent to God's commands. To say that stealing is wrong is to say that God forbids stealing. Thus, if God (that is, the God of near-eastern theism, worshipped by Jews, Christians and Muslims) is real, and if he issues certain commands, then there is a set of facts about how we should live. But if there is no such being, then there are moral obligations.

From this highly simplified claim, how might we proceed? Discussion of God's existence is not directly to the point here. Rather, we need to know what the exact relationship could be between the commands of a supreme being, and the commands of morality.

One way to proceed is to ask a very old question, posed by Socrates in Plato's dialogue *Euthyphro*.[8] In the work, Socrates is talking to Euthyphro, a conventionally religious man who believes that piety consists essentially in obeying the will of the gods (official Greek religion being polytheistic). Faced with the moral question about what to do with his father, who has left a servant to die in a ditch, Euthyphro wants to prosecute his father, because he thinks this is commanded by the gods. However, Socrates cleverly asks him whether *pious things are pious because they are loved by the gods*, or whether *the gods love pious things because they are pious*. Rephrased in a modern idiom, and within a monotheistic framework, the basic question is: if some act is right, and if God commands it, then is it right because God commands it, or does God command it because it is right?

This is a powerful challenge, for it seems to expose the divine command theorist to a dilemma (hence, the challenge is known as "Euthyphro's dilemma"). For suppose that we opt for the first possibility, or horn of the dilemma. Suppose for example that generosity and forbearance are good *because* God commands them. In that case, we have to admit that if God had not commanded them, they would not have been good. If God had commanded envy and spite instead, then those things would have been good. On the other hand, suppose that God commands or approves of generosity and forbearance *because* they are good. In that case, it seems that – logically speaking – God drops out of the moral picture altogether. For even if he exists, and approves of the things in question, it still seems that the reality of good and evil is logically independent of God's commands. In that case, the divine command theory would appear to be false.

Many sophisticated theists would favour the second horn of the dilemma, and admit that, logically at least, divine commands and moral requirements are independent of one another. This may be a sensible view, if they think some other basis for morality can be supplied, though whether it really represents the guiding spirit of the major monotheistic religions, in their traditional conceptions of God, is a moot point. I think that in some ways it is truer to this spirit to adopt the first horn. But this has some uncomfortable implications, for it appears to imply that, prior to God's commanding some action, there really are no moral requirements at all. In which case, God, so to speak, makes up morality as he goes along, in an entirely arbitrary way. He is not responding to morality when he forbids murder – he is creating it. But in that case, he had no prior reason not to command and forbid entirely different things. If he had commanded us to kill innocent people, then that would have been right. What this suggests is that for God himself, there is actually no difference between right and wrong. God himself is not subject to any prior moral constraints.

This potentially devastating objection to the divine command theory is tersely summed up by Bertrand Russell, as follows: "Theologians have always taught that God's decrees are good, and that this is not a mere tautology: it follows that goodness is logically independent of God's decrees".[9] For suppose it were a tautology to say that God's decrees are good – like saying that "a bachelor is a man who has never been married". In that case, to say that God decrees good things, and to praise him for this, would be empty of any real content. For it would be true by definition that God's decrees are good, and thus it would be no more informative to say that God's decrees are good than to say that God's decrees are God's decrees.

This raises complex theological issues. But its immediate interest is in what it tells us about the grounding of moral values or requirements. In many ways we are reminded of G.E. Moore's argument against the naturalistic fallacy. Moore was as strongly against the attempt to define moral goodness as that which God approves of, as he was against any other attempt to define goodness. For his open question argument can be used in all these cases. Just as it is a sensible thing to ask whether happiness is really good, so it seems sensible and meaningful to ask whether God is good, or whether we ought to obey his decrees.

But recall one important objection to Moore's argument. Some questions which seem open may not really be; the example of water and H_2O showed this. Similarly, although it seems to be an open question whether God's decrees are good, it may not really be at all. But surely it is not a tautology to say that God's decrees are good? It does not seem to be. But then again, it is not a tautology to say that water is H_2O, even though water is – and must be – H_2O. The same kind of thing could, for all we know, be true of the relationship between moral goodness (or rightness) and divine commands. It may not be *logically* necessary that God commands what is morally right. But it may still be necessary in some other, non-logical way.

This is at least an interesting possibility. It is a potentially devastating rebuttal of the potentially devastating Euthyphro dilemma. However, we should not be too excited by it. Even if the original claim of morality's dependence on theism can be interestingly refined, we still need some reason to believe that there is such a (refined) dependence. Even if the traditional Euthyphro challenge does not dispose of this more subtle possibility, it is still unclear why we should believe that it is true. The subtle view might be expressed by saying that it is not God's *commanding* something that makes it obligatory, but the fact that the command is issued by a being with God's nature. But intriguing though this suggestion is, we need to know why moral goodness (or rightness) should be in any way connected with God.

We should now briefly mention another way of attempting to ground the objectivity of value. This is that which derives from the Greek philosopher Aristotle's metaphysical biology, and has wielded great influence in "natural law" accounts of morality

– especially in the Catholic Church. The theory, however, makes no theological assumptions.

We shall discuss this theory in much more detail in Chapter 7, when we look at virtue theory.[10] But, in summary, the idea is that how a person should live, and the virtues he needs to live well, are objectively determined by his function as a human being. Aristotle believed that everything in nature had a specific function, and that a condition of flourishing for a living being was that it should live in accordance with that function. The same is even more obviously true of artefacts: for example, a boat is made so as to float on water, and it is ridiculous to think that what should count as a *good* boat is a *subjective* or *emotive* matter. A good boat is simply a boat that properly does what boats should. Something similar, although a longer story must be told about it, is true of men (i.e. males. Aristotle was writing before feminism. He did think that women had a function too, but not the same as men's). A good man lives well, and this living well consists in the flourishing of his distinctive function, which is rational thought. To do this he literally needs certain virtues. Whether this gives modern objectivists the sort of moral objectivity they want is a difficult problem (on the other hand, if it doesn't, this probably shows something wrong with what modern objectivists want). We shall defer discussion of all this to later on.

Moral facts and moral reasons

Let us hold on to the earlier idea that, according to an objectivist account of morality, our best moral responses are guided by considerations external to us, which dictate what moral commitments we should form. One way of trying to understand this idea is by invoking the doctrine of *moral realism* – the view that there are objective moral facts, which are facts about states of the world. But another way of understanding the concept of objectivity in morality is not by appeal to moral facts, understood as referring to states of the world, but rather to what Immanuel Kant called "pure practical reason", which issues judgements that are objectively normative for us. When we respond to practical reason, we are not being guided by beliefs about how the world is, morally speaking.

Rather, we are being guided by *reasons* which have some kind of objectively binding force.

We shall look at the details of Kant's moral theory later on (in Chapter 4). For the moment, the important feature of the theory is that it is reason, not perception, which gives us the content of morality. This reason is practical: it tells us what we ought (have reason) to do. The essentially practical aspect is seen in the fact that morality is a set of imperatives, derived from a supreme principle known as the *categorical imperative*. To construe morality as a set of rational prescriptions is supposed to avoid the problems of saying how a feature of the world can generate a reason for action. One of the main problems for moral realism, or at least popular varieties of it, is that it tries to combine the idea that moral convictions are *beliefs*, with the idea that moral considerations are also *practical*. This was problematic, because on a widely accepted account of human motivation, desires are required to motivate action – beliefs on their own are unable to do so. Now, it would certainly be wrong to say that the Kantian theory puts desire at the helm of moral motivation; nothing could be further from the truth. Nevertheless, by understanding moral utterances to be fundamentally prescriptive rather than descriptive of moral features of things, we make moral motivation less of a problem. For the Kantian thought is that prescriptions have their own internal logic. Some prescriptions (or what Kant calls maxims) can be shown to be irrational.

We shall look at some of the details later. They have been introduced only to suggest that there may be objectively valid reasons for action. In Chapter 1 we saw the distinction between hypothetical and categorical imperatives. Hypothetical imperatives can be objectively valid in a sense, but only conditionally; their validity depends upon the existence of certain desires (thus the imperative "if you want to avoid a parking ticket, do not park here" is valid only assuming that you want to avoid the parking penalties). But it is not this kind of imperative that interests us here. Imperatives that Kant called categorical are said to be valid for us, quite apart from any desires we might have. Perhaps Kant's theory fails to find a convincing example of such an imperative. But it is the concept of reasons for action which are not dependent on our desires which is important here.

How are reasons generated?

The thought that there may be obligations that are not dependent on desires will strike many people as odd. Some people hold the Humean view that reason alone can never motivate action; there must always be some desire or passion operating in the background. Others may protest that it can never be morally obligatory to do anything that has no bearing on anybody's desires. We should say something about this latter view to begin with, as it contains much potential for misunderstanding of what is at issue.

It may be that all moral requirements are related in *some* way to the desires of sentient beings. Nevertheless, what is morally incumbent on me, at some particular time, is often what I myself have no desire to do. If a colleague absent-mindedly leaves his vintage bottle of champagne in my office, I am obliged to return it to him, not least because he would want me to – but I may still want to drink it above all else. Perhaps I would have no reason to return it if he didn't want me to. Nonetheless, if he does desire the bottle himself, I have a reason to give it back. I still do not desire to; I do so, if at all, out of a sense of duty.

The basic idea is someone else's desire gives me a reason to act, just as my own desires give me a reason to act. To take a basic example: if I am in extreme pain, or am severely depressed, I have a reason to try to alleviate my suffering. This seems simply obvious. But now consider the implications. If I have reason to end my depression, then that perhaps suggests that depression is a bad thing. If something is bad, then that is a reason why it should not exist. But then, does it not seem that anyone has a reason to try to alleviate depression, whoever suffers from it? If my depression gives me a reason to cure it, then it surely can give another person a reason for helping me cure it, and it can give me a reason to help other people who are depressed.

This idea is, of course, highly disputable, and many philosophers would doubt that reasons can be generated quite so easily. But the thought is intriguing enough to merit exposition. The immediate point is that we are now invited to think of the reality and objectivity of moral value in terms of the *objective existence of reasons for action*. In saying they are objective we are saying that they give everyone who can act, a reason for acting – even if they have no desire to do so. I can have a reason to end someone else's suffering even if I am a sadist and like the thought of another's suffering. This idea makes a great deal of sense of the common sense idea that practical reasoning – reasoning about what to do – aims at something, that it strives to reach good reasons, and that these are not merely determined by present desires or beliefs. It brings us back to the notion of the objective guidedness of moral decision-making, whatever the exact nature of what does the guiding. It is, I suggest, in this concept of objective practical reason that we find the most fruitful account of the objectivity of morals.

So let us take it that, whatever the great metaphysical complexities behind it, we do have the concept of the guidedness of practical reasoning, in something like the way we understand the guidedness of ordinary empirical beliefs. In the latter case, what guides belief is truth; truth is what beliefs aim at. Now it is also attractive to think that something plays the role for practical reasoning that truth does for theoretical reasoning. The great question at the heart of the disputes about moral realism and objectivity is how we should understand such an idea.

Almost everyone accepts that there are reasons why we should do certain things. The simplest and least disputable source of such reasons is our own desires. Wanting to consume the champagne gives me a reason to do so: it is the explanation I would offer if I did in fact drink it. What causes more problems is the idea of objective reasons, which in some sense exist apart from desires. This is partly the familiar problem of whether we can be motivated to do something by what Hume called "reason alone", without desire. But it also brings us to a fundamental dispute about what the idea of the objectivity of (moral) reasons really amounts to.

Mackie's complaint about the objectivity of morality was that it would involve a strange kind of quality or entity. Blackburn similarly, while taking a somewhat different line from Mackie (he does not think, in fact, that moral commitments involve any error, as Mackie does[11]) still thinks that the picture of objective morality that the moral realist has in mind is an unintelligible one, or at least one which makes a mistake about explanation. On the other hand, realists such as Thomas Nagel[12] dismiss these charges, arguing that the anti-realist has set up a straw dog – a needlessly implausible account of what realism would involve. For Nagel, it is really a matter of there being objective reasons for action, and responding to such reasons is a matter of bringing "an external view into the determination of our conduct" rather than bringing our thoughts "into accord with an external reality" (*The View From Nowhere*, p. 139). However, since Nagel himself talks of there being true and false propositions about reasons for action, that would suggest that there can be true and false *beliefs* about such reasons – and that in turn makes it difficult to distinguish his position, in the end, from the straw dog he dismisses. Just what is the difference between saying that external reality contains objective moral facts, and saying that there are objectively valid moral reasons?

More on why the problem is thorny

Problems of this sort, which are really problems about the interpretation of the issue in question, are often found in disputes between realists and anti-realists. Take the concept of the past. The realist starts by saying the past is real, i.e. that there are true and false statements about the past. The anti-realist answers that this is fine, so long as you don't think the past exists in some inaccessible realm. The realist retorts that if the past is real, it must be possible for there to be facts about the past which will forever elude discovery. The anti-realist answers that everything a realist wants to say about actual past events can be said by the anti-realist – and moreover, the anti-realist has a common sense view of the past which doesn't involve a mysterious, undetected realm. The realist then says that of course he doesn't believe in a "mysterious" realm – realism is not like that at all; it is perfectly simple! And so on.

In spite of some differences, similar difficulties in interpreting the issue are involved in discussions of moral realism or objectivity. If we are to adjudicate between the parties, we need some mutually agreed account of what each of the positions really involves. This leads us to ask whether there is any substantial account of a realist position which is not – through its protestations of simplicity – really a capitulation to anti-realism.

Credible and incredible moral realisms

There is good reason to think this can be supplied. We should contrast the true account of realism, with a version of realism about value which most realists and anti-realists can reject. This false kind of realism maintains that moral values have *causal powers* in their own right. According to this conception, they share with Locke's primary qualities, such as mass, shape and size, the ability to bring about effects in the physical world. (The size of a car prevents it from getting into a certain parking space; the mass of an asteroid determines how big a crater it makes when it hits the desert). This kind of realism entails that moral reasons directly cause actions; that given certain other conditions, the addition of a moral reason is sufficient to bring about an action, in virtue of its moral properties.

But we must bear in mind another kind of explanation, which can be termed rational or personal, and which involves normative considerations rather than brute causal power. When I say that I apologized because I realized I had been unpleasant, or that you owned up to breaking your neighbour's window with a cricket ball, because that was the honest thing to do, the sense of "because" is normative: it refers to justification rather than cause. (I leave aside highly involved questions about the relationship of reasons to causes here). The honesty of owning up did not causally produce effects in the world; it had an effect in a different way, namely that you judged it a good reason for action.

A moral realist or objectivist, on my account, is someone who holds that there are good reasons for action; that these reasons are not simply generated by desires, and that we sometimes accept them as valid and act because of them. The realist need not say these reasons have their own causal properties. Now, if this account describes a genuine realism, then a certain objection to the doctrine can be silenced. The objector might say that since moral reasons are not part of the causal fabric of the world, they are not "really real" at all, and an anti-realist – perhaps projectivist – account should be accepted instead. However, our realist is now in a good position to challenge the anti-realist to say why only the causal, scientific perspective on the world is the one that yields access to "real reality". From a scientific perspective, it is true that values will not feature. But it would be confused to infer from this that the reality of value is incompatible with the truths of science. Rather, values are (at least on present assumptions) simply not in the domain of science.

Note that this is not a form of relativism. We are not saying that the best established theories of physics are only "relatively" true, and that if we deny them we are making no mistake. This confused position is sometimes held by people anxious to defend morality, religion or even New Age theories against the "cold", "materialistic" scientific view, but it is no part of moral realism. All the realist is doing is trying to come up with some theory to account, not for the physical behaviour of objects, but for the moral appearances most of us encounter. His position is that our moral experience is best explained by the existence of a reality by which it takes itself to be guided.

If an anti-realist now retorts: yes, many people do think there is a moral reality, and most of us engage in moral reasoning, but why on earth should we believe there is such a reality? – then we should admit that we cannot prove this. But that is what the appearances point to, and we should accept appearances until we have been given a reason not to – rather than the other way around. The typical anti-realist accepts certain moral claims, (e.g. "it is wrong to try to dominate or manipulate others"), but at the same time denies that this moral view is any reflection of an external moral reality (a notion he will probably claim not to understand). The realist should now point out that he has already made sense of the notion, since he understands what he means in condemning such behaviour, and understands why he condemns it. What more, ultimately, does he want?

Moral discovery

What probably underlies the anti-realist's position is a certain picture of moral *discovery*, which he associates with the realist position. On this picture, moral disagreement, which often seems irresolvable, would be authoritatively settled by appeal to some source of knowledge entirely independent of the feelings and attitudes of the proponents of opposing positions, and in such a way that they could all go away satisfied that at last they all know the truth. Since it is hard to imagine what it would be like to make such a discovery, doubt is cast on the objective moral facts which would thus be discovered. We are back with the apparent unverifiability of moral claims and the possibility of unresolvable moral disagreement which so impressed the anti-realist all along. The best realist answer, now, is to admit that some conceptions of moral discovery lack credibility, but still insist that access to moral knowledge, or at least well-grounded conviction, is so close to us that we fail to see it: namely, in our everyday feelings and rational deliberations about moral questions. It is in both feeling and in practical reasoning that we are brought into contact with moral reality. Furthermore, even if some disagreements cannot be settled, there is such a thing as persuasion and the emergence of a consensus, and this is not merely a matter of mesmerizing opponents into acquiring new feelings about moral issues. Progress in moral thinking is often slow and uncertain, but it is mere dogma to think that morality is, for this reason, at a special disadvantage compared with other areas of enquiry.

So a good case, even if by no means a conclusive one, can be made for moral objectivity – which here amounts to a kind of moral realism which upholds the objective reality of reasons for action. But if a good case can be made for this, then we have got somewhere with the most perplexing and fundamental problem of metaethics.

But do not heave a sigh of relief quite yet. We have not exactly got answers to all our questions. Even if there are objective moral facts, this alone does not settle pressing debates about moral theories of right action. It does not tell us what to do. It is to some of these questions that we can now turn.

Further reading

There is a wealth of scholarly literature on these issues, much of it technical and obscure. Good sources include:

Ayer, A.J. *Language, truth and logic* (London: Gollancz, 1936.) Reprinted many times. See Chapter 6.

Blackburn, S. *Spreading the word* (Oxford: Oxford University Press, 1984). See Chapter 6.

Brink, D. *Moral realism and the foundations of ethics* (Cambridge: Cambridge University Press, 1989).

Honderich, T. (ed.). *Morality and objectivity* (London: Routledge, 1985). This contains important essays, especially by Simon Blackburn defending "quasi-realism", by John McDowell defending an analogy between moral values and secondary qualities, and by R.M. Hare on ontology in ethics.

Hume, D. *A treatise of human nature* (originally published 1739–40), L.A. Selby-Bigge (ed.) (Oxford: Clarendon Press, 1978). See Book III. A classical source for "projectivist" views (although the term is Simon Blackburn's).

Sayre-McCord, G. (ed.). *Essays in moral realism* (Ithaca, NY: Cornell University Press, 1988).

Williams, B. *Ethics and the limits of philosophy* (Cambridge, MA: Harvard University Press, 1985). See Chapter 8.

Chapter 3

Consequentialism

So far much of our discussion has been on issues of metaethics, or philosophical questions about the nature of morality. The subjects of moral relativism and moral realism are central problems of metaethics, as they enquire into whether moral utterances can be true, and if so, whether they must be true (if true at all) for all people at all times. But to solve these problems is clearly not all philosophical speculation can offer. For as well as investigating metaethical problems, philosophy can also explore questions of moral theory. This is our main concern now.

Earlier in the twentieth century, many philosophers saw the role of their discipline in moral enquiry as somewhat cursory. For them, questions about the nature or meaning of moral utterances were properly philosophical, but as far as forming opinions on everyday moral problems was concerned, philosophy had nothing special to offer. It is perhaps no accident, at least psychologically speaking, that prominent philosophers who took this view (e.g., A.J. Ayer) denied that there were any objective moral facts. The resolution of problems in what is now called *applied ethics* – such as euthanasia, abortion or income distribution – was not, in their view, a matter of coming up with literally true answers – although some of them had strong attitudes or convictions about such things.

However, even if there are no objective moral truths, and even if philosophy has nothing distinctive to say about moral problems, an important area exists between metaethics and applied ethics. This is moral theory: theories of right action which purport to have relevance for problems like abortion, euthanasia and war. These theories are general: they aren't concerned with specific moral problems but they do underpin common positions on such issues. For example, suppose we are discussing the ethics of abortion. Some people say that human life is sacred and must never be deliberately taken, even before birth; others say a woman is always entitled to choose whether to have an abortion or not, while others still will say it depends on the consequences for all concerned. Hence, we quickly find ourselves asking whether, in general, we should always do whatever will bring about the best possible consequences. And then we find ourselves asking what counts as a good consequence (human happiness, perhaps? or the satisfaction of as many preferences as possible?), and hence open up the question of what sort of considerations are relevant to settling these matters. Thus, we start theorizing about what is good, and what makes an action right.

One of the most important and widely discussed theories of right action is consequentialism. According to this doctrine, what makes an act morally right or wrong is its consequences, and nothing else. Considerations of the motive of the act (such as kindness or malice), or the intrinsic nature of the act (for example, its being theft or deception) are in themselves unimportant, though both these things may themselves have further consequences. If something has been agreed to be good, then the basic moral requirement is to promote it. It may be possible to promote it only by producing something bad in itself, such as suffering. But we should do this, if the overall good achieved outweighs the bad.

Mill's "Utilitarianism"

The term *consequentialism* was devised to describe a view that says that the moral character of an action is determined solely by its consequences. This, as it stands, leaves it entirely open what is to count as a good consequence. Someone who thought that the only good thing in the world was the colour green, could couple this unusual moral conviction with consequentialism by maintaining that right acts are those that bring about more green things, and wrong actions (mowing the lawn, perhaps) are those that diminish the amount of green in the world. Classical utilitarians, however, believe that the ultimate good is something that most people actually desire, such as happiness or pleasure. (Most modern utilitarians take preference satisfaction, rather than happiness, to be the ultimate goal at which we should aim). The doctrine of *ethical hedonism* asserts that the only ultimate, intrinsic good is pleasure. This, in fact, was the view of the classical utilitarians, Jeremy Bentham (1748–1832) and John Stuart Mill (1806–1873). In what follows I am concerned with the theory as defended by Mill, though Bentham was really the progenitor of the doctrine, and applied it to legal theory as much as to ethics. Bentham notoriously claimed that, provided the quantities of pleasure yielded were equal, pushpin was as good as poetry. Mill is generally thought to have provided a more refined and sensitive defence of this hedonistic doctrine, and most discussion of classical utilitarianism is concerned with Mill's theory.

Mill's famous work *Utilitarianism*, published in 1863, elegantly explains and argues for utilitarianism.[1] The mainstay of the doctrine is the principle of utility, namely that "actions are right in proportion as they tend to promote pleasure or happiness". The term *utility* is not used here with its everyday meaning – it does not mean *usefulness*. For Mill, the utility of an action simply is its tendency to produce pleasure or happiness. Pleasure or happiness is the only ultimate good, the only good thing in itself, and pain is the only ultimate evil. Mill's utilitarianism thus combines the doctrine of consequentialism with that of ethical hedonism. The principle of utility is also known as the "greatest happiness principle" and it tells us to promote the "greatest happiness of the greatest number". Insofar as Mill endorses the traditionally accepted principles of morality of mid-Victorian England, he does so only because they happen to promote happiness or pleasure. He rejects the idea that actions are right only because God says they are, or because they have any inherent moral properties of their own. Even if utilitarians of Mill's persuasion can agree with some of the moral views of their opponents, they still disagree about the ground for those principles. A utilitarian might agree with them, for example, that we ought to acquire certain habits, such as truthfulness or honesty, but only because there is a better chance of promoting the greatest happiness of the greatest number with those habits than without them.

Some people think that the utilitarian philosophy is just a matter of common sense. Most of us want to be happy, and it seems irrational or superstitious to follow rules (such as "Thou shalt not commit adultery") simply for their own sake rather than for any human happiness they bring. In fact, many moralists are tempted by utilitarianism as offering a uniquely rational solution to moral problems, and this is one of its great attractions. But it is important to remember that in Mill's time, many critics received the doctrine as an outrage, thinking its hedonistic element "worthy of swine", as Mill puts it. Many of these critics were devout, and were unimpressed by Mill's claim that the morality preached by Christ was really a utilitarian morality. However, opposition to the theory does not come only from religious believers. There are questions to raise, as we shall see, about many aspects of the theory, including the nature of pleasure and happiness, the claim that only one thing is intrinsically good, and indeed the prodigious demands on our time that a thoroughgoing utilitarianism appears to make.

Pleasure, happiness and hedonism

Mill's theory is hedonistic: it maintains that the only ultimate value is pleasure or happiness. But when philosophers like Mill talk of hedonism, what they have in mind is, alas, something more sober than most of us might hope. It is not a doctrine that tells us to spend all our time in riotous living, but a theory about what ultimately has value. But even if cleared of the charge of encouraging us to binge on food, drink and sex, there are a number of philosophical difficulties with it.

To begin with, Mill seems to speak of pleasure and happiness as if the terms were interchangeable. Of course, they are not. It is possible to experience pleasure without being happy, and vice versa; the depressed person who takes to drink gains some transient pleasure from alcohol but is not made happy by it, and it is also possible to feel happy without there being any specific source of pleasure. Pleasure is also tied more specifically to some particular activity or feeling than is happiness. We take pleasure in certain bodily sensations, pleasure in music, in food, conversation, sport and good news, but happiness seems more general than this: it does not, for instance, attach to sensations. Many thinkers deny that happiness is a psychological state at all; although we talk of "feeling happy", the mildly euphoric feelings we have in mind are more closely associated with pleasure. What Aristotle called *eudaimonia*,[2] which he said was the ultimate good for us, is often translated as happiness, but it actually refers to well-being – an overall quality of a human life rather than a type of feeling that occurs during life.

Moreover, even the concept of pleasure is not as clear cut as it seems. It appears that pleasure is not, in itself, a feeling. Rather, it is a quality possessed by diverse feelings. The feelings we get from sinking into a warm bath on a cold day are pleasurable, as are the feelings we get from a cool shower on a scorching day, or the feelings we experience in sexual activity. Yet these are very different feelings, all sharing the quality of being pleasurable. It is nonsense, therefore, to talk of *the* feeling of pleasure, as if it were something to be counted alongside other feelings, like those of being tickled, or of warmth, or of sweet tastes.

A utilitarian need not feel challenged by this. She can accept the necessary clarification, and continue to maintain that the only thing which makes something good, whether a sensation, a perception or an activity, is its pleasurable quality. She might accept that there are many different sources and kinds of pleasure, but still hope that they can somehow be ranked in order of the amount of pleasure they yield. Perhaps it is usually more pleasurable to hear a piece of good news than to get into a warm bath. If so, she would recommend actions that promote the first sort of pleasure over the second, if given the choice.

Higher and lower pleasures

Mill, to be fair, is sensitive to some of these difficulties. Indeed, he devotes considerable space to trying to show that one common observation, namely that pleasures appear to differ in quality as well as in quantity, can be reconciled with utilitarianism.

Contemporary critics of Mill said there was something "mean and grovelling" about a moral doctrine that gave pleasure such an important place. Was there not far more to a good life than pleasure? Mill took the point, but thought it was better expressed by saying that some pleasures were higher, more elevated and worthy of enjoyment, than others. Mill himself clearly thought so. Indeed, more typical hedonists might even regard Mill as a bit of a prig – the mastery of Greek verbs held more excitement for him as a small child than the rougher pursuits of most boys. The important point, however, about higher and lower pleasures is that pleasures can be compared not only in quantity but also in quality. There are, in other words, not only greater and lesser pleasures but also better and worse pleasures.

As I shall presently suggest, this is almost certainly true. But the crucial question is whether to admit this is consistent with being a utilitarian. Mill's purpose in introducing the distinction is, of course, to rescue the claim that the only ultimate good is pleasure – for higher pleasures are still pleasures. But the problem is that we have to say according to what criterion of value we are to judge the quality of pleasures. If we remain steadfast utilitarians, we must apparently say that the only ultimate criterion of value for anything at all is its pleasurable character. We could, no doubt, add that certain pleasures have an additional, instrumental value if they are conducive to yet more pleasure, and thus favour them over pleasures that do not lead to further pleasure. But if we are utilitarians, the answer to our question must seemingly be that the quality of a pleasure must be measured in terms of its *quantity*. Any departure from this notion is a departure from the utilitarian doctrine.

Now, no doubt the utilitarian can still make something of the idea that there are higher and lower pleasures. By accepting the notion, he or she must (it seems) be employing the concepts of "higher" and "lower" in a descriptive and non-evaluative sense (or at the very least, not in a morally evaluative sense, although possibly appealing to aesthetic value). Thus, he or she might talk of the richness of pleasure in music, and contrast it with the simplicity of pleasure in the taste of brandy. A rich pleasure could be one which invites fruitful interpretation, and which can be better appreciated when thus understood, as contrasted with a simple sensuous pleasure which it makes little sense to speak of understanding in depth. Our utilitarian could even accept that on a scale of *aesthetic* value, some pleasures are of a higher quality than others. What is unclear is that this can have, for a utilitarian, any moral implications.

Are there bad pleasures?

If it makes sense to talk of higher and lower pleasures, might it not make sense to say that some pleasures are not only "lower", in the sense of being less complex and rich than others, but actually bad? I do not mean "poor quality pleasure", so-called pleasure that is not very enjoyable, such as what you get at dull parties with warm, sweet, cheap white wine served in plastic cups. I mean depraved or corrupt pleasures which may still be subjectively highly enjoyable. Does this idea make sense?

It is easy to find examples that might fit this bill. Sadistic pleasure, pleasure in humiliating and belittling others, or in coercive pornography are plausible cases. But a utilitarian will challenge the claim that these pleasures are bad in themselves. As a benevolent individual, who believes that pleasure should be promoted and pain diminished, he or she says it is bad if people are hurt, humiliated or coerced. Other things being equal, there should be no sadism or unpleasantness. But that doesn't mean that any pleasure is intrinsically evil. The pleasure enjoyed by the sadist is all right; what is not all right is its effect on his or her victims. If we could somehow allow the sadist to enjoy pleasures, while secretly protecting would-be victims from harm from the sadist, there would be nothing wrong, and everyone would be happy.

Think about the following illustration of this point. Imagine that once sex offenders are safely locked up, they are provided with virtual reality machines that enable them to experience all the pleasure of their past offences, but without harming any real people. The experiences seem just as real to them, but thankfully they are no longer a danger to anyone. Nor will they be – for let us also imagine that utilitarian judges have put them away literally for life, so they cannot offend again. Leave aside, for the moment, objections to the cost of installing the machines in question. Is there anything intrinsically wrong with such a situation?

I would imagine (and hope!) that you find this appalling. True – in a sense, everyone would be satisfied. But it is surely a mistake to judge pleasures solely on their actual effects in the world. We also take certain predilections to indicate a person's character. To derive pleasure from the thought of another's suffering is normally an indication of a flawed character. To take pleasure in what is evil can itself be evil, not because of its effects, but simply because of what it is.

In response, the utilitarian might insist that there is a confusion here, involving an equivocation with the word *pleasure*. He or she will say that we should distinguish the pleasurable, enjoyable *feeling* of some activity or fantasy, from the intentional object or *content* of such feeling. The second can be bad if it involves another's pain, but the first never is. To speak of "bad pleasures" is really to say that something bad has aroused a pleasurable feeling. But the feeling itself remains innocent.

However, although we can draw the distinction suggested, the utilitarian's claim is not convincing. For it seems to ignore crucial points about the nature of pleasure. True: at one end of the scale there are brute pleasures of sense, which are not about anything and have no particular object, and it may be that, other things being equal, the more of such pleasure, the better. But in the case of most pleasures, it is artificial and arbitrary to separate the feeling from the content, for the purpose of evaluation. It is odd to judge pleasure only in terms of its feel; we also speak of the appropriateness of pleasure, in the light of its object. Pleasure in a friend's good fortune is appropriate, pleasure in his or her ruin normally is not. The second pleasure may feel just as enjoyable, but that does not mean that it is good. Given the fact that some pleasures have content – they are about something – there is surely at least as good a reason to evaluate them according to their content as according to their feel. The utilitarian, I suggest, has not provided an adequate reason to think otherwise.

Perhaps our objections can be summed up as follows: whereas Mill's utilitarianism, in spite of various qualifications, regards a thing as good because it is pleasurable, a better account would say that many things are pleasurable because they are good, and that the goodness of something is often what legitimizes the pleasure. Sometimes, it is true, the goodness is hard to isolate from the pleasure. But this is not always the case. There are times when a thing brings us pleasure because we already value it. In that case, we can judge the goodness of the pleasure according to whether the thing we value is worthy of being valued – whether it is admirable or not.

Psychological hedonism

In spite of these problems, there is still something to be said for Mill's hedonism. It is hard to think of pleasure and pain as having no bearing on morality at all. If anything is wrong, deliberately causing needless suffering surely is wrong. Most of us do desire pleasure and the avoidance of pain, and it is because of this that pleasure and pain seem to have considerable moral importance.

But this leads to two other questions. First, although we often do desire these things, are they all we desire? Secondly, exactly whose pleasure do we desire? Does each individual desire only his or her own pleasure (and avoidance of pain), or are we motivated simply to avoid all pain and promote any pleasure, whoever experiences them?

The theory that claims that all we ever desire for its own sake is pleasure and the avoidance of pain is known as *psychological hedonism*. This theory generally assumes, moreover, that each person ultimately desires his or her *own* pleasure. This may involve the pleasure of others too, but only because it gives him or her pleasure in the end. Psychological hedonism underlies Mill's utilitarianism. It lies at the heart of his ethical hedonism – his view that pleasure alone is intrinsically valuable. If, in fact, pleasure is all that we do desire, it seems natural to infer that pleasure is the only thing that is ultimately desirable, or worth desiring.

However, whether this inference is valid depends on exactly how we interpret the claim that all each of us desires is our own pleasure. There are two ways it may be understood: as an *empirical* claim, or as a *conceptual* claim.

If the theory of psychological hedonism is to be understood as an empirical claim, then it is saying that, as a matter of contingent, psychological fact, all that anyone wants is their own pleasure. We could, in theory, discover someone who didn't desire their own pleasure – and if we did, we would have to admit that psychological hedonism was false. Thus, it is an empirical generalization that has held good so far, but could be falsified by further evidence. It is like saying that "all judges are Tories" or "all students are laid back". They are claims which, according to those who make them, may happen to be true but do not *have* to be true.

This is one way in which one could construe psychological hedonism, but in fact it is probably not the way most proponents interpret it. I suspect they would really construe the theory as a *conceptual* claim. That is, they would take it to be a kind of necessary truth that all we ever desire is pleasure. Pleasure is not only all we do desire, but all we can desire, as a matter of necessity. Any evidence that we desire anything else would be explained away in a fashion consistent with psychological hedonism. Imagine that I give five pounds to a vagrant, and when asked why I did this, I reply that I thought he needed the money to buy more alcohol, which brings him pleasure. A psychological hedonist will answer that I was really acting to bring myself some pleasure. The thought that this man's unfortunate life could be lightened by wine was pleasing to me, and I helped him in order to please myself. In other words, the appearance that I was acting for another's pleasure can be explained away; if his pleasure gave me pleasure, that only shows that I acted for my own pleasure. This is the explanation for even the most powerful seeming counterexamples, such as the fact that some people indulge in masochistic activities. In these cases, says the psychological hedonist, it is obvious upon reflection that such people gain intense pleasure from having pain inflicted upon them. Maybe the pain is real, but it is outweighed by a countervailing pleasure.

What is wrong with psychological hedonism

But brief reflection shows that psychological hedonism is actually a naïve and superficial theory, especially when construed as a conceptual claim about what we desire. Everyday appearances strongly suggest that we do not always desire our own pleasure above all else. Some of us are kind to lame duck acquaintances when it would be much more fun to be rude; some of us pay back our debts even though we could perhaps gain more pleasure from keeping the money and buying things we want. But cannot the psychological hedonist explain away such appearances? Don't we pay back debts only because if we didn't, we would feel guilty (and that is unpleasant), or because we are afraid of being caught? Yes: the psychological hedonist will say these things, and it is hard to prove him wrong. But *why* should he say this? What is the argument? There isn't one, in the end; the real appeal of the theory is that it appears clever and cynical.

This doesn't show that pleasure and the avoidance of pain are not important and common motives for action. A qualified empirical version of psychological hedonism may contain much truth, as far as a great many motives are concerned. But there is no reason to think it is a *universal* truth or a *necessary* truth. The concepts of desire and pleasure are closely linked in our minds, because so often, when we want something, we think of the pleasure or happiness it would bring to us. But that doesn't show that the only thing we ever desire is pleasure. On the contrary, to echo an earlier thought, the pleasure of getting what we want often comes because we attach an independent value to the things that we want, and manage to get.

Whose pleasure counts?

The psychological hedonism of Mill's theory is in ostensible conflict with another essential element of utilitarianism. This is that Mill's utilitarianism is rigorously committed to promoting the greatest happiness (pleasure) of the greatest number. Far from saying that the more pleasure *I* get, the better, I must if I am a utilitarian believe that my pleasure matters no more (and no less) than anyone else's. Further, I must try to increase the amount of pleasure in the world – it should be spread as widely as possible. From this it follows that certain sacrifices will often need to be made. If, to alleviate the suffering of ten people I need to make one person unhappy, then barring consideration of further, unpredictable consequences, that is what I must do. The person to be sacrificed may be me or someone I love, but as a utilitarian I must not flinch from that.

This brings out the consequentialist element in utilitarianism. In many ways this is more worthy of discussion than the hedonist element. As we shall see, consequentialism thrives even if Mill's hedonistic version of it founders. We do not have to be hedonists to be consequentialists. All we need believe is that there is a good or set of goods, whether or not pleasure is among them, and that actions are to be morally judged solely according to their productivity of these goods. Ironically, this shows that utilitarianism can be charged not only with being too lax (in upholding no absolute moral rules forbidding certain sorts of deed) but also with being far too demanding. Certain sacrifices are required for the greater good. Morality, on this account, significantly eats into your spare time.

The immediate problem this causes for psychological hedonism is that the psychological hedonist must produce some account of how moral motivation is possible, if morality insists on this strongly non-egoistic stance. Morality forbids me to behave as if my pleasure were any more important than anyone else's. Yet psychological hedonism says I can be motivated only by desire for my own pleasure. Thus, it would seem that morality demands what is psychologically impossible – in which case, it thoroughly discredits itself.

It must be said in fairness to Mill, that he does try to overcome the problem. He thinks that we can come to desire things for their own sake rather than directly for the sake of pleasure, but only because of an original psychological association of those things with pleasure. This does seem to be something of a departure from psychological hedonism, however – for even if things we desire for their own sake were originally associated with pleasure, it does not follow that we now pursue them for pleasure. To think otherwise is to commit the *genetic fallacy*: the mistake of confusing something with its origins. (Compare: man is descended from the apes; therefore he is really a hairless ape). But I shall not pursue Mill's answer in particular, since the interesting point is more general. This is that any such theory, hedonistic or not, must find some account of how ordinary people can acquire the motivation to live according to it. This problem is brought to the fore by the demanding nature of consequentialist theories. But first, we need to know something of what the normative, practical implications of consequentialism really are.

Surprisingly, although the general framework of consequentialism is clear, there are significant disagreements among consequentialists on the exact normative implications it has. Suppose you are now suddenly converted to consequentialism, having read what is above. What should your first act be, to show your newly acquired zeal? Should you write a generous cheque to Oxfam, in order to promote happiness and minimize pain? Should you give away your CD player to someone who would get more pleasure from it than you would? Or ought you at once to abandon philosophy and try to become a merchant banker, so that you can earn as much as possible and then give it all away to the needy? What about your old school friend whom you promised to see this evening? Can you justify keeping this promise, when you could be occupied buying hamburgers for down and outs? Some of these questions clearly turn on the difficulty of calculating the short and long term consequences of our actions. But there are deeper questions as well. One of these – concerning direct and indirect consequentialism – turns on the extent to which a good consequentialist should be consciously guided by consequentialist considerations. This is a complex problem and I merely alert the reader to it, rather than discuss it here.[3] But there is another division among consequentialists, concerning whether or not there is any place for moral rules in a consequentialist theory. This, and other issues, will be discussed not only in the light of Mill's utilitarianism, but also to much more recent developments of consequentialist theory.

Act- and rule-consequentialism

The disagreement over the place of rules may seem surprising, since we have seen that the hallmark of consequentialism (whether it is hedonistic, like Mill's version, or not) is the conviction that, in the last analysis, only consequences determine the morality of actions. So how could rules, such as "do not steal", have any place in a consequentialist framework?

Rule-consequentialists argue that it is possible both to embrace a consequentialist view of what makes actions right or wrong, and give an important place to moral rules. They believe that there is a good *consequentialist justification* for our adherence to certain rules. Keeping certain rules produces better consequences than trying to judge the consequences of each individual action. They stress that they are not "rule-worshippers", who advocate obedience to rules for their own sake. Instead, they advocate sticking to certain rules precisely because this is the best way to achieve the good. *Act-consequentialists,* on the other hand, believe that we should ask ourselves, for each individual act that we are contemplating, whether or not it promotes the good. Act-consequentialists who think the good is pleasure say that we should judge each individual deed according to whether it would produce a good net balance of pleasure and pain. If it would, then they would judge that the act was morally right. Otherwise, they would judge the act wrong. Hence act-consequentialists do not feel bound by rules telling them, for example, never to steal, lie or cheat. Of course, they might recommend that we should usually avoid doing these things, precisely because they usually produce bad consequences. They might even judge that in their own lives it is never right to do these things, for this very reason. But they do not hold to a *rule* that forbids them. For the only thing that can really determine the morality of an act is the consequences of that particular act.

The following trivial, though useful, example illustrates the case for rule-consequentialism. Good drivers know to stop at a red light. Even if they can see that the road is clear, they must still stop and wait until the light changes. They also know that there is an external point to the rule – that the rule doesn't exist for its own sake. The point of the rule is to promote road safety. They know that if everyone always obeyed such rules, there would be very few accidents. But at the same time, it is clear that rules are quite rough and ready things, and that even though the requirement to stop at red lights is justified in terms of road safety, it is obviously not always dangerous to drive past red lights. Why then should we follow the rule of never driving past them, even when it is clearly safe to do so? A plausible answer is this: that any attempt to refine the rules so as to take account of all conceivable exceptions would, in the end, collapse into the principle: "do whatever seems to you, in the circumstances, to be safe". And there would be far more accidents if everybody followed that rule (which is really no rule at all), than if they followed the existing rules. Thus we have a kind of rule-consequentialist justification for always stopping at red lights. This seems to provide a fruitful analogy with certain proposed moral rules. The fact that the odd lie may have good consequences is no justification for it, because a consequence of lying whenever the consequences seem to be good, is that very often you will tell lies when the consequences are not good. It may be that the easier it becomes to tell the lies that have good consequences, the easier it becomes to form a habit of lying. This will eventually cause you to lie when the net results are bad. It may also be said that since lying often comes from selfish motives, you will be tempted to think the consequences will be good when really they will not be. This, then, shows how a rule-consequentialist could justify a rule against telling lies.

Why should act-consequentialists disagree with this? It seems to be eminently sound. But they have a powerful response. Start from the rule-consequentialists' protestation that they are genuine consequentialists, and not deontologists or rule-worshippers. If this is so, then the justification for keeping a rule on any particular occasion must be that to keep it will produce good consequences. But in that case, rule-consequentialism collapses into act-consequentialism. If the rule-consequentialist is a genuine consequentialist, and if he or she can persuade the act-consequentialist that the net results of breaking a particular rule will be bad, then the act-consequentialist will agree that it should not be broken. But this only shows that there are cogent *act*-consequentialist reasons against the action in question; the idea of rules drops out as irrelevant. On the other hand, suppose that the rule-consequentialist admits that in some isolated case no harm would result from breaking a rule, but that it still should be kept because adherence to the rule does more good than general non-adherence. The act-consequentialist will then reply that this is no

longer a genuinely consequentialist position, since it advocates
something that cannot be justified by appeal to consequences. Even
if it is agreed that things are better if everyone always keeps the
rule than if no one keeps it, what is *still* better is for the rule to be
kept whenever it is beneficial to do so, and broken whenever it isn't.
This, then, is the point: the act-consequentialist has the resources
to say everything that the rule-consequentialist can correctly say
within a consequentialist framework. Indeed, he or she can even
agree that something like a rough system of rules is beneficial,
since it is clearly absurd to spend all your time calculating the
consequences of each act you are contemplating. But these mostly
beneficial rules cannot be absolute, because it is occasionally clear,
on consideration of consequences, that they should be broken.

In what follows, then, we shall be concerned with act-
consequentialism, since the recommendations of the alternative
are either contained within act-consequentialism, or else do not
constitute a consequentialist position at all.

Acts and omissions

A very important feature of consequentialism is its fundamental
denial of what is known as the act-omission distinction. Because
the ultimate criterion of moral requirement turns on the consequences of the courses we adopt, there can be no intrinsically
significant moral difference between *performing an action* which
results in certain consequences, and causing the same consequences to occur as a result of *omitting to perform* some action.
This, as it stands, needs quite detailed explanation – but consider
these cases first of all.

Imagine you are driving on a deserted country road when you
come across the aftermath of a serious accident that happened a
few minutes earlier (a solitary car hit a tree). It is doubtful that
any other traffic will pass the scene for quite some while, and it
seems that the driver of the crashed car is seriously injured. Your
intervention in getting help may well save her life. You have a
mobile phone and can summon an ambulance, and you can attempt first aid while you wait for it. Unfortunately, however, you
are late for a social appointment, and although you wish the crash

victim well, you decide not to intervene. Is this morally equivalent to harming the victim by your own careless driving, when the results might be identical?

Another example: you have just heard a TV appeal for urgently needed funds to alleviate the results of a natural disaster. Reliable statistics show that individual contributions can make a difference to the number of lives saved, and you are quite well off. You have given to charities in the past, but your son's education is now a pressing concern and you are keeping money aside for the extravagantly costly school he will go to (ten years from now). So you don't give to this appeal. People die who could have been saved with your money. Are you morally culpable? If so, are you as culpable as you would be if you directly act to cause the deaths of an equivalent number of people, say, by sending them poisoned food?

These examples illustrate the appeal of the act-omission distinction. Few people would really consider that in these cases, causing a bad outcome by omission is as bad as causing the same outcome by action – although I suspect that most of us would be much harsher on the driver than on the concerned parent. A tempting thought is that although it is morally praiseworthy to offer help, it is not a requirement. It is *supererogatory*, that is, it goes beyond the call of duty. Indeed, it is hard to imagine the transformation most of us would have to make to our lives if we did regard acts and omissions in such cases as morally equivalent. Empirically this may have an advantage, for the denial of the act-omission distinction is just as consistent with permitting ourselves more actions with bad effects, as it is with permitting ourselves fewer omissions with similar effects! But what are the relevant arguments here?

Problems with the distinction

The consequentialist case is indeed powerful, at least at first glance. Why is it wrong to drive carelessly? Because of danger to oneself and others. What is the danger? Clearly, that of causing death or injury. That is the bad situation we must avoid. But in that case, it is surely irrational to be less harsh on omissions with those outcomes than on acts with precisely the same outcomes.

The outcome is what makes the act wrong, so why doesn't it make the omission equally wrong?

One might uphold the act-omission distinction on the ground that moral responsibility for evils depends upon an agent being the *cause* of such evils. If I harm another by reckless driving, I am the cause of her injury, whereas if I just drive past after she has been injured, then I am not the cause. (After all, she would still have been hurt even if I had never come upon the scene at all).

This answer, unfortunately, is not convincing. Part of the problem is that the term *cause* is here being used in an over-simple way. When we investigate the causes of accidents, we are often just looking for a salient feature – maybe something unusual, or at least something we could reasonably have expected to have been different. Thus, if I could reasonably have been expected to be sober and careful while driving, but I was not, then my careless driving is seen as *the* cause of the accident. But if we broaden the concept of cause to include any condition whose absence would have resulted in a different outcome, then there is no limit to the number of causes we can enumerate: the state of the road, the weather, the alertness of the other driver. Similarly, if the injured driver in our first example dies after I ignore her, it could be true that if I had stopped to help, she would have lived. It is true that I am not the cause of the accident, but I am still able to make a difference to whether or not the accident is sufficient to cause her death.

This observation is strengthened by the fact that omissions can sometimes be intended to have certain outcomes. By withholding the truth from someone, I can intend that she persist in a false belief, to my advantage. By not treating patients, doctors can intend to hasten death. We are surely responsible, at least sometimes, for the consequences of our omissions. This is one reason why consequentialists deny that there is any intrinsic importance to the distinction between acts and omissions.

If the consequentialist is right, most of us should find it disturbing. But is she right? I suggest that she has some genuine insights, but that the overall framework is not rationally compelling.

Let us accept that there are times when omissions with certain bad consequences are morally as blameworthy as acts with the same consequences. There are occasions when deliberately withholding important information is as bad as lying, or when not helping someone in need is as bad as harming him or her actively. This is especially so when such omissions are intended to have these bad results. However, this doesn't mean that there is no intrinsic moral distinction between any set of acts and omissions that produce the same results. What it does show, I think, is something more qualified: that in certain instances where *the wrongness of an act turns on its consequences*, an omission with the same consequences is just as wrong. Obviously some acts are wrong merely on account of their consequences, and one doesn't have to be a consequentialist to accept this. (Don't forget that consequentialists think that the *only* thing that ultimately makes an act right or wrong is its consequences, and sane people can deny this, without thinking consequences never matter). However, it is possible that some acts are wrong for non-consequential reasons. Those who favour deontological (roughly: duty-based) theories of morality say that the wrongness of an act comes from the fact that it is a *lie*, or a *murder*, or an act of *adultery*, rather than from any consequences, or circumstances, of the act. Perhaps this sounds obscure, but the attack on the act–omission distinction has not dealt with this possibility.

Furthermore, even in those cases where consequences are the sole thing that make acts or omissions wrong, there are often sound reasons for coming down more harshly on agents who produce bad outcomes by their acts, than on those who merely omit to prevent these situations. This is because we are often concerned to evaluate agents as well as actions; to judge their character and motives. In general we judge malice to be worse than sloth, and whereas bad acts are often driven by malice, omissions with similar results are more often caused by sloth. The slothful individual may be perfectly easy-going and well-wishing (although shrinks from making any positive contribution to the good). He doesn't mind if others are happy. But the malicious man may well object if others are happy or fulfilled. Unlike the slothful man, the malicious man wants to increase suffering. Thus, bad acts often reflect more badly on the character and motives of the agent, than do bad omissions.

Consequentialists typically recognize that we judge people who commit bad acts more harshly than we judge those whose omissions produce similar results. But they can offer two different responses. One is that although our different judgements are *explained* by invoking motives, this does not *justify* the difference in our judgements. It is still irrational to think like this. Another response would be to accept the moral importance of the difference between malice and sloth, but account for that significance in ultimately consequentialist terms, saying that an energetically malicious person is likely to do more harm than an indolent one: hence, if we must choose, it is better to promote a slothful character over a malicious one. But these responses will not satisfy the non-consequentialist, who thinks that certain states of character, perhaps like certain acts, can have an intrinsic moral significance independently of their consequences.

Intention and foresight

There is another important way in which consequentialist thinking departs from various kinds of opposition. This is in the role given to *intention* in much non-consequentialist moral theory. Many opponents of consequentialism insist that a crucial consideration in determining the morality of an act turns not on its consequences, even if they are foreseen, but on whether its consequences were intended.

Imagine that I enjoy hearing others say derogatory, although amusing, things about mutual acquaintances. However, in order not to gain a reputation as a gossip, which could rebound on me, I always ensure that nothing of this sort is directly attributable to me. Instead, I deliberately provoke others to make these remarks by saying pleasant things about the mutual acquaintances, knowing that I will be amusingly contradicted. The consequence I intend is that others will say entertainingly rude things. On the other hand, imagine that I say the nice things about the acquaintances because I actually believe them, even though I know that I shall provoke the derogatory comments. In both cases the results are the same, and are known to be the same. Is there any moral difference between the two cases?

One difference is in the motive with which I make the kind remarks – in the first case it is malice and in the second kindness.

But another, and here more important, difference is in the *intention* with which I make them.[4] In the first case I intend to provoke nasty comments by disingenuously saying kind things; in the second I do not intend to provoke the nasty comments, even if I know this will result. At first glance, it appears perfectly clear that there is a great moral difference between the cases. But if there is, it doesn't seem to rest in the consequences, since they are exactly the same. This appears, then, to provide a potent counterexample to consequentialism.

The underlying principle the non-consequentialist invokes, in order to explain this moral difference, is known as the *doctrine of double effect*. The foreseen effects of deeds can be divided into those which are intended, and those which are merely foreseen and not intended. According to the doctrine, under certain circumstances it is permissible to perform certain deeds knowing that bad effects will ensue, even though it would always be immoral to perform deeds with the intention that these bad effects should ensue. A straightforward example occurs in discussions of the just conduct of war. According to a tradition known as the "Just War Theory", it is always wrong, in the conduct of a war, deliberately to target non-combatants such as children, those in hospital and prisoners of war. However, under certain circumstances it is permissible to launch attacks, even if you clearly foresee the likelihood of non-combatant casualties. If the enemy has built a hospital in the vicinity of a crucial command centre, then it may be permissible to attack the centre even though the hospital will also be damaged. The important thing is that the damage to the hospital is not intended, either as a means or as an end; what is intended is the destruction of the command centre, which is a perfectly legitimate target in the course of a just war.

Many thinkers side with consequentialists in sneering at this distinction. It is of little comfort to the hurt non-combatants, they point out, that their fate was merely foreseen and not intended. If you know perfectly well what the result of your action will be, how can it matter whether you intend it or not? The doctrine simply allows people to be indifferent to the "merely foreseen" outcomes of their actions. This is in fact a classic objection to the doctrine of double effect. Critics say that its main role has been to manufacture ridiculous justifications of indefensible deeds.

At a high level of abstraction, the doctrine does encounter diffi-cult objections. But many criticisms levelled against it are unjust. Its bad name partly comes from its association with Roman Catho-lic "casuistry" (the application of assumed moral principles to particular cases – a kind of Catholic method of doing applied ethics). Critics thought the doctrine just provided astute people with an excuse to do whatever they wanted to do anyway. How-ever, the fact that the doctrine can be abused does not prove it is unsound.

There is no doubt, of course, that it can be abused. It is abused, for example, when people confuse what is *desired* with what is *intended*, and conclude that as long as they don't actually desire the bad effects of their actions (or take positive pleasure in them), then they are permitted to produce those effects. This is a mistake, because the doctrine is concerned not with what we desire but with what we intend, and we often intend things that we don't posi-tively desire. Another abuse of the doctrine occurs when we con-fuse our intentions with our *ultimate goal*. Thus, we can be misled into thinking that as long as the ultimate goal is a good one, we can use nasty methods to reach it, and pass off these methods as foreseen and not intended. But this is a complete misunderstand-ing of the doctrine – in fact, it takes us in the direction of consequentialism! The important point is that, according to the doctrine, we intend both our ends *and our means*, and certain means may be impermissible even if they lead to valuable ends.

In short, the doctrine of double effect traditionally states that it is morally permissible to knowingly bring about effects that it would be wrong to intend, provided the following conditions are adhered to: (a) the guiding intention of the act must be permissi-ble; (b) the bad effects must not be intended in any way; (c) the bad effects must not be used as a means to the procuring of the good effect; (d) there must be proportionality between the good and bad effects of what is done.

When people try to exploit the doctrine for dubious purposes, they do so by violating at least one of these conditions. Believers in the doctrine of double effect usually think that certain acts are morally prohibited, perhaps in all circumstances; that there are deontological restrictions on certain acts. The doctrine does not itself tell us what these acts might be. But it tries to reconcile the opinion that certain acts are forbidden by their very nature, with the view that in some circumstances it is allowable to do things that produce the same consequences as the forbidden acts.

Advantages of the doctrine

But what can be said in favour of the doctrine? Much of its appeal is intuitive, in that it alone can make sense of certain other intuitions many of us have. In itself this is no proof, of course. Still, one intuition concerns the proper assignment of spheres of responsibility. Can we really be held morally accountable for all that we could, in theory, have made a difference to? To maintain this would, we quickly see, have two undesirable implications. First of all, it would in practice dissolve the notion of moral responsibility altogether. More importantly, it would make nonsense of things most of us treasure, such as personal integrity.

To see the first point, try to suppose that I am accountable not only for what I intend, but for all that I can foresee occurring as a result of what I do. How far into the future must my calculations go? This question is a familiar challenge to the consequentialist, who if consistent maintains not just that immediate results matter but that temporally distant ones do as well. One obvious problem here is of how these consequences can be calculated. But even where reliable probability judgements can be made, there are so many of such consequences that they simply drown the significance of what I specifically intend. To hold me morally responsible for all of these is to ignore the peculiar intimacy that exists between my character (what I am judged for) and my intentions. In particular, to make me responsible for the bad things that others foreseeably do as a direct result of the good things that I do is to dissolve the idea of responsibility altogether. Since the causal network involves such complex interconnections, it turns out that many more people are responsible for specific deeds than we at first thought; the result of assigning responsibility so promiscuously is that no one is really responsible for anything.

This point is made clearer by reference to the concept of integrity. Bernard Williams[5] is particularly noted for framing objections to consequentialism by reference to integrity. In a famous example, he asks us to imagine that a vicious general, Pedro, who is about to execute 20 innocent Indians to deter others from rebelling, offers a chance visitor, Jim, the opportunity to kill one of these Indians himself. If Jim takes up the offer, the general will spare the other 19. Otherwise, all 20 will die.

The consequentialist recommendation, it would seem, would be to take up the offer; after all, it saves 19 people who would otherwise die. But Williams' real objection is that a consequentialist would think that this is *obviously* the right thing to do – whereas if we could excuse or even defend Jim's killing the Indian, it is surely not obvious that this is the right course of action, or the only right course of action. Even more disturbing, in fact, is the thought that if Jim refuses, he does something seriously wrong. Yet if it really is obligatory to kill one innocent person to save the others, then it would seem that if the visitor refuses, and all 20 die, then he shares moral responsibility with the general for their deaths. This is surely incredible. Although Jim foresees that his refusal will result in 20 deaths, surely he is not morally responsible for them. The doctrine of double effect exonerates him. He doesn't intend them to die as a result of his refusal to comply with Pedro; he only foresees this with great distress.

But why should we look to this doctrine to account for his exoneration? One good answer is that by refusing to kill even one man, Jim retains his integrity. If he holds that it is absolutely wrong to deliberately kill innocent people, then he will appeal to the doctrine to justify his non-intervention to save the twenty. Although he can save them, he is not morally responsible for their fate: the general is. Their death is a foreseen but unintended consequence of Jim's refusal to kill the one.

Consequentialism and maximization

It is clear that the doctrine of double effect is unacceptable to consequentialists, because the emphasis on intention is incompatible with the consequentialist emphasis upon outcomes. But the deep reason why consequentialists find the doctrine wrong goes further than this. It is that the doctrine appears tailor made to cope with apparent moral conflicts. Such conflicts often occur when it is impossible to obey one deontological restriction – for example, against killing the innocent – without infringing another one – for example, commanding that you must always save life where possible. The doctrine can seemingly cope with some such cases, since the intrinsically bad outcome that it would be wrong deliberately to produce can be passed off as foreseen but unintended. The consequentialist objection, however, is to the very possibility of this kind of moral conflict. Since we must ask what course will produce the best possible outcome, the only times when there is literally no right answer to a moral question occur when the outcomes of different possible courses of action are simply equal in value. In that case, we do not have a deep conflict – we just have a choice.

According to consequentialists, not only is the doctrine irrational – its assumptions are wrong. There are no interesting kinds of moral conflict. Problems in deliberation arise more from empirical difficulties in predicting outcomes than from being faced with clashes of principles, or moral dilemmas. Thus, there is no need to devise a theory of obligation which exonerates you for some of the foreseen consequences of what you do, since the system of absolute, or nearly absolute restrictions to which it gives rise is wrong in the first place.

Moreover, not only does the consequentialist reject the idea of absolute or nearly absolute moral requirements which do not derive their force from considerations of outcomes. They often claim in addition that even on their own terms, deontological theories are mistaken. This is because they refuse to maximize the values that they themselves claim to endorse.

Agent-relative morality

This can be illustrated as follows. Suppose that Jim, if he refuses to accept Pedro's offer to kill one of the Indians, refuses because he holds that it is wrong in all circumstances to kill innocent people. Very well, says the consequentialist – refuse. But now look at the result. It is not only that 20 people die. It is that the *murder* of 20 innocent people takes place! Even if we don't confine our evaluations only to states of affairs, but include actions among them as well, it is plain that the result of Jim's refusal is that mass murder takes place. No one says that Pedro's killing of the Indians is permissible – no one holds that Jim's refusal actually justifies Pedro's action. So Jim's refusal, based on his conviction that deliberate killing is wrong, actually brings about a *larger amount of the same evil* (i.e. deliberate killing). It seems that to minimize the occurrence of an evil sort of action, Jim should do the decent thing and kill the Indian.

What this brings out is that people who believe in deontological restrictions are not committed to maximizing compliance with these restrictions – or at least, not if maximization would involve any deliberate infringement of them. They are opposed to infringing such principles, even if by so doing, fewer people infringe them overall. This shows that their allegiance is not based on impersonal considerations about how bad it is that someone or other infringes such principles. Rather, the restriction is *agent-relative*: they think: "*I* am forbidden to break them." That is the primary thought.

Is not everyone else also forbidden to break them? Of course. But it is not always my concern that they should not: it is their concern. To call a restriction agent-relative is certainly not to imply that there is some set of principles which applies only to me! That sort of moral solipsism would be a sure sign that something had gone wrong. It is really to do with the ineliminable character of a particular perspective of the agent, which we shall briefly try to make intelligible.

Subjective and objective points of view

A fruitful way of looking at this issue has been proposed by Nagel.[6] He sees the tension between the *agent-neutral* and the *agent-relative* moral outlook as a manifestation of a general tension between subjective and objective viewpoints on reality. Consequentialists try to adopt an objective or perspective-free view of reality, and are hence tempted to make moral judgements in accordance with the overall condition in which our actions leave the world. Any particular agent is only a tiny part of the whole, and if it is necessary to directly intend some intrinsically bad state of affairs in order to increase the overall good, then so be it. It may be necessary for consequentialists to devote all their efforts to producing something intrinsically evil – but we should think of the countervailing benefits.

As Nagel sees, the problem with this approach (which really gets to the root of the problem with consequentialism) is that it is difficult to see why this perspective-free conception of reality is the appropriate one to adopt. It is no less legitimate to concentrate on the point of view of individual agents. The point of view of the universe, or as Nagel calls it the "view from nowhere" is an abstraction: it logically cannot be the view of any actual individual. Yet it is only individuals who can act morally.

Thus, suppose that you are told, after consequentialist calculation, that your proper role in life is to focus on producing some intrinsic evil – say, by informing on your spouse for the secret police – because this will somehow minimize the overall occurrence of this sort of evil. Within your perspective, the intention to hurt someone very close to you will loom large – it will become the centre of your life. Will you not feel that something is wrong here, even if the good overall outcome could somehow be demonstrated (which in practice, it almost certainly couldn't be)? Is it not part of the essence of evil that it should repel? Just why should the perspective of the universe, or the view from nowhere, be the right point of view to adopt?

The separateness of persons

This suggestive thought leads to another, which also gets to the root of what is wrong with consequentialism. This is, as John Rawls puts it, that the theory cannot accommodate the "separateness of persons".[7]

Rawls' remarks actually arise in discussion of the political arrangements one would expect consequentialists to support. But his remarks apply to the purely moral sphere as well. In politics one would expect consequentialists (in the context, utilitarians who want to maximize happiness) to endorse social arrangements that would simply maximize the amount of happiness on a purely disinterested basis, favouring no one over anyone else. Yet this

seems to have the logical result that if some good can be maxi-
mized only by wholly taking it away from a small number of
people, then this should be done. In other words, what matters is
merely the amount of happiness (or other good) in the world; the
distribution is irrelevant. Even though, in Bentham's words, each
is to count for one and no one for more than one, this alone does not
guarantee either distributive or retributive justice.

Now consequentialists, or utilitarians, try to adopt a particular
perspective when they deliberate: the perspective of a hypothetical
figure known as the *impartial benevolent spectator*. In deciding
how to act, we must ask what this spectator would do, having
taken due account of all the preferences involved. But as we have
suggested, this impartial benevolent spectator does not and cannot
occupy the point of view of any real individual. The separate points
of view of actual people cannot be merged into some larger, unitary
perspective – there simply are irreducibly separate individual
points of view. This thought is behind Rawls' criticism of classical
utilitarianism, and it leads crucially to grave difficulties with the
utilitarian conception of justice. It is here that the most pressing
conflicts are to be found between utilitarianism and a great deal of
"common sense morality".

Justice, ends and means

Williams' example of Jim and Pedro should provide a clue to the
problem here. It is made more acute when we consider whether
utilitarians can make sense of desert and of retributive justice
generally. Thus, suppose that as a result of a serious wave of
terrorist crimes, the government and police secretly agree that,
since the terrorist group in question is extremely efficient and
ruthless, and its members very hard to catch, innocent but likely-
looking people should be framed for these crimes. Petty criminals
known to be on the fringes of terrorist circles, and in whose guilt
the public would readily believe, are charged with major crimes
and the evidence rigged. Suppose (what is empirically, perhaps,
implausible) that the public's outrage can be propitiated in this
way, and confidence in successful detection maintained. Should
this course be contemplated?

Of course, many utilitarians will be among the first to say that the case is unrealistic: such a policy would not remain secret, the long term effects on the police and judiciary would be bad, the real criminals would still be at large to commit more crimes. But this does not satisfy the opponent, who thinks that utilitarians are rejecting this course for the wrong kind of reason, allowing themselves to support such a course in principle. But it is the very principle that is wrong – we should not accept that it could *ever* be right to frame the innocent.

For many non-utilitarians, this notorious case illustrates a general feature of utilitarian thinking which we shall look at in some detail in the next chapter. This is that utilitarian, or more generally consequentialist morality is willing to treat rational beings as *mere means to ends*, rather than as – in Immanuel Kant's terminology – "ends in themselves" (see Chapter 4).

This objection underpins both the Pedro case and the innocent prisoner case. Can it ever be legitimate to make use of a person in order to further some end, *without his or her consent*? If Jim kills an Indian in order to save 19, he seems to be making use of the man he kills. He uses his death as a means to saving others. Now, in itself this may be unobjectionable. If one Indian were to offer himself to die in order to save the others (maybe because they include his family) then non-utilitarians might take a different view – unless they object point blank to all deliberate killing of people. But some thinkers object to utilitarianism, not because they believe there are deontological prohibitions on particular kinds of act such as killing or stealing, but because utilitarianism fails to respect people's *autonomy*. If the Indian were to offer his informed consent to be killed, then that might be a different matter. Although his death would be a means to saving others, he would not be treated as a mere means. He would now share with Jim the goal of saving the rest of the Indians. That would be an end he autonomously embraces.

The worry about utilitarian "justice" is closely connected to the Kantian concern not to treat others as mere means. Indeed, it is (I think) highly plausible that the most fundamental requirement of justice is that people should be treated as ends rather than as mere means. Many paradigm examples of injustice, such as exploitation, murder and many deceptions, involve using people in objectionable ways. There may be more to justice than this, and more to morality than justice. But a strong case can be made for holding that justice necessarily respects individuals as ends, and this suggests that at its core, utilitarianism has no defence against the charge of being prepared to tolerate massive injustice.

Concluding remarks: utilitarianism and practical rationality

There are many immediately attractive features of consequentialism. It prescribes courses of action without fear or favour, giving equal weight to the pleasures and suffering of all people, and in many versions, non-human creatures as well. Especially in its hedonistic versions, it values things that almost all of us actually do want, such as happiness or pleasure. It relies on no non-secular authority, and seems to avoid some of the mysterious features of some opposing views, such as the deontologists' obscure insistence that some scts are wrong in themselves or because of their nature. More fundamentally, the theory presents itself as uniquely rational and simple. It appeals, for this reason, to people who think of themselves as hard-headed and practical, interested in results rather than fancy theorizing and spurious scruples. In classical versions it displays a genuine concern with suffering, and unlike some of its rivals sees cruelty as a major vice. It also challenges vested interests in areas where a self-serving moral mentality flourishes. However, it is not persuasive overall. There is no convincing argument for its central claim that only consequences have ultimate importance, and it can, in principle, make moral recommendations that ought to strike the decent person as repugnant. For these reasons, we should look elsewhere for a theory of the right and the good.

Further reading

Bentham, J. *An introduction to the principles of morals and legislation* in J.H. Burns & H.L.A. Hart (eds) (London:

Athlone Press, 1970). The classical statement of a hard-line utilitarianism.

Hare, R.M. *Moral thinking* (Oxford: Clarendon Press, 1981). Clear and useful as a statement of his "two-level utilitarianism", which has not been discussed in this chapter but is an important attempt to reconcile our ordinary decent intuitions about morality, with a utilitarian conception of the basis of morality.

Lyons, D. *Forms and limits of utilitarianism* (Oxford: Clarendon Press, 1965).

Mill, J.S. *Utilitarianism*. In J.S. Mill and J. Bentham, *Utilitarianism and other essays*, A. Ryan (ed.) (Harmondsworth: Penguin, 1987). The most readable and well-known classical exposition and defence of utilitarianism.

Scheffler, S. (ed.) *Consequentialism and its critics* (Oxford: Clarendon Press, 1988). A very useful collection of recent, though tough, articles.

Smart, J.J.C. & B. Williams. *Utilitarianism, for and against* (Cambridge: Cambridge University Press, 1973).

Chapter 4

Kant's ethics

In the last chapter we saw that one of the most important objections made against utilitarianism is that it permits the treating of rational beings as mere means, rather than as ends. A related idea was that it cannot take on board the *separateness of persons*, since it is interested only in producing as much good as possible and is indifferent to how this good is to be distributed among persons. So important do these notions seem to some thinkers that whole new ethical theories can be built up around them. These are what are known as Kantian theories, deriving originally from Immanuel Kant (1724–1804).

Kant's works on ethics are many. His longest such work is the *Critique of practical reason*, which is the second of his three major Critiques. But his most fundamental ideas are found in a much shorter work, the *Groundwork of the metaphysics of morals*. Here, the central themes of his whole ethical approach are introduced and summarized, so effectively in fact that many writers feel this is his most important contribution to ethics. I shall try to show how, in this work alone, Kant succinctly produces an approach to practical reasoning whose ideas can still teach us much, even if there are significant flaws. In particular, I shall try to show the importance of Kant's ideas for the themes of the last two chapters on the objectivity of morality and consequentialism. With respect to the first in particular, there are valuable insights to be gained as to the true nature of the problem.

Kant was a great system builder. His aim was not merely to produce a moral theory that was internally consistent and which accorded with as many ordinary practical intuitions as possible. It was also to put morality on an entirely rational foundation. He tried to discover the a priori basis of morality – that is, a foundation for morality in reason alone, independent of contingent human consensus and the attitudes and desires of actual people. His contribution is thus distinctly in opposition to those theories, current at the time he was writing, which stressed the role of moral sentiment and desire for moral commitment and motivation. For example, contrary to David Hume, who had argued in his *Treatise of human nature* that "Reason is, and ought only to be, the slave of the passions" (D. Hume, 1978: 414), Kant argued that morality and rationality coincided. To be moral is to be rational, to be immoral is to be irrational. The passions may or may not impel us to go against the imperatives of morality, but moral awareness is not a state of desire or inclination.

There is much in Kant's theory that rewards exploration. It is partly for this reason that what is loosely known as Kantian ethics is really a cluster of approaches that broadly owe something to Kant, but which are developed in ways that go beyond anything Kant said. Some theories broadly describable as Kantian are in fact in mutual tension. In this chapter we shall look both at some elements of Kant's doctrine but also at some of these offshoots of it, as the latter have great contemporary importance, especially in the ongoing debate about utilitarianism.

The supreme principle of morality

What is this principle of practical rationality that Kant thinks can be discovered a priori? Kant calls it the *categorical imperative*, and it is formulated in several ways. The initial formulation is known as the Formula of Universal Law, and states that "I ought never to act except in such a way that I can also will that my maxim should become a universal law."[1] A "maxim" here is a subjective principle on which I act. Kant's idea is that an act is morally wrong if I cannot prescribe ("will") that not only I, but everyone else too, should act similarly in the circumstances. I shall not be able to will my maxim as a universal law if I cannot also will the consequences of everyone following it. Thus, to use one of his own examples, if I am wondering whether to obtain a loan by making a false promise of repayment, I must ask myself whether I could will that the principle involved (i.e. that I should escape difficulties by false promising, whenever I am in need) can be willed as a universal law. Kant thinks it cannot be, for:

> by such a law there could properly be no promises at all, since it would be futile to profess a will for future action to others who would not believe my profession or who, if they did so over-hastily, would pay me back in like coin; and consequently my maxim, as soon as it was made a universal law, would be bound to annul itself.[2]

That is, a universal law of lying promises would cause the collapse of the institution of promising – in which case, in turn, there would be no lying promises. The principle that I should make a lying promise thus annuls itself.

Kant produces other examples of maxims annulling themselves, and it is generally agreed that some of them – for instance, one ruling out suicide – are unconvincing. But what is philosophically important is Kant's method. If only a few of his moral injunctions are persuasive, and can be shown by this method, then that is significant. The crucial thing about this method is that, in spite of reference to consequences, it is in no way a consequentialist approach. It is therefore important to separate Kant's *formula of universal law* from other, familiar appeals with a superficial resemblance to it.

One such argument appeals to people in petty authority, and proceeds thus: don't tell lies, ignore gas bills, take free rides (and so on), because once you start doing these things, everyone will start doing them – and where would we be then? (Somewhat better

off! you might retort). This is a straightforward appeal to consequences, and suggests that somehow *my* breaking some rule might
cause *everyone else* to do likewise. But this warning is obviously
ridiculous. Fortunately, it is not Kant's point. Kant doesn't claim
that my making false promises will cause others to do so as well,
and thus cause the breakdown of promising. He is asking rather:
what *would* I be committed to accepting, if I willed false promising
as a universal law? If what I would be committed to would annul
the maxim I was planning to adopt, then I should reject that
maxim. No appeal to likely results is needed for me to know
that I must not make false promises; this rule admits of no exceptions and can be reached independent of observation of the
world.

Closely related to Kant's claim that moral principles can be
worked out a priori is his equally important doctrine that the only
motive to action which can confer moral worth on the agent is the
motive of duty. To be morally praiseworthy we must not only act in
accordance with the moral law – we must do what is right
because it is our duty. If we help others in distress only because
we feel natural sympathy for them, or if we repay our debts only
because others will not trust us again if we do not, then our
actions lack moral worth. Such deeds conform to the moral law,
but are not motivated by it. One who acts merely out of desire or
inclination shows no evidence that he adopts morality as a
motive, and would act rightly even when it went against his
desires.

Many critics say this is absurd, and that it reveals Kant's theory
to be harsh and excessively rigorous, allowing no place for human
feelings. Even if we do not admire the man who repays his debts
only out of self-interest, surely we should admire the one who
helps the stranger because he is distressed by his suffering? Kant's
reply involves a complex background theory of free will and autonomous action, and denies that any action can be free (in the
way required for moral worth) if it arises merely from natural
inclination. People have different temperaments and natural dispositions, and some are by nature or nurture more benevolently
disposed than others. Thus if real moral praiseworthiness depended upon such natural inclinations, then it would seem to
depend upon a kind of luck beyond our control; the luck of being

born with a pleasant nature. This itself raises a very important issue in ethics which we shall look at in more detail later on. But more superficially, Kant can rightly stress that his theory does not condemn feelings of sympathy – in fact, he says they are "beautiful". The point is that they do not confer *moral* worth upon the agent. There is nothing wrong with doing your duty and taking pleasure in it, provided that the motive is still a sense of duty – that is, provided that you would still do it even if you felt no inclination to do so.

The formula of the end in itself

This emphasis on pure practical reason, both as the source of moral principles and the proper motive to follow them, has an implication which takes us to the very heart of Kant's moral outlook. This is formulated thus: "Act so that you treat humanity, whether in your own person or in that of another, never as a means only but always at the same time as an end."[3] This is known as the *formula of the end in itself*, and is another way of stating the *categorical imperative*, or supreme principle of morality. It captures the essence of what, according to latter day Kantians, is wrong with consequentialist ethics. This *formula* absolutely forbids us to treat rational beings as mere instruments to our ends, without respecting the fact that they too have ends. It is ingeniously derived from the claim that reason is the source and motive of morality, because it demands that I respect reason as a motive in all rational beings. I must treat others as embodiments of the moral law, themselves able to formulate and follow the categorical imperative. To treat them as mere means is to use them for ends to which they could not in principle assent.

This is, of course, quite different from treating people as means and ends simultaneously, as we all do in countless everyday situations. In hiring a taxi I employ the driver to get me to where I want, thereby making use of him – but I do not treat him as a *mere* means, since I collude with his own end of making a living by getting people to their destinations. There is nothing wrong with using people as means, in itself. But I must not override another person's autonomous moral deliberation. If I want someone to do something. I must offer him reasons to which he can assent. The offer of payment may constitute such a reason. It may be that by paying him, I treat him as an end. I acknowledge that he is suspending his rational projects in order to serve me. I also furnish him with the means by which he can continue with his rational projects. At all events, I must neither coerce him nor deceive him, for both those actions treat him as a mere means.

A reasonable question, at this point, concerns the relationship of the two versions of the categorical imperative that we have discussed. The first version told us to act in such a way that we could will that everybody else should act likewise; the second stressed that we must always treat others as ends. It is, to say the least, obscure how these two formulations are related. A brief answer is as follows. Creatures who are ends in themselves derive this status from the fact that they are autonomous deliberators, able to act for reasons rather than merely from causes. (For this reason, Kant thinks that animals are not ends in themselves, and that it is absurd to try to treat them as if they were. They can only be treated as means). To treat a person as a mere means is to subvert the principle of autonomous deliberation within him. But it now becomes clear that to will as a universal law that rational beings should be treated as mere means is also to will that *I* should be treated as such – in other words, as a being who is not capable of rational deliberation. But this puts me in the position of rationally willing the destruction of my own capacity of rational deliberation. The maxim thus undermines itself. I cannot rationally will the subversion of rational willing.

The categorical imperative thus stands in obvious contrast to the principle of utility favoured by utilitarians. The fundamental moral principle of Kant is "always treat others as ends", whereas that of utilitarians is "maximize, or at least increase utility". Kant's system gives rise to a number of "deontological constraints", in other words, duties and obligations that are binding in themselves and not in virtue of their results. Admittedly, given the abstract nature of the categorical imperative, there is latitude for dispute over what duties there really are. But utilitarian, or in general consequentialist, morality has no place for deontological constraints. This much should be clear so far.

Freedom and morality

So Kant's theory contrasts with consequentialism at the practical level. But it also contrasts at the purely theoretical level with the Humean account of the source and motive of moral behaviour. We have seen that Hume insisted that the source of moral appreciation is in the passions (feelings, emotions, attitudes) rather than in reason. Hume, indeed, makes two points in clear contrast to Kant: we cannot determine our moral duty by reason alone, and reason alone, unaided by the passions, can never motivate an action. Hume thus offers what may be called a "naturalistic" account of ethical awareness and motivation. What we call the moral features of states are on a continuum with the rest of the natural world – they are not divinely determined or inspired, nor are they located in a realm of pure practical reason, cut off from the world of cause and effect. A simple picture of Hume's basic outlook is summed up in the projectivist picture of values (explained in Chapter 2). The world contains natural states of affairs, with their own causal powers, and some of these produce sentiments in us which we proceed to call moral, and which lead us (if we are philosophically naïve) to posit real moral properties in the world. Deeds done for the sake of others, for example, spring from sympathy, which most of us naturally possess to some degree.

Hume, then, was a thoroughgoing naturalist, but with Kant, the story is complex, ingenious and somewhat ambiguous. Ostensibly, Kant shares a number of the convictions of the eighteenth century Enlightenment of which he and Hume were major figures. For example, he rejects a great deal of natural theology (the attempt to produce rational arguments for God's existence, that do not depend on alleged revelation). He also fiercely denies that divine commands can be the source of the obligation to be moral. (An argument in support of Kant's view on this is expounded in our earlier discussion of the Euthyphro dilemma in Chapter 2). Moreover, he believes in the pervasiveness of cause and effect in the natural world, and counts human passions and inclinations as elements in the causal chain. On the other hand, he thinks that moral motivation is something quite other than the operation of desire, that the content of morality can be known a priori, and that – most importantly – if we are to think of ourselves as capable of moral motivation, we must think of ourselves as possessing a radical kind of free will. None of this fits easily with the naturalistic picture of Hume.

The issue of free will is the central problem here. Kant believes that if I ought to do something, then it follows that I can do it. He has a famous maxim "ought implies can". Morality thus implies freedom, but freedom of a special kind. For Kant, to act freely is both to act according to reason and to be motivated by it. This is in stark contrast to action prompted by desire or inclination. Such action is not free in the sense that interests Kant. Of course, there may be a sense in which desire-prompted action is free – at least in so far as you are not prevented from acting on your desires. But desire is part of the realm of causality, and acts as a causal, rather than a rational, explanation for action. To be genuinely free your actions must be explained in a mysteriously different way.

This insistence underlies Kant's *formula of the end in itself*. To treat another person as a mere means is to subvert his free will or *autonomy*; it is to cease to respect him for what he essentially is, a rational being capable of formulating the moral law for himself and adopting morality as a motive. As we have just seen, another way of putting Kant's point is like this: there would be a contradiction if reason were to permit the undermining of itself, as would happen if we tried to bypass a person's rationality and use him as a mere instrument. This is why such a maxim cannot be willed as a universal law.

Persons – to use the word now in a special, Kantian sense – have a unique worth, precisely because they are able to formulate and act upon the moral law. This is what gives them *dignity*, rather than *price*. An object has a price that corresponds with the value of its use. If it is needed for something important, then it has a high price. But persons are not *for* anything in the way objects are; they may not be used as mere instruments. What about the view of autonomy that underlies this idea? This brings us to one of the most obscure aspects of Kant's moral theory, his theory of free will.

As we saw, Kant occupies an uneasy position between rationalist metaphysics and Humean naturalism. This is especially shown in his theory of free will. One of his difficulties arises because he believes that the empirical world is governed by causal laws. (The details of his argument need not detain us here). Human beings are clearly part of nature, part of the observable world, so it follows that they are also entirely governed according to causal laws as well. In so far as we exist in the natural, empirical world, it is our desires which cause us to act. There would be no problem for Kant if he had said that freedom was just the ability to act unhindered upon our desires, but he emphatically denies this. There is thus a great mystery of how he is able to allow that we have free will of the kind he thinks indispensable if we are to be ends in ourselves.

The two standpoints

His answer is that we are able to view ourselves from two different standpoints. There is the standpoint of the *phenomenal world*, the natural world of cause and effect, the world which is presented to us in sensory experience. There is also the standpoint of the *noumenal world*, a mysterious world of "things-in-themselves", of which – at least, *as* noumenal – we can have no experience. Seen from this standpoint, when we do our duty for duty's sake we are acting with *noumenal freedom*, with our actions not causally explained but rationally justified. The distinction between the noumenal and the phenomenal world plays a large part in his theory of knowledge as well. He claims, roughly speaking, that appearances (phenomena) are all that we can experience, but that we must postulate a world of noumena, or things-in-themselves apart from appearance, of which we can say nothing except that we must postulate it. This is not, it should be noted, literally *another* world – it is the same world considered from a different standpoint. This notorious distinction is carried into his moral theory. As phenomenal beings, we are causally governed, but we must postulate a noumenal aspect to ourselves, which we cannot understand except from a practical point of view. That is, the fact that we deliberate morally forces us to accept that we are noumenal as well as phenomenal beings, but beyond that, all is silence.

It is probably fair to say two things of this theory: one is that it is a brilliant attempt to make sense of our most sophisticated intuitions about morality and freedom, the other is that, almost by its own admission, the theory is incredible. Two difficulties stand out in particular. The first is that we are given no idea of how the deliberations in the noumenal realm (or in the self, conceived as a noumenal entity) can produce any effects in the phenomenal world – which after all is what our deliberations are meant to do. If the relation is not causal, then what is it? How can a reason for action produce any effect unless it is also a cause? Or perhaps it doesn't produce effects – in which case, how can we attribute changes in the phenomenal world to agents? The other objection is that this idea of the dual standpoint is itself obscure, and threatens to yield contradictions. To say that an action is, as phenomenal occurrence, *caused*, but as noumenal occurrence, is *not* caused, seems to imply that it is both caused and not caused, which is contradictory.

A sophisticated attempt to get round this might suggest that all talk of causes must be relative to a certain description – for instance, to events or actions described in physical terms – and that the Kantian idea of the dual standpoint only claims that human actions are causally determined *to the extent* that they are phenomenal events. There are other valid ways of describing them which do not invoke causally relevant properties, but this does not imply that the same events are both caused and uncaused. The idea is that the causal relations hold between actions and their antecedents in virtue of their being phenomenal events, rather than in virtue of their being noumenal deliberations. (Compare: the asteroid makes a crater of a certain depth in virtue of its mass and volume, and not in virtue of its colour. But this does not make the asteroid both causally efficacious and *not* causally efficacious. One and the same object has both a certain mass and a certain colour, but it is in virtue of its mass alone that it makes the crater). Perhaps, then, one occurrence – say, a moral deliberation – is caused in virtue of its phenomenal properties, but not in virtue of its noumenal ones. To pursue this further would take us into difficult issues in the philosophy of mind. It is enough to say that this move will not get us out of the problem. For to say this of what comes before an action is to say that its phenomenal (perhaps physical) features are sufficient to produce the action. In that case, it becomes unclear how Kant's noumenal self and its deliberations gain a foothold in the world at all. Can we really say, given the sufficiency of phenomenal causes to bring about the action, that the action would have occurred differently if only different noumenal deliberations had taken place? It seems that we cannot say this, in which case Kant's theory of the dual standpoint remains in difficulty. At best, the noumenal self shadow-boxes the phenomenal self, but has no explanatory power.

The good will

Nevertheless, the idea that moral principles must be formulated and adopted in a noumenal realm, apart from causes, is still pivotal to Kant's theory, and to some highly attractive normative conclusions he supports with it. We have looked at one such, namely the *formula of the end in itself*. There is another view Kant holds as well, which we should now look at.

At the very beginning of the *Groundwork*, Kant famously asserts that only one thing is able to be good in itself, without qualification, and that is the "good will":

> Intelligence, wit, judgement and any other *talents* of the mind we may care to name, or courage, resolution or constancy of purpose, as qualities of *temperament*, are without doubt good and desirable in many respects; but they can also be extremely bad and hurtful when the will is not good which has to make use of these gifts of nature . . .

Qualities of temperament, such as moderation and coolness, often help us do our duty and are part of the make-up of admirable people – but they can sometimes be put to bad use. A "scoundrel" may be all the more effective in his misdeeds, and therefore all the more objectionable a character, if he is also "cool". Thus coolness is not good *without qualification*. This is Kant's way of saying that whether it is good depends on other circumstances. Such, however, is not the case with the good will, with willing to do one's duty for duty's sake. No external circumstance can deprive this of its moral value. Even if it fails to achieve its intended effects, its value remains unassailable.

We seem to have an idea of what Kant means, since similar thoughts are part of the moral assumptions of most of us. Claims like "we mustn't blame her, since at least she did her best" capture the flavour of the idea. "The thought is what matters" and "the intention is what counts" again, however loosely, are Kantian thoughts. But some clarification is required. To start with, Kant says that certain things normally thought virtuous, like temperance or courage, can sometimes come to the service of mischief (the apparently courageous terrorist might be a modern example). But we might answer that the good will can sometimes lead to disastrous results as well. You can try to bring about some good, yet fail and bring about something undesirable instead. Why not conclude that the good will is therefore not good without qualification? Maybe, to put it differently, we should sternly say "it isn't enough to try, if you want to win moral praise. You must succeed as well."

Kant's explanation for the difference (even if it is not a successful defence) is that only practical reason is ultimately action-guiding, although its operation can be facilitated by traits of character such as courage. Action is explicable in terms of maxims, or principles – that is what makes it intelligible, rather than just causally explicable. Thus when we want to assess an agent's worth when he performs some deed, we try to identify the guiding maxim. Indeed, only thus is the deed traceable to agency. But it is clear that a good maxim can fail to produce the intended effect, if factors outside the agent's control get in the way. Non-culpable factual error, as well as sheer bad luck, can turn a good intention into a bad effect. But Kant says – and surely this does accord with a well-grounded intuition – that when this happens, the agent is not to be blamed.

> Even if, by some special disfavour of destiny or by the niggardly endowment of a step-motherly nature, this will is entirely lacking in power to bring about its intentions; if by its utmost effort it still accomplishes nothing, and only good will is left ... even then it would still shine like a jewel for its own sake as something which has full value in itself.[4]

The good will and moral luck

This brings us to a concept which has recently generated interesting discussion. It is that of moral luck. We can be lucky in all kinds of ways – in our parents, education, talents and income. But can we be morally lucky? Or is it a necessary truth that our *moral* praiseworthiness or blameworthiness cannot be determined by luck?

Kant firmly denies the existence of moral luck (though he does not use the term). The seat of moral worth is in the will; if the will is good, then the agent is good – and the goodness of a good will cannot be taken away by external circumstances. This is connected, it is clear, with the doctrine of the noumenal self; seen as apart from the unstable world of empirical causes and effects, it is immune to the assaults of chance. But what is moral luck? Is Kant right to reject the notion?

Two kinds of case suggest the existence of moral luck. One kind seems to show that actions are justified by their *actual*, rather than intended results. The other kind suggests that the proper judgement of a person's moral character is determined by factors which are significantly (though not completely) beyond his or her control.

The point of the first formulation, then, is that it is the *actual* results that matter morally, even when these are not the intended ones. Suppose there is an armed insurgency aimed at getting rid of a bad political system. On this account of moral luck, the justification for the insurgency depends, partly at least, upon whether it actually achieves its aim without costs comparable to the evil it seeks to destroy. If it does, then we should judge it more favourably than if it just increases human suffering without achieving its primary aim. In fact, whatever our theoretical positions, this is how many of us do think of these things: many people think the nuclear bombing of Japan in 1945, involving the deliberate killing of about 100,000 non-combatants, was morally justified because it actually caused the Japanese to surrender. If they had not surrendered, many people's moral judgement of the deed would have been different. It cannot be stressed too much that this is not just a psychological remark. We are not merely saying that people look favourably upon things that happen to produce good effects, even

103

though there was considerable risk when they were done.[5] Rather, such people believe that whether the deed was *morally* justified can only be determined later, by seeing what actually happened. It is in this sense that the Allies in August 1945 are said to have been morally lucky: it turned out (was a matter of luck) that they had done the *morally* right thing.

The other example of moral luck concerns the idea that people's moral blameworthiness or praiseworthiness can depend upon what actually follows as a result of something they do, or omit to do. This is clearly linked with the first example, but this time stresses the role of luck in the assessment of agents. Here it seems that moral luck is extensively written both into popular attitudes and into the law. Thus – mistakenly according to a Kantian – those who murder are thought worse than those who attempt murder but fail, and those whose negligence leads to accidents are blamed far more than those whose equivalent negligence happens not to cause an accident.

An example: a ferry disaster

An excellent example is the *Herald of Free Enterprise* disaster at Zeebrugge in 1987. This passenger ferry turned on its side shortly after leaving the port, and most people on board were drowned. When it was discovered that its bow doors had been open when it set sail, allowing water into the car deck, scapegoats were naturally sought. Eventually the company that owned the ferry was found guilty of corporate manslaughter for negligently allowing the doors to be left open. Yet this was no doubt only one of countless occasions when ships have set sail with doors left open. Nobody would attach much moral blame to those who act with equal negligence, but whose negligence does not cause disasters. It looks as though the ferry firm was just morally unlucky on this occasion.

However, upon reflection, this presents some mysteries. Why are you so much more to blame if your negligence happens to cause a disaster than if it doesn't? For surely, what you have done, or omitted, is exactly the same in both cases. It just happens, due to circumstances directly beyond your control, that in one case you causally contributed to an accident and in the other case you didn't. Now, someone will of course retort what you did in each case was *not* the same – in one case you caused a terrible disaster, and in the other you didn't. In defence, you might say that the only thing you did was leave the bow doors open – even though this caused the disaster, you did not bring about the causal connection between your original omission and the disaster. That is, although your omitting to close the doors caused the ship to sink, sinking the ship is only very misleadingly described as something you actually did – at least for the purposes of moral evaluation.

This is really the heart of the problem. How are our actions (or omissions) to be separated from what results from them? What is this core of action for which we are responsible, and how is it to be cut off non-arbitrarily from the actual consequences? Kant's solution is radical. For him, all moral worth arises from an inner condition of the will, which can retain its worth or corruption even if it doesn't achieve its aims. But upon reflection it is hard to separate this inner state of will from all the contingencies surrounding it. Kant's appeal is to a rational faculty whose deliberations (when conducted according to the moral law) is immune from the effects of causes or contingent conditions. Are we really left with anything at all, once such contingent, empirical conditions have been removed? Does not the good will of Kant's system turn out merely to be nothing at all?

This vexing problem can be solved only by carefully distinguishing the different forms that moral luck is supposed to take. I suggest that there is enough truth in Kant's theory to justify rejecting some forms of moral luck, but we probably cannot eliminate the notion of moral luck altogether.

How should we determine our moral status, after we have done some particular deed? The Kantian idea is to strip away all the attendant and subsequent conditions over which we had no direct control, and investigate the maxims, which of course include what we intended to achieve by the act. What if the maxims themselves (or more prosaically, our intentions and values) are determined by external factors? How then are we supposed to discover the "real" person?

Another example: the Greek junta

The following example illustrates the point above. In Greece, in 1967, there was a military coup followed by seven years of government by an incompetent, but ruthless junta. Like most such governments, its power was maintained by the widespread use of torture. The recruitment of the torturers, however, was subtle. Youths were chosen from within the regular army and subjected to several months of brutal training, during which they were badly roughed up and humiliated. However, at the end of this period they were suddenly treated with respect, given uniforms and told that they were now the security police. They now had the job of torturing and murdering others, which they all did. When the junta collapsed, many of these men were arrested. A few repented, but most did not. It seemed that they had committed dreadful acts and that they should be punished. They had not been recruited because they were already particularly brutal – in fact, repressive régimes usually avoid recruiting naturally sadistic people. If they had not been recruited, they would probably not have turned out the way they did, whereas if others had been recruited, most of them would have turned out the same way. Is it fair, then, to attach moral blame to them, if we know that we ourselves would probably become like them under the same conditions?

This is the problem of moral luck at its most intractable. On the one hand, it was not the fault of the recruits that they were selected for this training, and there is no reason to think they were originally worse than anyone else. On the other hand, if we cannot form moral judgements about them, given their circumstances, how else will we formulate a just moral assessment? Will we not end up having to take into account their childhood, their schooling, early experiences, country of origin and perhaps inherited dispositions? If we carry on down this road, will we not end up stripping away everything that makes them the people that they are? In which case, whom exactly are we judging?

You might protest that these people still had free will, and that whatever the *influences* on them, each was still able to choose not to become a torturer. Even if most people in their circumstances do end up committing brutal acts, there are always a few who do not. This is an important point, but its significance is not quite what those who make it think it is. The problem with simply saying that it is possible to stand firm, even if most people do not, is that it suggests that the people who do end up committing brutal deeds should be judged by the rest of us, according to a standard that the rest of us are very unlikely to measure up to ourselves. If most people (by definition) are not exceptional, this is as true of the judges as of the judged. On the other hand, the point about free will is still important, because it is only on the supposition that those being judged are rational agents, who cannot fail to make decisions, that we adopt moral attitudes towards them at all. (We do not adopt these attitudes towards animals.) Thus it seems, in cases like this, that we have to accept that luck cannot make the moral assessment of agents illegitimate – not, at least, if we are to continue with the vast bulk of our everyday moral judgements. The likely alternative is that if we continue discounting circumstances which contributed to making them what they are, we shall not end up with a revelation of their "real" nature – we shall just end up with nothing at all.

There is, on the other hand, a type of moral luck which really does present serious problems. Think again of the ferry at Zeebrugge; does it not seem unfair that companies or individuals be prosecuted when the consequences of negligence are disastrous, but not when there are not? Are you a worse person, just because your negligence happened to lead to something appalling? It is cases like these that bring out the full force of Kant's position. There are many practical reasons for not treating people the same, whatever the consequences of their mistakes or negligence, but there may be no good moral reasons. From a practical point of view, if we tried to hold people responsible for all that *might* have resulted from their mistakes, there would be no end to the list of accusations – and few of us would manage to exculpate ourselves. Most drivers, for instance, make mistakes of the kind that can cause serious accidents in unlucky circumstances, yet for them to remember them all and feel guilty about them, as if they had caused people's deaths, would soon lead to conscience-fatigue. Rather, to feel guilty about something you have brought about, there must precisely be something you *have* brought about, so that your feelings of horror about the situation can translate themselves into the pain of guilt. There still seems something

107

unsatisfactory about attaching more blame to a bad driver who causes a casualty than to one who does not. Here is where a belief in moral luck really does appear misplaced, and Kant's basic idea is correct.

Kant and the objectivity of moral judgement

It is here that it is worth pausing to consider some of the metaethical aspects of Kant's ethical theory. Strictly speaking it is difficult to separate the normative and the metaethical elements in the theory, as it is a seamless web with mutually dependent parts. But we find in his ideas some interesting materials with which to approach the thorny matters we investigated in Chapter 2 concerning the objectivity of moral judgement.

Those who maintain that moral questions have objective answers want to say, roughly, that our best moral judgements are guided by something external to themselves, and that practical reason, like theoretical reason, should aim for truth or at least something analogous to truth. Naïvely, they want to say that utterances like "it is wrong to exploit people as mere means to your ends" are true, much as the utterance "the south pole is in Antarctica" is true. But beyond this very general commitment, as we noted, there are difficulties in formulating the issue uncontroversially. Moral realists maintain that there are moral facts, and that moral utterances like the one given above can be true in virtue of reporting such facts. According to some realists, these moral facts are about the existence of moral properties, whether these be construed as properties of being *good* and *evil* or, in a naturalistic vein, as virtues (like courage, industriousness, kindness). Not all moral objectivists want to call themselves moral realists in *that* sense, and to understand their point it is helpful to turn to Kant. This, perhaps, will illuminate some quite difficult ideas we discussed in Chapter 2.

Kant is adamant that we do not come by moral requirements through perception, or through the passions. The idea held by some recent moral realists, that moral awareness is somehow like perception, is contrary to Kant's view. Also opposed to it is the Humean, naturalistic account of how we get our moral commitments. We cannot verify experimentally that some action is bad. Goodness and badness, rightness and wrongness are not features of the world that can appear in any explanatory hypotheses purporting to account for moral appearances. In much the same way, freedom is not something whose reality can be established by observation of the world, for the universality of causal laws must be presupposed if anything is to be observed at all (Kant argues for this conclusion in his *Critique of pure reason*). However, both freedom and morality must be presupposed if we are to make sense of ourselves as agents. We cannot fail to see ourselves as agents who have to make choices, and many such choices can be made intelligible only by invoking justifying reasons, rather than causes. Of course, many of our choices are just explained by desires, combined with beliefs about how to satisfy them. Kant's great claim is that practical reason is not exclusively like this – there are categorical reasons for action whose binding character is borne upon us simply because we are rational beings. Morality is objective, in the sense that it makes rationally inescapable demands which do not depend for their validity upon desires or opinions that people just happen to have. Awareness of the moral law is inseparable from our rationality. Reason and morality coincide, and immoral action is contrary to reason.

The point is obscure, and many philosophers question the alleged distinction between moral realism and moral objectivism. The distinction, in fact, is reflected in Kant's theory of knowledge, in which he distinguishes *objectively real appearances* from noumena (thing-in-themselves). If we are just trying to make some sense of it, the analogy with Kant's view of freedom is helpful. As an agent, I cannot but think of myself as free and able to determine my actions by my rationally worked out maxims. Given this, I cannot but see my maxims and actions as guided by categorically valid requirements: the question "what ought I to do?" is forced upon me as a precondition of being an agent at all. For Kant, freedom and the moral law must thus be seen as presuppositions, or standpoints which cannot be independently justified, but are nevertheless inseparable from our view of ourselves as agents. It is thus not in the empirical world that we find evidence of the moral law, but in reason, which yields us the categorical imperative. This is really Kant's fundamental claim about the nature of ethical reality; the fundamental normative claim he gets from it, as we have seen, is the *formula of the end in itself.*

The significance of Kant's ethics

We have seen much that is attractive in the ethical theory of Kant, as well as much that is implausible and overstretched. One of the merits of Kant's ethics is not so much that it finds correct solutions to the problems it discovers, but that it is unusually perceptive of what the problems are. There is a fundamental problem about free will (which we shall discuss in Chapter 6), namely, how can a world governed by causality also contain genuinely responsible agents? Kant sees this problem, but also perceptively suggests that it is really a difficulty of reconciling two different standpoints on one world. That he ends up with no plausible solution does not take away from his insight into the problem. Another historically important feature of Kant's theory is that it combines the thinking of the Enlightenment with an unyieldingly rigorous moral code. He holds that religion cannot be the logical basis of ethics – yet the secular ethic he embraces has all the strictness of a typically religious ethic. (It was this feature of the system that led the German philosopher Nietzsche, a century later, to call Kant a "catastrophic spider", presumable on account of the systematized complexity of the intellectual web he had spun.) Yet another reason for studying Kant is his ingenious attempt to reconcile the autonomy of the genuinely moral agent, with the objectivity of the law he autonomously embraces. Intuitively, we might at first think that to be autonomous – that is, self-ruled – our morality must be "up to us" in some way that detracts from its rigour; or that moral truth must be subjective. Not so for Kant, for autonomy is rule by reason (rather than desire), and rule by reason entails the free adoption of objectively valid moral principles.

The ethics of Kant has given rise to a cluster of approaches to ethics that have been broadly labelled Kantian. Important Kantian themes such as autonomy, deontological ethics (based on concepts of duty rather than the quality of outcomes), and the dignity of the rational person are to be found in these approaches. One set of approaches is labelled contractualist (or contractarian), and its main idea is that morality is that set of principles to which rational beings could all freely agree. It is to these ideas that we now turn.

Further reading

Hume, D. *A treatise of human nature* (1739–40) L.A. Selby-Bigge (ed.) (Oxford: Clarendon Press, 1978).

Kant, I. *Groundwork of the metaphysic of morals* (London: Harper and Row, 1964). Translated and analysed by H.J. Paton. Also published under the title *The moral law* in the Philosophy series of the Hutchinson Library.

Kant, I. *Critique of practical reason* (Indianapolis, IN: Bobbs-Merrill, 1977). Translated by L.W. Beck.

Kant, I. *Critique of pure reason* (1781), translated by N.K. Smith (London: Macmillan, 1929).

Nagel, T. Moral luck, In *Free will*, G. Watson (ed.) (Oxford: Oxford University Press, 1982) pp. 174–86. A clear and searching essay on moral luck, partly in reply to an essay on the same theme by Bernard Williams (see below).

O'Neill, O. *Constructions of reason: explorations of Kant's practical philosophy* (Cambridge: Cambridge University Press, 1989).

Paton, H. *The categorical imperative* (London: Hutchinson & Co, 1947).

Scruton, R. *Kant* (Oxford: Oxford University Press, Past Masters series, 1982), Chapter 5. This book lucidly explains other aspects of Kant's philosophy as well as his ethics, and thus helps to make his ethical doctrine more intelligible.

Spinoza, B. *Ethics* (1677) trans. A. Boyle in Everyman Library no. 481 (London: Dent, 1910, 1959, 1963). This work of the famous seventeenth century philosopher provides a useful comparison with Kant's ethics and helps to place Kant in a historical perspective, rather than as an isolated figure in the history of ethics.

Williams, B. Moral luck. In Williams, B. *Moral Luck* (Cambridge: Cambridge University Press, 1981).

Chapter 5

Contractualism

Amid all the obscurities of Kant's ethical theory, one intriguing idea stands out. This is that a *supreme principle of morality* can be worked out a priori, which dictates that rational beings must always be treated as ends in themselves. It is not wrong, according to Kant, to use rational beings as means to our ends, provided that we do not treat them as mere means, by coercing or manipulating them into courses of action to which they could not in principle consent. This principle can be known a priori precisely because to reject it would involve subverting the capacity for autonomous (i.e. moral) action in another person. No *moral* maxim can ever prescribe the subversion of *moral* deliberation in another agent.

This formulation of the categorical imperative is possibly Kant's most valuable contribution to normative ethics. It has a ring of truth, even if other details of his theory are open to question. It also plays an important background role in another cluster of theories that we shall proceed to examine. These are contractualist (sometimes known as contractarian, or social contract) theories. Contractualism gained influence in the late seventeenth and eighteenth centuries and is associated in particular with Thomas Hobbes[1] and Jean-Jacques Rousseau[2], although the germ of the idea is found in Plato[3]. The general idea is that morality is devised by rational beings for mutual advantage. It is to be seen in terms of an agreement between people, which they enter into because they have more to gain from doing so than by not doing so. Modern contractualists sometimes contrast their theory with "intuitionism" and moral objectivism, and offer their own theory as the only possible basis for moral commitments. These same philosophers also deny that there are any intrinsically action-guiding properties in the world (here they agree with Mackie's moral scepticism). Rather, moral judgements and practical decisions have, in their opinion, a much more intelligible basis. It is this that we shall discuss below.

Hypothetical contracts and moral obligations

The idea of a contract poses no particular difficulties. In law, a contract is an agreement freely entered into by at least two parties, each of whom hopes to derive a net gain from complying with it, provided the other also complies. Agreements are not always written or explicitly stated. It is more usual for the contractual nature of certain transactions to be simply assumed. I go to a restaurant because I prefer to eat out than to cook at home, and the restaurant charges me for the meal. I consider it a net gain for me to eat out and pay; I prefer this to not eating out and not paying. The restaurant owner, similarly, is more than happy (unless he is in eastern Europe during the communist period) to provide a meal on the understanding that he is paid. I take my place on the tacit understanding that I shall pay at the end, and both of us are content.

Contractualism in ethics sees moral obligation as founded in agreement, but with an important qualification. For, unlike in the restaurant, where the parties are aware of the implicit agreement, contractualists do not claim there ever *was* an agreement entered into by moral agents. (And they can see that even if there had once been an agreement, it would still need to be constantly renewed by successive generations). However, according to the contractualist this is not fatal to the theory. For the content of morality is determined by what rational people *could* agree to, because it works to their mutual advantage. Ordinary, explicit contracts are meant to produce both benefits and burdens for each contracting party. In the restaurant case, the benefit I gain is the meal and the burden is that I have to pay. Morality, too, distributes benefits and burdens to us all, but we can agree to abide by it precisely because all parties to the moral system have more to gain from it than to lose.

Consider these brief illustrations. We might want to know why morality forbids theft or murder, to take relatively uncontroversial examples. The answer is that we all have more to gain from a rule prohibiting these things than from the absence of such a rule. The restriction on my freedom to steal or kill is amply compensated by the fact that others are forbidden to steal from me or kill me; it is a burden that I am more than willing to shoulder, in return for the benefit of security for me and my possessions. The same, if to a more limited extent, goes for co-operative exercises. I may have more to gain from offering my particular skills for the benefit of others, on the understanding that they do for me what I cannot do for myself, than from a set-up where no one helps anyone else. The gain for me again outweighs the loss.

This is a plausible, orderly and rational theory on first consideration. But for many critics, it has some disturbing implications. For although it provides grounds for the intuitions of everyday morality under certain circumstances, it seems sharply to diverge from them under other circumstances. Its assumption appears to be that "opting in" to morality makes sense from a self-interested point of view, because you are compensated by the fact that others have opted in as well. But suppose that you are self-sufficient, intelligent and strong enough not to need the help or the restraint of others? Why then should you concern yourself with the rules in question? This is a challenge to which the social contract theory will need to respond, although different answers are given by different kinds of contractualist.

Hobbes and the state of nature

The social contract theory, as we have presented it, claims that the demands of morality are such that self-interested people could agree to obey them, provided that others do so as well. It thus tries to answer that most embarrassing question of moral philosophy, "Why should I be moral?" But so far it has made no mention of categorical moral requirements, of the importance of treating others as ends in themselves, or of natural sympathy. Neither has it mentioned any divine law, or natural law, or objective rights or duties. This presents a bare and grim account of the basis of moral obligation. But pre-theoretical unattractiveness does not provide a refutation of it, and we shall need to examine the idea on its merits.

The theory of Thomas Hobbes (1588–1679) provides the basis for it. Writing after the tumult of the English Civil War, which marked the end of monarchical rule by divine right, he was concerned to furnish an ultimate philosophical justification of political power in the absence of such a theory. His writings also offer a rational basis for compliance with morality. Although he believed that the moral law was in fact issued by God, he offers a secular basis for it as well.

Start from the idea of the *state of nature*. This is a philosophical fiction which refers to a pre-political condition of mankind, in which there are no laws, no government and no accepted social rules. Everyone can do as he or she pleases. There are no sanctions or police or courts. For Hobbes (who was perhaps thinking of the mayhem of civil war), this situation is dire. Scarcity of natural resources leads to conflict, since people's needs are equal and everyone tries to grab the scarce resources for himself and his family. Moreover, altruism and sympathy are limited; people naturally care for themselves and those close to them, but have little concern for others. As he points out in the *Leviathan*, the sorry result of all this is a constant war of each against all. There is "continual fear, and danger of violent death, and the life of man, solitary, poor, nasty, brutish, and short".

One cause of the constant conflict in the Hobbesian state of nature is the approximate *equality of strength* of human beings. This is an important fact that explains the need for agreements between them. In an insecure and dangerous world, where fear and selfishness rule men's hearts and vital resources are limited, there is fertile ground for competition and bloody conflict. If men have roughly the same degree of strength (some compensating with wits for what they lack in brawn) and if self-interest is a dominant motive in all of them, then everyone will feel insecure: even when they have acquired what they need, they will have to protect it from theft. Even those who have been successful in their quest for dominance will feel insecure, and will watch out for other strong and cunning people.

The only way out of this sorry state of affairs is by having enforceable agreements of non-violence and respect for posses-sions. Two equally powerful and resourceful people each have something to gain from agreeing to leave the other alone, provided the other does the same. This, then, is the tough-minded implica-tion of the Hobbesian picture. It is only on the assumption that enough men are approximately equal in strength that morality gets off the ground at all. The need to escape the state of nature creates a reason to form agreements only with people of roughly equal power. There is no need to bargain with signifi-cantly weaker people, since you can get what you want from them without needing to enter agreements with them. Neither is there any point in trying to bargain with significantly stronger people, since they can get what they want without needing to give any-thing up.

The Hobbesian solution is for all to agree to be governed by an absolute ruler, who enforces agreements between the rest of us. Only by giving absolute power to the ruler do we relieve ourselves of the need to be continuously vigilant in case we are harmed or cheated. Hobbes' primary consideration, we should bear in mind, was political. He was trying to find a basis for political obligation towards a ruler or state, following the end of absolute monarchy in England after the execution of Charles I. To have such a ruler, according to Hobbes, was to the advantage of the strong, for it would spare them the worry, if they ever entered into agreements with their rivals, that their rivals would renege on such agree-ments whenever they could get away with it. The absolute ruler would preserve peace, which is to everyone's advantage. However, the importance of Hobbes' theory, as we have indicated all along, is not only political. It suggests that a rational basis for the observance of moral constraints can be found in self-interest.

The contractualism of Gauthier

In our own day, the Hobbesian contractualist tradition has been taken up by David Gauthier. In various works, in particular *Morals by Agreement*,[4] Gauthier argues that a contractualist approach is the only theory that can provide us with genuine reasons for action. He thinks that morality is in a "foundational crisis", because we no longer accept that there are objective values, or objective justifications for moral constraints. To a certain extent, moral behaviour coincides with our natural sympathies, but these are limited and will not get us very far. Morality presents us with constraints – it tells us to do or not do certain things. But what grounds can be offered for the constraints urged upon us by morality?

According to Gauthier, it is senseless to think that there can be genuine reasons for action that make no ultimate reference to the desires or interests of the agent. At the same time, morality does impose real restrictions on our pursuit of our desires. Can morality, then, offer us any genuine reasons for action? It might seem not, but in fact it can. The reason for this echoes Hobbes' idea: that it is better for each person that *everyone* (including him or her) should follow certain restrictions, than that *nobody* (or few people) should follow these restrictions. The important point is that if I try to evade some restriction on me, for example, if I try to steal another's car, I am unlikely to be the only one behaving like this. I might get my car stolen. Of course, if I were the only person to flout the restrictions, then things might be fine for me. But we need to take the *choices of others* into account when we work out what courses of action are good for us.

The prisoners' dilemma

A classic way of putting this point comes in a notorious puzzle known as the *prisoners' dilemma*. I shall borrow from the account given by J.L. Mackie[5], which has been adapted from its usual form in order to make it easier to follow. Suppose that two guards have been assigned to protect a military post against oncoming enemy fire. Each fears for his life, and would much rather run away (imagine that the military ethic of courage and solidarity leaves them unimpressed since they are unwilling conscripts). Now imagine that each guard reasons as follows: "Either my comrade will stay put, or he will run away. If he stays put, he will provide protection for me against enemy fire if I run away. If he runs away, then I shall be a real fool staying put, since I shall be all the more vulnerable to enemy fire. So whatever my comrade does, I had better run away." Now this reasoning seems to be dictated by self-interest. The problem, however, is that the other soldier is thinking exactly the same thing. The result is that both run away, and each ends up with a *worse chance of survival* than he would have had if they had both stayed at the post.

The lesson is clear: you are better off individually if everyone keeps agreements than if everyone defects. But what makes it seem a dilemma is that if you decide to keep trust, others might still take advantage of you. The best outcome for you individually (and remember, you are assumed to be entirely self-interested) is one where *others* co-operate and *you* defect. It is always going to seem rational to renege on agreements once the compliance of others has been irreversibly secured. Now a society might get round this just by drilling a habit of co-operation into its members. But this seems tantamount to brainwashing, since no real argument is produced, at least as far as completely self-interested people are concerned. Can a real argument for compliance with agreements be found?

Gauthier thinks such an argument is available. It is true that there is a short-term advantage to be had in breaking agreements unexpectedly once the compliance of others has been obtained. But if people know that you are like that, they will stop entering into agreements with you. That is, the long-term benefits of co-operation are only available to those disposed to keep trust. You also get more opportunities for beneficial co-operation if you sometimes forego short-term gain. You become a welcome partner in joint activity.

There are more details in this theory, and we have skated over some of them. But one further remark is worth making, which foreshadows our later discussion of the virtues (Chapter 7). This is that although, for contractualists, compliance can be ultimately justified in terms of self-interest, such compliance will be easier if you are not always trying to calculate what is to you personal advantage. Rather, it should become second nature. Once it has done so, we can say that you possess a *virtue* – the virtue of justice. That is, you have a standing disposition to keep trust. We shall see later how it is argued that those with virtues do better out of life than those without them.

Kantian contractualism

The Hobbesian contractualist theory is pessimistic and tough-minded. It is pessimistic in that it portrays the pre-moral state of nature as full of fear, pain and violence. It is tough-minded, in that it is not based on any prior idea of the equality of human *worth*. It is, on the contrary, equality of *strength* that brings about the need for an agreement to be ruled. It is mainly in this respect that it differs from another type of theory, sometimes known as Kantian contractualism. As so often happens when these theories are named, there is only a loose connection with the figure after whom they are named. But there are enough affinities between this version of contractualism and the central elements of Kant's moral theory to justify the label.

We have seen that the crucial feature of Kant's theory of obligation centres around respect for persons, based on the fact that persons (in this special, Kantian sense) are ends in themselves. Humanity must always be treated as an end, because no one could rationally will that rationality and moral deliberation be subverted, which is what happens when we treat rational beings as mere means and not as ends. From this we may infer that all moral principles must be such that all rational beings can agree to them. No fully rational being would agree to the subversion of his own rationality, since this could not be rationally willed without contradiction. Thus, the principles or maxims which guide our treatment of others must be ones that they themselves could rationally and autonomously accept.

The crucial idea behind Kantian contractualism is precisely that genuinely binding moral principles must be ones to which any rational being could agree. This, however, is not the trivial claim it seems to be. A celebrated way of bringing out its meaning is contained in the contractualist theory of John Rawls, the best known recent defender of Kantian contractualism. His *A theory of justice* is a systematic attempt to defend a certain conception of *justice*, and is fundamentally a work of political philosophy. Since moral arguments are clearly relevant to questions of a just state or society, his theory can be fruitfully applied to many general areas of moral controversy as well.

The "original position"

Rawls sets up an hypothetical scenario called the "original position". This is an imaginary position that rational agents are in before they enter society. In it, they are all behind a "veil of ignorance": they do not know whether they are going to be rich or poor, intelligent or stupid, physically strong or weak; indeed, they know nothing about the particular qualities they will have except that they will be rational beings with basic human needs. Rawls believes that we can find out what a just society would be like by discovering what kind of society people *in the original position* would opt for. In other words, what kind of society would they agree to enter, if they didn't know what their own individual qualities and circumstances would be in that society?

A pivotal assumption is that people in the original position will make their choice self-interestedly, just as, in the actual world, people's views about justice are at least partly produced by self-interest. The whole point of the veil of ignorance is to prevent special pleading to one's own advantage, when deciding what social arrangements are just. For instance, if I already know that I shall be wealthy, I shall be tempted to opt for a system in which I am not made to give it away to the less fortunate. If I already know I shall be relatively poor, I shall probably favour a system in which wealth is more evenly distributed. However, a self-interested choice in the original position may be very different from a self-interested choice when my circumstances and qualities are known. For Rawls, whatever is wrong with unadulterated self-interest in the actual world is rendered innocent by the veil of ignorance, or, put differently, the enactment of self-interested choices made in the original position results in fairness in the actual world. (Rawls in fact call his conception of justice "justice as fairness").

Interestingly, the method can be applied as a test for justice in many other spheres too: for example, you might use it to reach an account of sexual justice, asking what rational contractors would decide concerning the relative position of the sexes if they did not know whether they would be male or female once the veil had been lifted. In such a position, would they opt for a society in which one sex had many more advantages than the other, or would they opt for one in which the sexes were roughly equal, all things considered? It seems likely that they would opt for approximate equality, or at least, for an inequality that is to everyone's advantage. This Rawlsian method can thus be used in support of a certain type of feminism – though it raises important questions about the nature of sexual equality, and the possible mutual benefits of assigning men and women into separate spheres. These questions must here be left on one side.

Since the present chapter concerns a theory of ethics, we shall not become too involved, either, with the details of Rawls' conception of social justice. But it is important to note one principle that he defends. This is the *difference principle*. It states that differences in wealth should be permitted only to the extent that they make the condition of the poorest better than it would have been otherwise. So although inequalities are allowable, Rawls' theory has a strong egalitarian thrust: there is a restriction on how much inequality can be permitted. It thus appeals to those who see a close connection between fairness and equality. This principle is supposed to be one that rational persons would opt for, while still in the original position.

This Kantian contractualism can be extended to cover aspects of morality apart from justice. We might apply it to interpersonal relations in general, asking what agreements we could all have reason to make. It appears that basic moral requirements of non-maleficence and keeping trust have a clear contractualist basis. Each of us has more to gain from a world in which no one tells lies (except perhaps in unusual circumstances) than from a world in which everyone lies whenever they feel like it. The burden on each of us of not lying is amply offset by the benefits of not being lied to. The same applies to theft and assault. Indeed, a certain core of morality, captured in fact by those of the Ten Commandments that do not mention God, for example, do not steal, do not bear false witness, can be given a credible contractualist basis. Of course, there may be far more to morality than this – and it is a plausible criticism of contractualism that it cannot justify enough of morality. But at least something important is achieved if the theory can justify these core elements.

For what would rational agents opt?

There is something appealing about Rawls' device for determining justice. People often do support practices and institutions that are unjust when they have a lot to gain from them. But how convincing is Rawls' theory? Rawls asks us how we would like the least fortunate in society to be treated, if we ourselves were among them, and expects the answer to yield the *difference principle*, but there are notorious difficulties with the argument. One central difficulty concerns what people *would* opt for if they were behind the veil of ignorance. One might remark that since no one has ever been behind such a veil, it is idle to ask what they would do if they were in that situation. There is simply no evidence upon which to base such a judgement. Now this retort is unfair to an extent, because we could recast the device as telling what options it would be *rational* for a self-interested person to take. However, there is a better way of putting the challenge, and it turns on the problem of what choice would really be rational.

Rawls believes that in the original position, the contractors would bet conservatively. Their chief concern would be to make the worst that could happen to them, as good as possible – even if this would mean foregoing the chance of the enormous benefits that could accrue from a higher-risk strategy. This betting option is known as *maximin* – it maximizes the value of the worst outcome (i.e. it aims for the maximum minimum). Suppose that you are offered the chance to gamble, and that you are already in a tolerable, but not very desirable, situation. You are told that if your gamble pays off, you will be exceptionally well-off, sexy, popular, or whatever you want to be. However, if the gamble does not pay off, you will be in a wretched state of misery and hardship, much worse than your present condition. Would you gamble? Obviously, this depends on the relative likelihood, as well as the appeal, of each alternative. It is irrational to gamble if the odds of the fortunate outcome are extremely low, but it may be rational if the odds of the fortunate outcome are above a certain level. How great the odds must be (if they can be calculated at all) before it becomes rational to gamble will be judged differently by different individuals. Cautious people will bet far more conservatively than those who like a strong element of risk in their lives. Most people will agree, however, that there is some level of probability below which it is foolish to gamble. To give up your boring and poorly paid job, hoping that your national lottery ticket is about to win the jackpot, is not a shining example of prudence. Here, betting conservatively is the best option, to ensure that your least desirable fate does not fall below a certain level.

The problem, however, is that it is not obvious that the conservative, maximin strategy is *always* the rational one to adopt. It is almost certainly false that most people would, in fact, adopt it. One might argue that, if we are not allowed any prior knowledge of how society is going to turn out in respect of wealth distribution, then the rational course is to embrace the maximin strategy, in case there will be many people in dire circumstances. In Rawls' scenario, no one is allowed to know how probable it is that they will turn out to be among the poorest; this knowledge is entirely denied to the contractors. This seems to rule out taking a rationally calculated risk of poverty, based on the supposition that there is a much higher probability of a much more desirable outcome for oneself.

However, there is another reason for doubting the unique rationality of the maximin strategy. This is that the rationality of the maximin strategy partially depends on how attractive the best outcome would be. Imagine that the people in the original position have to choose between the following two societies. Choice 1 is a society in which the minimum income per head is £6,000 per annum, and the maximum is £40,000. Choice 2 is a society in which the minimum income is £5,000 and the maximum £5,000,000. In view of the relatively small difference between the worst outcome in each society compared to the best, it is hard to see why maximin would be the rational strategy here. It would surely be more rational to opt for Choice 2, if that gives you the chance to earn five million pounds. This is not to say that it is admirable to want to be very rich, or that there aren't factors that make for a desirable life apart from money. But the example does show why, on certain assumptions about what self-interested people would choose, the maximin strategy is not uniquely rational. It is only if the worst outcome is so bad that anything even worse would, in some sense, be absolutely intolerable, that maximin can be a rational bet.

Impartiality and "moral irrelevance"

The supposed appeal of Rawls' device is its emphasis on the impartial nature of moral concern. It is crucial that the hypothetical contractors do not know their own future place in the world, for only then can they avoid the temptation to favour themselves over others, and devise ingenious rationalizations for such self-preference. The thrust of Rawls' idea is that morally irrelevant features of persons – such as their height, their intelligence or the social position of their parents – should have no role in determining their opportunities. So Kantian contractualism, as found in Rawls' theory, stresses the importance of impartiality for the moral point of view; its slogan might be "morality as impartiality".

Further investigation, unfortunately, suggests that the position is not quite so simple. For what exactly is meant by *morally irrelevant*? Is it morally irrelevant to my success and prosperity in life that I am hard-working? Is it irrelevant that I have talents, such as a talent for writing saleable novels, for enterprise or for music? Any believable theory of just acquisition and reward would make reference to the talents and effort of the contributing parties. There may indeed be hard questions about the importance to be given to innate ability, as compared to sheer slog, in deciding what goods people are entitled to – but this is irrelevant here, since the hypothetical contractors behind the veil of ignorance know neither whether they will be naturally talented, nor whether they will be industrious. They will opt to make the lot of the *least* talented and motivated as good as possible, rather than do the same for those who are the *most* talented or motivated. But it is not clear why this is a requirement of the fairness that the veil of ignorance is supposed to guarantee.

But isn't there something important captured by Rawls' device, even if we should allow that talent and effort should be rewarded (and even rewarded to a degree that goes beyond what is needed to make the lot of the worst off as good as possible)? Is it not a patently unfair society that takes account of your racial origin or the occupation of your parents in deciding what your life chances should be?

This is hard to deny. However, although the veil of ignorance device may well yield this conclusion, the conception of moral irrelevance that underlies (say) the commitment to racial equality seems already to have been *assumed*, rather than demonstrated, by Rawls' device. It is because such things as race, intelligence, parental income or physical strength have *already* been deemed morally irrelevant, that the veil of ignorance is introduced in the first place. In other words, however reasonable this view may be, it is not one that can be derived from the veil of ignorance device, since it is the guiding assumption behind the introduction of that device.

The theory does have some merits, admittedly. Crucially, it rules out appeals to the mere *identity* of persons, when deciding how certain goods are to be distributed. It rules out, that is, a policy telling us to "maximize the chances of the most talented and industrious, provided that Piers Benn is among them; otherwise not". That is plainly something that self-interested contractors in the original position cannot agree to (apart from Piers Benn). Furthermore, if the contractors were told that there was to be manna from heaven that they could distribute in some agreed way, one would expect each of them to favour a principle ensuring that they *all* get at least some of it, as this is the only way that each contractor can be sure that *he or she* will get some of it. But beyond this, too many other plausible moral considerations, especially the moral desert, are unaccounted for by the device. Most importantly, the device assumes the very thing it wishes to explain, namely a controversial conception of what personal factors are morally relevant to what you should get out of life.

Contractualism and utilitarianism

Our discussion of the political aspects of Rawls' contractualism has been something of a digression. Its purpose is to provide a model of how ordinary moral positions, as well as political ones, might be grounded. We have considered certain difficulties with Rawls' version of contractualism, but it has one attractive feature, which is firmly rooted in Kantian ethics. This is that it gives a theoretical basis for respecting what Rawls calls the "separateness of persons". As we saw in Chapter 3, Rawls mounts an influential criticism of utilitarian ethics, based precisely on the objection that utilitarianism cannot accommodate this separateness.

It is always useful to compare and contrast contractualism with utilitarianism. The basic standpoint that the utilitarian tries to make his or her own is that of the impartial, benevolent spectator. The dominant rival to this standpoint is generated by Kantian contractualism, which adopts the standpoint of the hypothetical rational contractor. For the utilitarian the question to ask before adopting some course is: what would be recommended by the impartial benevolent spectator? The contractualist, by contrast, asks what the self-interested rational contractor could agree to in the original position.

Some applications

Imagine, now, that they are asked to decide whether the freedom, happiness or even the life of one person is to be sacrificed for the good of a much larger number. Now the benevolent spectator will simply weigh up all the preferences of all concerned parties and ask which course would satisfy the greatest number of preferences. This could well yield the conclusion that the sacrifice of the one for the many is justified. The hypothetical rational contractor, however, would ask *to which course could I freely agree*, if I am ignorant as to whether I would be the one sacrificed. The agreement we should expect, so it seems, is that while each will refrain from harming others in exchange for not being harmed himself, he will not agree to advance the interests of others if this would involve a significant sacrifice of his most fundamental interests, such as life and liberty.

One might, in reply to this, claim that rational contractors would in fact agree to some fundamental sacrifices of interests, in order to promote a greater number of similar interests. For, given the admitted harm of losing one's life or liberty, the utilitarian approach at least seeks to minimize the overall occurrence of this harm – and given this, we might expect contractors in the original position to opt for a system which has a greater likelihood of requiring others to sacrifice themselves, than of requiring them to sacrifice themselves for others. But the insight the contract theory has really latched onto is that discussed earlier (see Chapter 3): that the perspective – that is, the perspective of the impartial benevolent spectator – from which the utilitarian issues moral prescriptions is inappropriate, since it is not, and cannot be, the perspective of any actual person. We are all, in a way, at the centre of our own worlds, and there can be no such thing as a "view from nowhere". At least, although we *can* adopt this viewpoint, we cannot use it to show that the sacrifice of the few for the many is compensated for in any morally important way.

It may be that the utilitarian and the contractualist have merely reached a stand-off, so far. The utilitarian insists, understandably, that there is *some* sense in which it is better for a greater number of people to have their preferences satisfied than a lesser number; although the contractualist still insists that all moral principles must be such that a self-interested person could in theory agree to them. When such stand-offs are reached, it often happens that each side simply points to seemingly repellent implications of the other's theory. We have amply seen how this might be done against utilitarianism, but there are also significant objections to contractualism based on the same manner of reasoning.

A practical example: contractualism and animals

To show that our rather arid discussion does have interesting practical implications, I shall discuss some practical matters in which moral philosophers have been taking an interest since about the mid-1970s.

One notorious objection to contractualism is that it accords no direct moral standing to beings who cannot enter into agreements. Morality is a system that rational agents enter for their mutual benefit, and moral requirements can be justified by appeal to what we could all freely agree. This has radical implications for the moral standing of sentient beings which, for one reason or another, are not rational. This class seems to include the severely mentally retarded, the senile, new-born babies, foetuses and people in comas. It also includes non-human animals, about whose moral status there is much recent discussion. The arguments that emerge in the debate illuminate important issues in moral theory.

Consider what a utilitarian will say about the moral status of animals. A classical utilitarian such as Bentham, who regards pleasure as the basic good, and suffering as the basic evil, is not interested in the species membership of creatures which enjoy pleasure or suffer pain. *All that matters is that they can suffer.* If pain is bad, then it is bad whoever or whatever endures it, and there can be no more reason for discriminating against sentient non-humans, when deciding whose pain should be alleviated, than for racist discrimination against the members of a particular ethnic group. Bentham's principle that each must count for one, and none for more than one, can be extended to include sentient non-humans. It is, moreover, irrelevant that animals might have a lesser capacity for suffering or a narrower range of suffering available to them, due to their lack of certain concepts (they cannot have an abstract fear of death, for example, even if they can be terrified when they are hunted). The point is that *to the extent* that their suffering is comparable to that of humans, it should be taken no less seriously than human suffering.

Contractualism, however, suggests something altogether different. If morality is just a human construction devised to facilitate relations between human beings, and if hypothetical contractors would freely agree to its practical exhortations, then beings which cannot enter into such agreements have no moral standing in their own right. Only rational agents can be contractors – even hypothetical ones – and no beast is rational in the required way.[6]

Now it could be objected that some rational agents in the original position might decide to *represent* the interests of animals and weigh them alongside their own. However, this would be a radical departure from the contractualist idea, which depends essentially on the contractors in the original position being exclusively self-interested. Since no rational agent would have a self-interested reason to object to animal pain, the idea that such contractors, when behind the veil of ignorance, would decide to represent the interests of beasts seems an arbitrary addition to the hypothetical position. One could – in answer to this objection – construe the veil of ignorance as involving ignorance of the species to which the contractors will belong, and then imagine the contractors asking themselves how they would like to be treated if they were (non-rational) beasts. But the problem with this manoeuvre is that the fact that they *are* rational agents is already implied by our description of them as hypothetical contractors. We cannot allow that they be ignorant of whether or not they will be rational, even if we can allow ignorance of a range of other things, such as their sex, intelligence and social class.

If contractualism is true, then, it seems to imply that animals have no direct moral standing. But can we take this implication seriously? This moral position on animals is surely very questionable. True: to allow them *equal* moral standing to humans might also be implausible, but to allow them no moral standing at all is too extreme an alternative.

Contractualist responses

Some contractualist writers[7] try to soften the impact of this conclusion by arguing that we ought, indeed, to refrain from treating animals exactly as we please – but not because the animals possess direct moral standing. Rather, certain ways of treating animals express a cruel nature. To torment dogs for amusement is a sure sign of having an undesirable character, even though the dogs are not strictly speaking victims of a moral wrong. Plenty of examples can be given of actions that are objectionable because of what they reveal of the character of the agent. Consider a man who mutilates the corpses of his enemies. Even if corpses, not being persons, cannot be wronged, there is still something repellent about mutilating them for fun or out of spite. Surely a warped and twisted moral character is displayed in this activity? We would also fear the other things this man might do; someone who delights in hurting dogs or mutilating corpses is unlikely, we might suppose, to be a model of justice and benevolence towards living humans. It is for this kind of reason, according to many contractualists, that we should not be entirely heedless of animal suffering.

But this argument does not carry much weight in the end. If it claims that people who hurt animals show a propensity to hurt people as well, it needs to be backed up by evidence. But from what we know of people who compartmentalize their moral concerns, the evidence appears weak. People can behave appallingly to the members of "out groups" but impeccably towards those who belong to their own group. On the other hand, if the claim is that hurting animals reveals a bad character, *irrespective* of its connection to a tendency to maltreat people, then this needs to be defended. If there is nothing inherently wrong with hurting dogs for fun, then why should doing so reveal a bad character?

It appears that contractualism cannot accommodate at least one moral intuition that decent people can be expected to have. Of course, it is open to us to conclude that this intuition is a mistake and should be abandoned. But there is at least food for thought about the overall credibility of the theory.

Another practical example: contractualism and respect for nature

In a similar vein, philosophers opposed to contractualism point out that it fails not only with respect to animals, but also that it cannot justify widely shared moral sentiments concerning the natural environment. By making the human individual sovereign, the theory cannot allow that we might have a duty to display respect for the natural world – for the biosphere, plants, trees and rivers. According to the social contract theory of obligation, if these elements of the natural world have any value, they have it only instrumentally, in that they enhance the lives of human beings.

Thus, there is no inherent wrong in despoiling the environment, tearing down rainforests or destroying areas of natural beauty if these activities enhance human life. (Of course, they may well not; it is precisely this point that many "green" sympathizers make when they warn of the dire effects on humans of excessive economic growth and the consequent depletion of natural resources. But this point is entirely consistent with denying that nature has any *inherent* value). Yet many thinkers, and not only modern-day "deep ecologists" feel a sense of reverence for the natural world; some of them also feel that a proper appreciation of beauty and sublimity is necessary if we are to cut ourselves down to size and not imagine that we are, or should become, masters of the universe. The object of this reverence is hard to describe, since it is not necessary to suppose that nature itself has a mind or a rational purpose, and nature does not, in the contractual sense, have rights. Yet we may still have duties with respect to nature, as we also may towards many other beings with whom we cannot now enter into contracts – such as the dead, the unborn, or even nations. We might indeed have duties to ourselves, even though we cannot violate our own rights in a contractual sense. Theists, moreover, will say that our obligations to God do not come from any contractual arrangement with Him, but from His greatness and the fact that He created us. Of course, contractualists may insist that these moral concerns are irrational, but by saying this, they ignore vast areas of the moral experience of human beings.

Conclusion: contractualism and moral intuitions

Even if we should reject the social contract theory's claim to have the whole truth about morality, there are still good things about it. There is much to be said for Kantian contractualism, which maintains that acceptable moral principles must be theoretically capable of gaining the agreement of all rational beings. For this is an implication of Kant's *formula of the end in itself* – perhaps the most fruitful contribution of his ethical theory. Moreover, the question "what would you agree to if you were behind the veil of ignorance?" is often a useful one to pursue, since in many situations it is an efficient way to reach an intuitively acceptable answer. But does it really say enough? Can it capture certain moral ideals – such as unconditional love for strangers – that many people find intuitively compelling?

This idea of moral intuition brings us to something we often mentioned but did not really examine. In ethical debate we often encounter philosophers who reject certain moral views because they do not accord with their intuitions. But isn't this empty rhetoric? How can my intuitions provide me with any reasons? To pronounce "I intuit the matter *thus*" seems strangely empty. Surely, the fact that I *do* believe something hardly *justifies* me in believing it. Appeal to intuition could be expressed even more grandly; I might reach a decision on an important matter by going away and "consulting my conscience". But what is the difference between doing this, and simply consulting myself? Hardly surprising that I get the answer I was looking for!

The whole question of what justifies moral claims is very complex. A sharp way of putting the challenge is to imagine that I have made a claim to some moral *knowledge*, and that I am pressed on what entitles me to call it knowledge. To know something is more than just to believe it, or even to believe it correctly. Something else is required. What else might be needed is hotly debated, but according to a useful traditional account, no belief, even if true, is knowledge unless the belief is properly *justified*. On this account, then, my intuitive moral judgement cannot express moral knowledge unless it is properly justified. But now how can a moral intuition be justified? To splutter "because that is how it seems to me!" is merely to restate the intuition. And that seems a lame *justification* for the intuition.

In fact we can rise to this challenge. We might first point out that almost everyone has moral intuitions, and it would be strange if we were all wrong. Even those who challenge the authority of intuitions, when they are wearing their philosophical hats, still continue to entertain them. We could ask them whether this causes a tension in their minds. If so, can they resolve the tension by taking no notice of their intuitions?

They might say they can. They could draw an analogy with hallucinations. A few people who have hallucinations can learn to discount them, once they know that they are hallucinations. They continue to *see* what isn't there, but they know it isn't real.

However, in the case of moral intuition – *judgement* may be a better word – it is hard to see how a similar thing is possible. That is, it is hard to see how there could be a moral *impression*, analogous to the visual content of an hallucination, which is easily separated from the making of a moral judgement. Admittedly, some people have guilt feelings, often about sex, that they consciously judge to be irrational. I suspect it is better to describe this as cases of internal conflict, rather than as cases where an impression of the wrongness of some action is dismissed as altogether misleading.

Furthermore, the supporters of intuitions help their case by admitting that intuitions are not infallible or beyond criticism. That would be an absurd view. Rather, like ordinary perceptions, they are fallible but still reliable. We quite properly make perceptual judgements, even though persistent challenges may ultimately produce an exasperated, "Well, that is how things seem to me!" The challengers end up dismissing *any* reply that is offered. They win only by fixing it in advance that no response can ever meet their standards.

Much more can be said about this. But it is relevant to our discussion of contractualism, and indeed utilitarianism, in that it suggests that we should sometimes challenge the practical conclusions of moral theories by pointing out their intuitive unacceptability. It has particular relevance to contractualism, because contractualists like Gauthier take it as read that there are no objective values and no special moral sense. They regard the contractualist approach as the only way of placing morality on a secure footing. But to rely entirely on a theory, like contractualism, leads to a lop-sided conception of morality and threatens to generate absurdities. This is not to deny that contractualism has some important insights to offer. It is better to be a contractualist about some aspects of morality – for example, justice – than about the whole of morality. Perhaps what we really need is a hybrid moral theory that is contractualist about certain things, but Aristotelian or utilitarian about others. Without such a qualification, it appears that what contractualism regards as the enlightened process of cutting down the awkward intuitive obstacles to our vision of the moral horizon, is just as likely to end up in the laying waste and flattening of those intuitive judgements and moral allegiances that make the moral life intelligible to us.

Further reading

Carruthers, P. *The animals issue* (Cambridge: Cambridge University Press, 1992).

Gauthier, D. *Morals by agreement* (Oxford: Oxford University Press, 1986).

Gauthier, D. Why contractarianism? In *Contractarianism and rational choice,* P. Vallentyne (ed.) (Cambridge: Cambridge University Press, 1991), pp. 15–30.

Hobbes, T. *Leviathan* J.C.A. Gaskin (ed.) Oxford: Oxford University Press, 1996.

Midgley, M. Duties concerning islands. In *Ethics*, P. Singer (ed.) (Oxford: Oxford University Press, 1994), pp. 374–87.

Rawls, J. *A theory of justice* (Oxford: Oxford University Press, 1972).

Rousseau, J-J. *The social contract* Christopher Betts (transl.) (originally published 1762) (Oxford: Oxford University Press, 1994).

Scruton, R. *Animal rights and wrongs* (London: Demos, 1996).

Chapter 6

Free will and the moral emotions

Theories of moral obligation have featured prominently in our discussions so far, in which we tried both to examine important accounts of the basis of moral obligation and, if more briefly, to raise some doubts about trying to base moral judgements entirely upon theories. There is, however, a more nebulous area of moral philosophy upon which we have scarcely touched, but which is of great importance. It is also an area where conflicts between theory and everyday practice come to the fore. The conflicts are not so much between moral theories and their potential clash with ordinary judgement, but between more general kinds of theories – concerning human nature, or determinism, for example – and our interpersonal responses.

Hume wrote of the agreeable feelings we experience when we encounter what we take to be good. In a similar way, most of us react with moral feelings, not only to actions but principally to *persons*. We undergo reactions such as admiration and blame towards others and ourselves. Feelings of pride or of guilt are reactions to our own deeds and characters, just as feelings of gratitude and resentment are among the reactions we experience towards others. We not only formulate judgements about right action when we think about morality – since inseparable from this, at least psychologically speaking, is the fact that we experience special reactions to agents; we do such things as praise and blame, admire and condemn.

Of course, our attitudes towards agents are far more richly textured than this, but they illustrate something both inseparable from the moral life, and deeply problematic. How can these attitudes – or as P.F. Strawson names them, these "participant reactive attitudes" – be justified?[1] Are they, indeed, in need of justification, and if so, what kind of justification is required? Is it enough that they are a useful influence on conduct, or promote respect for persons, or do we also need a convincing theoretical justification? These rich but dark areas are our present subject of enquiry.

Participant reactive attitudes

Apart from noting the importance of these attitudes in our inter-personal lives, we should remark on the kind of objects onto which they are directed. For example, resentment is more than a feeling we have when something goes wrong for us. When we are hurt or harmed by a natural disaster, we do not usually think we can blame anyone for it, nor do we think resentment is appropriate. Of course, people do sometimes experience something like resentment in these circumstances; they try to find someone to blame in some way (perhaps it was someone's responsibility to warn of the impending disaster, like a hapless TV weather announcer who is blamed if he or she failed to predict a gale), or they might even attempt to blame God. Many of us have a psychological need to seek someone to blame. When we do this, we conceive of the object of blame in *personal* terms, ascribing culpable intentions or motives to it. This is made clearer by the fact that our attitudes to people who harm us by mistake is usually different from our attitudes to those who cause us equal harm, but on purpose. If someone jostles me in a crowded place, obviously by accident, I ignore it. If, on the other hand, it seems deliberate, I resent it. The physical discomfort may be quite insignificant, but what I resent is the *attitude of the other person towards me*. It is because my adversary conceives of me as a fit object of contempt – itself a participant attitude – that I react as I do towards him or her.

Hence, at least some participant attitudes depend on the belief that their objects themselves entertain participant attitudes. We do not blame or resent dangerous dogs that attack children; we just have them destroyed (unjustifiably, in some cases). We do blame some people for their actions, because we take it that certain attitudes and motives explain their behaviour.

It seems clear that there is an important underlying difference between creatures which are objects of these attitudes and those which are not. Even if it is difficult to draw precise lines, or to give a full set of necessary and sufficient conditions for being a proper object of participant attitudes, we can usually see when they are appropriate and when they are not. It is fairly clear that most human beings do, in fact, form intentions, have desires and ends, and entertain interpersonal attitudes towards others. If this much is clear, then why do such attitudes towards these people generate a problem?

We should distinguish between local problems and global problems here. Of course, there are always local hard cases. Should we – indeed, can we – form participant attitudes towards people with psychopathic personality disorders, towards schizophrenics, or towards young children? These specific questions assume, in a way, that the answer to the global question has been reached. They assume, that is, that there is no problem in general with entertaining these participant attitudes. But is this right? Is it justified, even in the most seemingly normal cases, to praise and blame, admire and condemn? To see whether that assumption is correct, we shall have to ask that large question.

The spectre of determinism

One of the traditional challenges to our participant attitudes is based upon *determinism*. There have, historically, been different ways of formulating the challenge; the problem that exercised

many medieval philosophers was that of reconciling human freedom with divine foreknowledge and power, while, in a scientific
age, the problem has been that of allowing for human freedom in
a world that supposedly runs in accordance with causal laws. It is
useful to begin with the latter problem.

Some people object to calling people good, bad, praiseworthy,
blameworthy, and so on, because they claim that all human actions (and intentions, desires and emotions) are *causally determined*. According to the thesis of universal causal determinism,
everything that happens – including all human actions – happens
as a result of causal laws which, in conjunction with all the antecedent conditions, ensure that everything happens as it does.
Thus, if all actions are performed as a result of causal laws and
prior conditions, then they could not be other than they are. There
is no important difference between the physical laws that govern
the behaviour of matter, and the laws, however they are to be
described, that govern human behaviour. Just as water must boil
at 100 degrees centigrade in normal atmospheric conditions, so all
human behaviour must occur as it does, since it is likewise subject
to inexorable laws. We may not know what these laws are, and we
may not be able to make accurate predictions of behaviour. But
that does not mean these laws do not exist.

If this is true, then how can people genuinely do other than they
do? If they cannot do other than they do, it surely does not make
sense to make them objects of participant attitudes. To blame
people is justifiable only if they could have acted other than they
did. If causal determinism is true, then (it is said) they could not
have acted other than they did. And in that case, it is wrong to
blame them. Not, of course, that you can be blamed for blaming
them!

Many people will accept that if causal determinism is true for all
that occurs, then no one can ever act otherwise than they do.
But for exactly that reason, they will reject causal determinism.
For what could be more obvious than that most of us, most of the
time, are able to do other than we do? If determinism implies
that we are never able to do other than we do, then determinism
seems certainly false. For anything that implies a falsehood is
itself false.

The case for determinism

In his defence, the determinist is likely to claim that causal determinism is an assumption we actually do make with respect to most things in nature, and that there is no particular reason to exempt human actions from the causal nexus. We know perfectly well that water always boils at 100 degrees centigrade at sea level under normal conditions, that objects fall when dropped, that physical regularities allow us to predict the behaviour of physical entities. Indeed, without these assumptions, it is unclear how we could understand the world or act in it. Causal assumptions underlie almost all of our predictions, and these predictions are necessary for successful planning. This applies not only to the strictly physical world, but also to the human world. We notice rough psychological regularities that permit us to predict people's behaviour with reasonable accuracy; we try to influence such behaviour using methods that often work. How would any of this be possible unless some kind of determinism were true? Many who resist determinism do so because they think they know, from experience, that there are genuine alternatives they can choose from when they act. But this familiar feeling does not refute the case for determinism provided by our general observation of the natural world. Whatever else we human beings are, we are made of physical stuff, and physical stuff obeys causal laws. Whatever else actions are, they involve physical changes, and as such have physical causes sufficient to produce them.

This, then, is how a determinist might defend his position. Although it is enough for present purposes, it is worth briefly noting two possible variants on it. First, the determinist might allow that the causal laws governing events are statistical rather than strictly deterministic. In the light of physical theory since the advent of quantum mechanics, most physicists hold that at a subatomic level, determinism does not hold true. But for practical purposes (says the determinist) this is irrelevant, because at the macroscopic level the world is *as if* strictly determined. The same regularities hold, allowing accurate predictions. Secondly, our determinist need not believe in materialism (or "physicalism") – that is, the view that all that exists is physical. It is convenient to lay out the case for determinism in materialistic terms, but determinism does not imply materialism. He or she might say instead that even if there is more to reality than physical reality, this is no reason to deny that determinism holds for non-physical events as well as physical ones. For example, if thoughts, desires, acts of will and so forth are literally immaterial occurrences, there may still be deterministic relations holding between these immaterial occurrences. Indeed, our observation of the psychological regularities in the world might suggest that, whether or not mental events are ultimately physical, they are still determined.

We have, then, a coherent case for determinism, which deserves to be taken seriously. It challenges our participant attitudes. The version we have considered suggests that we should try to give up these attitudes, since they are founded on a false belief in human free will. Of course, if we don't give them up, we cannot be morally blamed for not doing so! There is also a thorny question, if this kind of determinism is true, of whether we actually have the *choice* of whether to give them up! As we shall see, determinists are not without answers to these problems.

Compatibilism

Before assessing the case for determinism, however, it is important to present a well-known and popular way of trying to escape some of the apparent implications of determinism, without having to deny determinism itself. In the stark and hard version above, the determinist is portrayed as claiming that if determinism is true, then our participant attitudes should be jettisoned as far as possible (we shall leave on one side the interesting question of what *possible* means here). However, there is a tradition associated with many major philosophers – among them Hume, Mill and Ayer – which simply denies that human free will is in conflict with determinism. This view is known as compatibilism, since it claims that free will is compatible with determinism. If it is correct, then it may be possible to rescue the participant attitudes, even if determinism is true.

How can free will be compatible with determinism? At first sight there appears to be an obvious conflict, since it seems that free will

142

entails the ability to act other than you actually do; whereas if causal determinism is true, then all events are necessitated by their causes, in conjunction with the antecedent conditions. However, compatibilists have various replies to this. Some of them, though a minority, deny that free will entails the ability to do other than you do. They say that you can do things freely, without being able to do anything else. For example, you might freely stay in a room, without realizing that you have been locked in and could not leave if you tried. The basic idea here is that even though you cannot but stay in the room, you still choose to do so – and it is this that makes you free. (Complex variations on this theme involve sinister science fiction characters, who stand by ready to manipulate your brain patterns if you show any sign of being about to do something they don't want you to do, but who otherwise leave you alone. In such cases, it seems that you act freely even though you could not act otherwise).

However, it is more common for compatibilists to insist that being causally determined, and being able to act otherwise, are in fact reconcilable. Put simply, they argue as follows:

Imagine that there are two mutually exclusive courses of action open to you, A and B. When you claim that although you did one thing (A), you were nevertheless able to do the other thing (B), this claim can be analyzed as follows: that had you *chosen* to do B, you *would* have done B. The basic idea is that free actions are those that are at least partially determined by your own choices; free actions are those that are done, not *regardless* of your choice but *because* of it. This is what is stressed in the idea that "could have done otherwise" entails "would have done otherwise if you had so chosen". The point is that, provided your choices (or perhaps desires or will) are themselves part of the causal chain, the resulting actions are free. On the other hand, things you do (if *do* is the right word here) regardless of, or without, such choices, are not free. In other words, the enemy of free will is not causation, but compulsion. Thus Hume, for example, claims that freedom is the ability to act or not act, according to the determinations of the will.[2] How the *will* comes to be the way it is, and whether it is itself causally determined, is not germane to the issue of human freedom.

This theory is certainly attractive, especially as it seems to find room for something that surely is a necessary condition of free will, namely, the determination of our actions by *us*. In the spirit of compatibilism, we might ask: what more can we want than this? Why should we require that human desires, choices and so on should themselves be uncaused? Even if they are uncaused, it is hard to see how this can get us any more substantial kind of freedom. For after all, whether they are caused or not, it cannot be ourselves who are responsible for them in the way the opponent of compatibilism (the incompatibilist) seems to require, because that would mean that we choose our choices, and choose our choosing of our choices, and so on – thus setting off an infinite regress.

Incompatibilist reservations

However, the matter may not be as simple as that. For an incompatibilist will insist that there are genuine explanations of actions and decisions that are *not causal explanations*, and that genuine free will requires that our actions be explicable in these special ways.[3] Compatibilists, for their part, point out that this is obscure, if it is meant to be an account of a meaningful sort of free will that goes beyond what compatibilism can already accommodate. But the incompatibilist idea is easy to express superficially; it is that decisions should be explicable by *reasons* rather than wholly by causes. To explain why a rock fell off a cliff and landed on my toe requires only causal notions, to do with gravity, mass and the like; but to explain why *I pushed* the rock off the cliff requires quite different concepts. Here you would not talk only of neural circuits in the brain which caused the nerves in my arm to enact a movement, which in turn moved the rock. You would invoke quite different explanatory factors: you would invoke my reasons, which include my motives, beliefs and desires. Actions do not become intelligible in human terms unless they are explained in terms of reasons. This sort of account, which incompatibilists believe is not reducible to a causal account, is the key to understanding how human actions might be *neither* causally determined *nor* purely random.

The dispute now starts to focus on whether complete causal explanation of action is compatible with genuine and true explanation by reasons. Those who think they are incompatible say that if there is a complete, sufficient causal explanation for all decisions, then even if this causal process is accompanied by reasons, these reasons cannot really be part of the explanation of the behaviour in question; they would be incidental or "epiphenomenal" to the whole process, since all the explanatory work would be done by the causal process. Compatibilists, on the other hand, will want to know why the reasons in question cannot also be the causes of the behaviour. There is indeed an important debate in the philosophy of mind about whether reasons are causes, and we should now give some attention to it.

Causality and rationality

The debate about compatibilism is closely linked to that of whether rationality in general is compatible with a purely causal account of mental processes, especially those associated with choosing and evaluating options. The link is clear, for the in-compatibilist places much importance on the rational explanation of action, which he contrasts with causal explanation. Explanation by reasons – or what some philosophers call *personal explanation* – is heralded as the only way through the prongs of *Hume's Fork*. This *fork* is a notorious dilemma. It states that all actions are either causally determined or else occur at random, and that neither alternative gives the incompatibilist what he wants. It is clear that the incompatibilist defender of free will – that is, the *libertarian* – does not think that all actions occur at random, but that at least some of them are intelligible in the light of rational considerations. He or she might allow that many actions can be quite reliably predicted; but only on the basis of what is known of people's characters and freely adopted habits rather than on the basis of causal laws.

In a similar vein, libertarians are likely to deny that rationality in general, which governs not only practical decisions but the formation of factual beliefs, can be reduced to causal processes. Consider the process of forming a belief on the basis of evidence and inference. When asked why I hold this belief, I refer to the relevant evidence and to principles of sound inference. Suppose I believe in the eventual victory of socialism over industrial capitalism. If someone asks me why I believe this, I might cite the works of Marx and Lenin and argue for their cogency. Perhaps the reasons I produce are bad ones, but I do at least think that they justify, and not merely cause, my drawing the conclusions I do. On the other hand, if I answer: "I believe that the dictatorship of the proletariat will eventually replace the forces of bourgeois industrial capitalism, because I was hypnotized at school by a bogus Latin teacher and told to believe this", it becomes unclear that I really *believe* it at all. For it is paradoxical to retain such a belief while simultaneously admitting that the explanation for my holding it is completely non-rational.[4] Admittedly, I might, having been hypnotized, subsequently come across what I think is a persuasive reason for holding the belief. Perhaps I would not have stumbled upon this persuasive reason had I not been hypnotized; maybe the hypnotist instructed me to go and look for such a reason. All the same, it is paradoxical to give my reasons for a belief – that is, to justify that belief – merely by referring to the occurrence of an entirely non-rational process. Facts about how I came to hold a belief are not, in themselves, any evidence whatever for its truth.

What is the moral of this, for the question of whether human rationality is compatible with the hypothesis that the explanation for human belief formation is entirely causal? The thoughts above are analogous to the libertarian's objection to the compatibilist account of freedom. Remember that the compatibilist maintains that provided our choices (or desires, motives, etc.) are essential ingredients in the causation of our actions, it does not matter whether they themselves are causally determined. The libertarian, on the contrary, thinks it matters very much, and draws an analogy with factual belief-formation to show why. He thinks it is not enough, for us to be genuinely rational agents, that our beliefs be true; after all, beliefs implanted by hypnotists might also happen to be true. Likewise it is not enough that our practical choices be (in some sense) rational, or that they cause our actions, for the real locus of human freedom must be in the formation of the choices themselves.

But now we reach a basic difficulty with the libertarian, or more generally, the incompatibilist position. For the compatibilist will argue that the incompatibilist requirements for freedom cannot, even in principle, be fulfilled – even granting the dubious premise that they are intelligible. He will insist that the demands of rationality are perfectly well satisfied if our beliefs and practical decisions conform to certain rational requirements, irrespective of whether a causal process led them so to conform. For what more could we reasonably want? Thrusting the prongs of *Hume's fork* in our faces once again, he will insist that ultimate responsibility for our beliefs and choices, of the sort that the incompatibilist demands, is necessarily unobtainable. Even if I can account for a certain decision I take by citing all the rational considerations in its favour, I still need to explain how it came about that I found these considerations persuasive and not some other ones. It is futile to try to account for my choices in terms of prior choices, and those prior choices in terms of still prior ones, because unless the regress is infinite (which is clearly unsatisfactory), there must be some point where the buck must simply stop. But if the buck must stop somewhere, then I cannot be *ultimately* responsible for the way I am and the choices that I make. So does it really matter whether or not there is a deterministic explanation for the way I am? Is it really preferable that there should be no explanation at all? As far as defending free will is concerned, it is quite hard to see why such randomness is better than causal determinism.

Moreover, the compatibilist has another card to play. As I suggested earlier, part of the debate concerns whether reasons can also be causes. If they can, then that suggests that the incompatibilist insistence that free actions be explained rationally and not causally is based on a false opposition of reasons and causes.

Of course, the apparent opposition is easy to see. Whereas causes make me do things, reasons explain why *I should* do them. In other words, reasons are normative – they are justifications. There may be a sufficient reason why I should do something, but I may still not do it. But if there is a causally sufficient condition for my doing something, it follows that I do it. That is what *sufficient* means here: "enough to make happen".

But what does this show? Certainly, the meaning of the word *reason* is different to the meaning of the word *cause*. Reasons are identified as reasons in quite different ways to the ways in which causes are identified as causes. To establish that some factor in a situation is a cause of some other factor may require careful observation and experiment, whereas to establish whether some consideration is a reason for some action requires rational normative reflection. But all of this, though important, does not show that reasons are not causes. Consider this parallel: diplomats are easily identified as such by the cars they drive and the houses they live in, whereas spies are identified as such only with great difficulty, through careful observation of their movements. But this obviously does not mean that no diplomat is a spy. It may be that a particular reason for an action is also its cause, but that it can be identified as a cause only through some complex observation, whereas it can be identified as a reason just by reflection on the situation.

But what does it mean to say that reasons are causes? Does it mean that some fact about an action – for example, that it will further some end of mine – can cause me to perform it? How can this be? The idea that there is some causal account, or even causal law, linking my reasons and my actions, appears obscure at first. The difficulty is lessened if we say that it is my *recognizing* something as a reason, that causes me to act. This is made plausible by the fact that we sometimes act for reasons that are bad, or that refer to non-existent situations mistakenly thought to be real. A lunatic jumps out of the window to avoid being eaten by a hungry bear that he thinks is chasing him. His action is not *caused by the bear's chasing him*, since this is not happening. It is really his entertaining the idea that causes him to act.

One helpful illustration of this would appeal to "physicalists", who believe that all mental states are physical. Suppose that every mental state, including the entertaining of reasons, is identical with some highly complex physical state. In that case, it seems possible that the mental states involved in thinking a certain course of action a good one to pursue, are identical with a set of complex brain processes that cause the action in question. So the recognition of reasons acts as a cause at the physical level. There is, of course, more to action than mere physical movement, but action involves physical movement, and an extremely complex set of neurophysiological processes is involved in producing it. If these processes, or some of them, can be identified with mental processes, including normative deliberation, then we have one interesting account of how an agent's reasons for action may also be the causes of his action.

Do these observations help the case for compatibilism? If my reasoning and decision-making are identical with highly complex brain processes, and if these processes cause actions, then it looks as though we have an interesting way of seeing how action can be free (because rational) yet also caused. Of course, as we saw in the hypnosis example, not just any cause will do. If hypnosis causes me to adopt beliefs that a fully rational person would adopt, this process is still not a rationally appropriate way to acquire them, even if the beliefs are rational, in the sense of being in accordance with the best available evidence and arguments. However, the process of weighing up arguments and thinking about alternatives may still be a causal process. For the compatibilist quite reasonably distinguishes between different types of cause, arguing that while some types are incompatible with genuine rationality, other types are perfectly consistent with it. Is it not fair to maintain that if my beliefs (and any choices that arise from them) are caused by the appropriate perceptions and internal deliberations, and if these in turn are caused by rationally connected perceptions and deliberations, then the requirements of rationality have been satisfied?

There is certainly much to be said for such a view. Unfortunately the matter is probably not as simple as that. It is hard to dispel the incompatibilist suspicion that if there are causal processes underlying action which coincide with the proper normative considerations, the latter cannot do any real explanatory work and can only shadow-box a causal process that is sufficient to produce beliefs and actions on its own. To go into more detail here would be to embark on a somewhat uncertain philosophical expedition, which would largely consist in the laying out of the moves and counter-moves. My own suspicion is that the compatibilist–incompatibilist debate, and the debate about reasons and causes, reach a stand-off at this point. Incompatibilists go on claiming that compatibilists have redefined free will in order to buy a cheap victory, and compatibilists go on claiming that they alone can say all that anyone can meaningfully say about free will. It is, then, in a spirit of disappointed agnosticism that we can return to the topic of determinism, uncertain whether the participant attitudes ought to be abandoned if determinism is true.[5]

Determinism again

Modern physics, we are frequently told, is fundamentally indeterministic. The old mechanistic idea of the universe, especially popular in the eighteenth century under the influence of Newtonian mechanics, has apparently been supplanted. Furthermore, scepticism about universal causal determinism could be entertained even before the advent of quantum theory, for determinism was never really an empirical claim but a metaphysical one. There are certain observable regularities, of course, but this is an inadequate basis for the ambitious metaphysical thesis of determinism. What is meant is this: that as Hume pointed out in a celebrated discussion of causality, mere *empirical regularity* in nature does not warrant, or even help us understand, the belief in *natural necessity*. On the other hand, this metaphysical notion of causality is entrenched in common sense thought, and it is perfectly reasonable to rely on causal regularities in a rough and ready way, without committing ourselves to a particular view about whether everything that happens is governed by deterministic laws. In short, there does not seem to be a case for the determination of human thought and bodily behaviour that is strong enough to make us abandon the participant attitudes, even if incompatibilism turns out to be true.

This brings us back to the participant attitudes themselves. Having sketched some of the background problems, it is essential to look again at reactions such as pride, admiration, respect and resentment, for it appears that the human world and moral thinking as we know it would be unrecognizable without at least some of these person-based responses.

These attitudes towards persons are extremely wide-ranging. The very possibility of such things as friendship, love, forgiveness, empathy, anger and sexual desire depends upon our adopting a participant rather than a detached point of view on their objects. The extent to which these ways of responding to persons pervade the human world cannot be overstated, and they include, but also go beyond, our moral responses. On those infrequent occasions when we do adopt the detached or objective attitude towards people, this detachment usually arises because we have detected something abnormal about the people in question – psychosis, perhaps, or extreme immaturity. We tend not to blame psychotic people for unpleasant things they do that are generated by their delusions, since in an important sense they do not share our world. This is the tragedy of many types of mental illness – sufferers cease to be intelligible to us, and in our eyes they almost become objects rather than persons. We come to see them as objects of scientific study rather than beings with whom we can genuinely interact on a personal level. We can fight them, if necessary, but we cannot quarrel with them.

Strawson, in his well-known article, emphasizes that such cases must be the exception rather than the rule, and that no acceptance of causal determinism could ever abolish the participant attitudes in most of our dealings with others. We shall return presently to Strawson's approach, but before doing so it is important to examine one popular justification of these attitudes, and certain practices which arise from them, which tries to bypass the issue of determinism altogether. This rationale may broadly be called *consequentialist*, although I do not suggest that those who adopt it must be thoroughgoing consequentialists in all other respects.

Consequentialist justifications

An obvious place to start is with punishment. We punish persons; we do not punish animals. At least, even if we sometimes act towards badly behaved animals in a way that resembles punishing them, it is not with the sort of motives for which we punish persons. We are not interested in getting the creatures to see themselves as *fit* objects of punishments, or in inducing shame in them. (Dog owners may be protesting at this point that their pets look distinctly guilty when caught doing things they shouldn't, and you may have noticed the way that cats always seem to be smiling. But much as it is important to develop *quasi*-personal relations with pets, the smiles are unfortunately just the way cats' jaws are made). Thus, foremost in our minds, at least for many of us, when we punish persons is that they deserve it, and perhaps (which is a connected thought) that to inflict suffering on them is a proper expression of a certain moral anger we feel towards them. This moral anger can be felt only towards beings we take to be morally responsible for their behaviour.

Now, in contrast to this natural way of looking at the matter, we might imagine someone proposing to punish people, not because they really are morally responsible for their actions, but in order simply to modify their behaviour and deter others from acting likewise. We might even do this because those being punished *think*, however mistakenly, that they deserve it and will not be able to feel forgiven until they have suffered. Furthermore, when particularly loathsome criminals get away with their crimes, there is public outrage, and this fact also could help justify their punishment. What nevertheless is absent from this account is any hint that the fate of those being punished is deserved.

If we criticize this attempt at justification, it is not because such considerations are irrelevant to the rationale of punishment. Rather, it is because it ignores the role of many punishments as an expression of disapprobation and indignation towards offenders. Punishment, I am suggesting, is fundamentally intelligible only when there is the notion of *moral desert* at its core; when those ordering it see it as a response to a person, justified because of what he has done. This, of course, is not to say that anyone really does deserve anything. If they do not, then whatever the peripheral merits of the pragmatic theory of punishment, the activity loses a rationale that is essential to it.

It is an interesting psycho-social fact (we might wryly remark here) that the "nasty" participant attitudes are, at least in sophisticated circles, a good deal less popular than the more congenial ones. Many decent people unthinkingly dismiss retribution and moral anger as barbaric or nothing but revenge. It is less common to find gratitude, forgiveness, sexual love or friendship similarly denigrated. Yet they too are participant responses which likewise depend – at least as far as *making sense* of them is concerned – upon a certain view of persons as being irreducible to purely scientific categories. Gratitude is an excellent parallel. If I express my gratitude to someone who went out of his or her way to help me, purely out of kindness, it is not because I sneakily think that my response will encourage future help. If that is my main thought, then it is not gratitude that I am expressing. Genuine expression of gratitude must spring from a sense that the gratitude is merited, and that its expression is appropriate independently of any consequences it may produce.

Thus, whatever we say, in the last analysis, about the ultimate justifiability of the participant reactive attitudes, they constitute an integral part of the realm of appearances, which we cannot just give up. For the most part, persons cannot fail to appear to us in this way. Behaviour such as reciprocation and punishment presents itself, almost unavoidably, as a response to personal, moral beings. Such behaviour is rational and intelligible to us only in terms of notions like *desert*.

By contrast, the way the emergence of such behaviour is *causally* explained may well, for all we know, refer to quite different kinds of thing: for example, Darwinian selection. Perhaps reciprocal behaviour confers some sort of evolutionary advantage upon those who practise it, and that is why it persists. Explanations like this are acceptable, provided they do not pretend to explain the inner meaning, or intentionality of such interpersonal responses. To do that, it is wise to look at the appearances themselves rather than search for the underlying causes.

A remaining disquieting thought

There is still a worry. We have suggested that the participant attitudes are deeply rooted and that practices such as reward and punishment are truly intelligible only by reference to them. We have also failed to find any decisive deterministic argument showing that these attitudes should be abandoned, or at least are irrational in some way. But we haven't exactly answered the (incompatibilist) determinist either; the verdict on these claims has instead been like the Scottish judicial verdict of "not proven". What would be satisfying, if it could be achieved, would be the success of some argument showing that the determinism issue is really irrelevant to the issue of our participant attitudes. Something like this has been attempted by Strawson (see Note 1).

Strawson, freedom and resentment

Strawson's attempt to rescue the participant attitudes is subtle. He emphasizes, as we have just done, the indispensability of inter-personal responses in intelligible human relationships and also delineates a range of conditions under which it seems right to suspend such attitudes. For instance, there are sometimes circum-stances that can remove a person, on a particular occasion, from blame, while leaving in place his membership of the moral commu-nity. Thus, if you are under great stress, your uncontrolled temper may be looked on with indulgence. There are also more radical cases where it seems appropriate to suspend the participant atti-tudes altogether, as we might towards some psychotic people. The important point, though, is that misfortunes like madness are incapacitating – they deprive you of your ability to think and act with an eye on reality. But the theoretical commitment to deter-minism – whatever that might ultimately amount to – is decidedly not a conviction that all persons are incapacitated in that sense. We think of these conditions as abnormal, and we require there-fore a backdrop of normality against which this judgement can be made.

But why, we might ask, should we not accept this yet still advocate the abolition of the participant attitudes? True, psycho-ses and the like are unusual and especially noticeable types of incapacitating condition, but why should ordinary causal deter-minism hamper genuine responsibility any less? Strawson's general answer here is, to a certain extent, the avoidance of an answer: he maintains that a sustained objectivity of interpersonal attitudes is not something humans would be capable of, even if they believed there were some theoretical grounding for it. We just *cannot* give up these attitudes; it is therefore useless to ask whether it *would be rational* to do so if we believed in determin-ism. Indeed, such a question can seem meaningful only to someone who has

> ... utterly failed to grasp the purport of ... the fact of our natural human commitment to ordinary interpersonal atti-tudes. This commitment is part of the general framework of human life, not something that can come up for review as

particular cases can come up for review within the general framework.[6]

Furthermore, even if we had to face the question of what it would be rational to do if we came to accept determinism, we could answer that question only in terms of the gains and losses to human life that would ensue if we abandoned the interpersonal attitudes. This is one of the most important points: it stresses the given nature of the interpersonal responses as a necessary condition for meaningful human relationships and institutions. It also seems to hint, at least for a reader who really understands Strawson's suggestions, at the unintelligibility of a sincere attempt to abandon these attitudes. Of course, there is nothing wrong with trying to modify and control some of them, if only because this might be required by the "better" among them. But the whole framework cannot be given up. It thus seems that no theory that implied that the framework should be given up could ever be more convincing than the fact that giving up the framework is not a serious option.

If this is correct, then there are two possibilities with respect to determinism: either it is compatible (in some sense) with the framework of interpersonal attitudes, in which case we need not fear for that framework, or it is not compatible with it, in which case we have excellent reason for rejecting determinism. Of course, so far that argument has proceeded by mounting a powerful case for the interpersonal attitudes, independently of separate consideration of arguments which would, if sound, undermine it. However, we cannot forget that these responses are implicated in meaningful social relationships, and such relationships would be seriously impoverished by any attempt to undermine them wholesale.

More importantly, such an attempt would fly in the face of the way we must – from a first-person point of view – understand ourselves. Whatever my philosophical views about determinism, I cannot fail to see myself as an agent with reasons and values which can explain my actions. I have ends as well as desires, and am capable of evaluating my desires. I can also form "second order" desires – desires concerning desires. If I am a compulsive gambler and waste away most of my salary in casinos, I can still strongly *desire not to desire* to do this. Among the good reasons for suspending our reactive attitudes with respect to certain people is the discovery that there has been an incapacitating breakdown in their practical reasoning; they cannot rationally evaluate options, or form second order desires. This might be true of the severely mentally impaired and the insane. More controversially, it is sometimes said of psychopaths, who, although not insane or lacking in intelligence, seem unmoved by ordinary moral considerations. The important consideration is that these conditions somehow disable the agent from making moral decisions. Where the agent was able to make moral decisions, and exercised wrong choices, it may be that condemnation is in order.

Furthermore, it is by treating people as moral beings, at least partially, that we enable them to become so. The moral development of children largely occurs precisely because those they interact with *treat* them as moral agents. The special difficulty with young children, of course, is that they are not yet morally mature, and therefore are not proper objects of the full range of participant attitudes. It is therefore unjust to hold them fully responsible for what they do. However, it is by treating them as having some responsibility, however qualified, that we cause them to become more responsible. Indeed, by praising or upbraiding them for doing things of which they do not yet have a full moral understanding, we get them to acquire such understanding. It is only then that they can learn to understand questions of practical reason, such as "what should I do?", "what sort of person will I be if I do this rather than that?"

Final reflections

The difficulties in this whole topic cannot be overestimated, and I have some sympathy with any reader who thinks the threat of determinism has been treated a little evasively. It is, though, important to see what life would be like without participant attitudes, in order to judge how credible the rational case for such abandonment could be. I have also echoed some distinctly Kantian themes that emerged in Chapter 4, especially concerning Kant's attempt to answer the question of free will by appeal to practical reason, and the perspective of the moral deliberator. There is a strongly Kantian flavour to Strawson's approach, which I have treated sympathetically, but the mysteries in Kant's answer to these problems remain, and our best hope is that while Kant has failed to give us a real solution to the problems of free will and moral responsibility, he has shown us what the problem really is, and how it might, at least in principle, be resolved.

Further reading

Ayer, A.J. Freedom and necessity. In *Free will*, G. Watson (ed.) (Oxford: Oxford University Press, 1982), pp. 15–23. A very clear statement and defence of compatibilism.

Frankfurt, H. Freedom of the will and the concept of a person. See Watson (ed.), 1982, pp. 81–95. Introduces the concept of first- and second-order desires, to which I briefly alluded.

Honderich, T. *How free are you?* (Oxford: Oxford University Press, 1993). A readable introduction-with-teeth to the issue, which takes the implications of determinism seriously.

Hume, D. *An enquiry concerning human understanding* (1748) L.A. Selby-Bigge (ed.) 3rd edn (Oxford: Clarendon Press, 1975). See Section VIII. A classic statement of compatibilism.

Strawson, P.F. Freedom and resentment. See Watson (ed.), 1982, pp. 59–80. As we have seen, this is a subtle essay that throws the issue of moral responsibility and determinism into a new light.

van Inwagen, P. *An essay on free will.* (Oxford: Clarendon Press, 1983).

van Inwagen, P. The incompatibility of free will and determinism. See Watson (ed.), 1982, pp. 46–58. Difficult, but rewards close study.

Watson, G. (ed.) *Free will* (Oxford: Oxford University Press, 1982).

Chapter 7

Virtue

Much of our discussion so far has been centred around two important issues in moral theory: that of whether there can be any objective basis for our judgements of right and wrong, and good and bad, and that of whether there is any credible theory that can determine what we ought to do. The first question is metaethical: it asks about the status of moral claims. Can they be literally true or false? If not, is there some other way in which they can be justified? Can there be a moral system which is objectively binding on all people in all places and at all times? The second question, as we have seen, concerns moral theory. Is there some theory – for example, "always promote the greatest happiness of the greatest number" – that can determine our duty? Both these questions have taken us to the heart of contemporary moral philosophy, and both leave us with seemingly intractable puzzles. On the one hand, it is initially hard to understand how evaluative judgements can be objectively true; on the other hand, even leaving the objectivity question aside, it is hard to see much resemblance between dominant theories like utilitarianism and the way most of our moral reasoning actually proceeds in everyday life. For most of us, the important moral questions we face are not about what to do when faced with the choice between causing one death and causing five, or between torturing a terrorist to gain life-saving information, and refusing to torture the terrorist at the risk that his hidden bomb goes off. They are really more like: should I open a bottle of wine tonight, or finish this chapter? Should I, out of benevolence, omit an unflattering detail about someone in a reference I write for her? What might be useful is some credible account both of the nature of morality and the nature of the good life that can speak to ordinary life.

It is in this spirit that from about the late 1950s there has been a revival of interest in specific *virtues and vices* and the centrality of virtue in moral philosophy. In what follows we shall be guided mainly by the question of whether virtue theory, as it is sometimes called, can contribute anything to morality that cannot be captured by some other approach. We should also bear in mind the problems we discussed in Chapter 2 about the objectivity of morality. For it is possible that a theory of the virtues, and the good life virtues make possible, can provide the kind of objectivity we were seeking for moral claims. Whether this is so is a question we shall postpone until the end.

Aristotle's ethics

Virtue theorists place a special emphasis on virtues and vices and give relatively little explicit attention to moral rules and principles. For this reason we might contrast virtue theory with *action-based theory*. Whereas for the Kantian, the central question of morality is "what ought I to do", for the virtue theorist, the really important question is "what kind of person ought I be?" This is not to say there is any strict incompatibility between these two approaches. Indeed, the extent to which they are in conflict is an intriguing question to which we shall return. For the moment, let us just say that there is a difference of emphasis and priority. Our task is to see if anything interesting comes out of the idea of the virtues.

Contemporary virtue theory is greatly inspired by the Greek philosopher Aristotle (384–322 BC). For it is in Aristotle's

Nicomachean ethics[1] that we find a highly detailed yet lucid treatment of the subject. In contrast to Kantian and utilitarian approaches, Aristotle is not concerned to discover a supreme practical principle telling us what to do, or to derive any secondary moral rules from such a principle. He is concerned with the sort of people we must be if we are to live the good life. If we can become like this, through proper moral education and practice in making right decisions, then we shall live the good life.

But what is this good life? Here we need to introduce Aristotle's account of human nature and human fulfilment. The opening words of the *Nicomachean ethics* are "Every art and every inquiry, and similarly every action and pursuit, is thought to aim at some good; and for this reason the good has rightly been declared to be that at which all things aim." Some goods are chosen for the sake of other goods, and these in turn may be chosen for the sake of yet other goods. But it cannot be that everything is chosen only for the sake of something else – that way the whole process goes on to infinity. There must be something that is chosen for its own sake, and this must be the chief good. To know the nature of this good is the aim of all ethical enquiry. Since it is the chief good, it is nonsensical to go on asking why it should be pursued; someone who needs to ask that question has not understood what it is. However, it may not be possible, on the spot, to give to someone who does not recognize that good a reason why he should pursue it. To know what the good consists of, you must have received the right kind of moral education and formed your character in the right way. This is a long-drawn out process that centres on the education of desire.

The good for man: happiness

According to Aristotle, the chief good for man is *eudaimonia*, which is usually translated as *happiness*.[2] It is something "final and self-sufficient, and is the end of action".[3] It is desired for itself alone, and cannot be made better by the addition of any other good. This eudaimonia is not exactly a psychological state, such as a feeling of euphoria, but is really a condition of well-being, or faring well. No doubt there is a connection between feeling happy and having your life go well. But it is the idea of your life going well that captures the idea of eudaimonia; we might say that in such a state you flourish.

Of what does such flourishing consist? The answer to this is found by discovering the function that man uniquely performs, and that sets him apart from all other living creatures. This brings to light an important element in Aristotle's philosophy; everything in nature has a function or characteristic activity, and man is no exception. The function of the eye is to see, the hand to hold, similarly each part of the body has a function, or is "for something". Aristotle thinks that man's function cannot be mere biological living, since animals and plants also do this. It cannot consist in perception either, since some animals also are perceivers. It must, says Aristotle, consist in that which is unique to us, as human beings. This is the life of our rational element. It is "activity of soul exhibiting excellence, and if there be more than one excellence, in accordance with the best and the most complete".⁴ For only human beings enjoy this.

The connection between man's function and his good (or happiness) is this: that just as an eye flourishes if it does well that which it is for, so a man flourishes and is happy if he does well that for which he is for. This is brought out in a slightly opaque way, as follows: ". . . if we say 'a so-and-so' and 'a good so-and-so' have a function which is the same in kind, e.g. a lyre-player and a good lyre-player . . . if this is the case . . . human good turns out to be an activity of soul exhibiting excellence . . .".⁵ For every activity there is an appropriate excellence, and all activity aims not only to perform its appropriate function, but to perform it as well as possible.

Some initial difficulties

Before linking this with a theory of the virtues, it is worth giving Aristotle's theory a helping hand by first conceding certain well-known criticisms of it, and then trying to show how something important may still be retained in spite of them.

A first, obvious objection is to the idea that man is *for* something; that he has a function. True (the critic says), there are things that man does, and many of these are guided by some kind of reasoning. But this is no ground for thinking that this is his function, independently of the plans and activities that he actually values. In other words, the mere fact that there are certain things he can do and sometimes does, is a poor ground for thinking this is what he *should* be doing. Secondly, even if we allow that man does have a function in this sense, it by no means follows that it is an activity that is unique to him. The mere fact that man alone lives according to a rational principle does not imply that this is what he is for, and that his good consists in doing this well. Thirdly (the critic continues), it is obvious that men do many things, apart from thinking, that no other creature can do. Competition, sport, artistic endeavour, as well as less edifying activities like mass murder and torture are also unique to the human race. Why should the life of the rational element in us be given special importance? Either we include all these activities under the heading of *rational activity*, in which case the idea becomes vacuous, because it leaves too many different activities from which to choose, or we narrowly restrict the activities that are to count as exhibiting man's rational function, in which case we are still left with many other activities apart from rational ones, each of which can claim to constitute the function of man, since no other creature can engage in them.

Aristotelian rejoinders

These points have some merit. But they do not fatally damage Aristotle's theory. The first criticism gains particular plausibility from Darwin's theory of evolution by natural selection, which has forced us to be more careful than Aristotle could be in claiming that anything in nature literally has a purpose. Modern Aristotelians should accept this theory, or lose entitlement to serious consideration. The explanation for the existence of eyes and ears is not literally given in goal-directed terms. Eyes did not literally develop *in order* to see; they *exist*, and they *do* see (or better, enable their bearers to see). They are the product of hundreds of millions of years of adaptation, which itself may not be guided by any purpose at all. However, even admitting this, it is clear that the distinct causal contribution of the eye is that it enables vision, and it seems appropriate to talk of eyes that do not enable vision as being defective or damaged. Seeing is what eyes do best, at least relative to human interests. So there might likewise be something that humans do best, such that they flourish when they do it well.

What this thing is could be linked, moreover, to our interests as rational beings and not only to our interests as biological beings. Aristotle gets his ideas about function from his metaphysical biology, but it is important not to construe his ideas about human well-being in purely biological terms. Our rational capacities owe their existence to biological evolution, but once they are in place, they can generate rational interests that can even go against our interests as biological entities. Self-sacrifice, for instance, might be in our interests as rational beings, even if our chief biological drive is to survive.

The second point perhaps has more force – it is difficult to see why the function of man (even allowing that there is one) must consist in what is unique to him. However, we may be understanding the idea of a *rational principle* somewhat too narrowly in making this criticism. Thinking is not to be sharply opposed to perceiving or experiencing emotions and sensations. Perception itself essentially involves understanding as well as raw experience, and emotions also can have a rational element, in that they are often *about* something. So although both humans and animals perceive and feel, humans' way of doing all these things might be unique. It is over-simple to say that humans and animals enjoy roughly similar sense experiences and differ only in the ability to reason. For the rationality that is distinctive of humanity pervades all aspects of our lives and is not limited to purely abstract reasoning. This does not make the idea of the rational principle vacuous through being too inclusive. The fact that rationality is manifested in such a variety of activities does not imply that the concept of rationality itself is vague or over-inclusive. Aristotle's theory, incidentally, backs this up: in fact he goes on to say that even if the best life is one of contemplation, you can lead a good life just by displaying practical reason in all your many types of dealing.

Virtues and needs

We can return to the idea of man's function and good to see how these ideas connect with Aristotle's account of the virtues. One important point is that virtues are not just *good* or *admirable* in some abstract way; they are needs. We all need the virtues – that is, we need to possess them ourselves, rather than merely profit from the possession of them by others. For Aristotle, they are needed in order to be happy. Happiness, he tells us, is an activity of soul in accordance with perfect virtue. To lack virtue is therefore to lack happiness, which is the good.

What is meant, in general, by saying that one thing is needed for something else? Sometimes there is a straightforward means-end relation. A man might, in this sense, need to be hard-working in order to realize his ambition to be rich or famous. What he values is the end result alone, but he knows that he will not get it unless he cultivates a habit of work. In this case, he does not value industriousness for itself – he may prefer, other things being equal, to do as little as possible. So in this case, there is only an accidental relationship between the means and the desired end; if he could attain the end without the bother of working, he would do so. But it is not in this sense that we need the virtues in the Aristotelian scheme. Rather, there is an internal relationship between virtue and happiness; virtue is a *part of happiness*. Virtue is needed for happiness, but not in a simple means-end way: there could not, even in principle, be any happiness apart from virtue. The good for man – happiness – is to live according to a rational principle. Virtue is a disposition to choose well, according to this rational principle. Man fares well – in a state of eudaimonia – when he lives and chooses according to it.

The virtues and the mean

Virtue, says Aristotle, is a state of character. It is not a passion, like anger or fear, or a faculty, like the capacity for anger or fear. Neither is it virtuous or vicious – *per se* – to feel such emotions. The important thing is that in respect of these feelings, virtue is the *mean state* between excess and deficiency. This is Aristotle's famous *doctrine of the mean*. At times he calls virtue the intermediate state between too much and too little, but makes it clear that this is not a matter of being literally at the mid-point between two extremes. Rather, where the mean is to be found depends on the circumstances and must be discerned by careful judgement.

Some examples should illustrate this well. Anger, for instance, can be virtuous, provided that it is experienced in the right degree, towards the right object and at the right time. Pleasure, too, is virtuous when taken in the right things and in the right degree. Aristotle calls the *excess*, the *deficiency* and the *mean* by different names. Thus liberality is the mean with regard to disposing of money, while prodigality is the excess and meanness the deficiency. In matters of honour and dishonour, "the excess is known as a sort of 'empty vanity', and the deficiency is undue humility".[6] With respect to courage, the excess is rashness and the deficiency cowardice.

The nature of the virtues in Aristotle's ethical theory has sparked off much controversy. The basic virtues of courage, justice, temperance and wisdom (what medieval thinkers called the *cardinal* virtues) have an important place both in Aristotle's scheme and in later Christian and secular thought. To get on in life we all need these virtues: courage because we could all face dangerous and fearful challenges, temperance because the ability to forswear or postpone the gratification of desire is essential to getting what we really want, and to lasting happiness. There are other virtues noted by Aristotle, such as *megalopsuchia*, often translated as *pride*, which are not valued by later thought. Aristotle does not value humility, though he does condemn boastfulness. Medieval Christian philosophy condemned pride as one of the seven deadly sins, though megalopsuchia is not the Christian sin of pride, which requires the Christian God as its context. Perhaps it is closer to the modern managerial virtue of *assertiveness*, much extolled today. It is also important to note that Aristotle's system takes hierarchy, including slavery, for granted. The highest virtue could be possessed only by males of a high social standing, and signs of such virtue apparently included a measured pace and a bass voice. But these outrages against the spirit of modernity should not prevent fruitful discussion of the content and structure of Aristotle's theories.

Pleasure and desire

The rational principle that determines the mean, however, cannot be reduced to specific moral rules, or even general principles like "always treat others as ends" or "maximize the good". Right decisions depend on perception of individual circumstances. This does not mean that there are no absolutely forbidden actions, such as murder or adultery. However, we do not become virtuous (and therefore happy) by learning rules forbidding these actions. We gain virtue, and hence learn to make right decisions, by cultivating certain dispositions – and in particular by educating our desires.

Aristotle describes desires and appetites as an irrational element in the soul, but this is interestingly qualified. For although our desires do not in themselves grasp a rational principle, they can nevertheless respond to it. Moral virtue is a state of character that is acquired by moulding one's desires in the right way. It is not a matter of reason overriding desire or trying to ignore it. On the contrary, for Aristotle, the motive to all action, whatever its moral character, is desire. Virtue is fundamentally a matter of having the right desires, towards the right objects and in the right degree. This explains why Aristotle makes a distinction between acting virtuously, and acting in conformity with virtue. "Actions, then, are just and temperate when they are such as the just or the temperate man would do; but it is not the man who does these that is just and temperate, but the man who also does them *as* just and temperate men do them".[7] In other words, the agents must be in the right condition when they do them – in particular, action must spring from a firm character of the proper kind. Virtuous deeds must be second nature. They must have firm dispositions to the right kind of choices, and these dispositions are expressed in their desires.

From this we can see the importance of the education of character – the acquisition of these firm dispositions. According to Aristotle, this does not come naturally but must be taught. To this extent, there is some similarity between acquiring virtue and acquiring skills such as mastery of a musical instrument; both require practice before the appropriate habits are acquired. You get the dispositions by first of all acting as if you already had them – you train yourself to do the right things, and gradually you gain a standing disposition to do them. When you have this disposition, it will be second nature to choose according to the rational principle that defines the good life. Reason and desire will be in harmony, and inner conflict (which, incidentally, is plausibly regarded as a major cause of unhappiness) will have been removed. Moreover, a sign that the virtuous disposition has been acquired is that you take *pleasure* in performing virtuous deeds and are repelled by the thought of vicious ones. This attractive doctrine is in stark contrast to that of Kant, who as we saw (Chapter 4) insisted that pleasure in right action contributes in no way to its moral worth, and that no action with genuine moral worth can be explained solely by reference to the desires of the agent. It is surely better to take Aristotle's position on this, for much as we can muster some admiration for those who act solely out of a sense of duty and take no pleasure in doing their duty, we tend to think better of agents who like to do what they ought, because their good deeds express their real character.

What this suggests is that the fundamental question of morality, for virtue theory, is not: what ought I to do? but rather: what dispositions should I acquire? Once we have answered the second question, we may be able to answer the first. When confronted with a certain choice – say, between divulging a friend's confidence in order to be entertaining, or keeping quiet – the crucial question concerns what the person with the relevant virtue would do. Loyalty is an indispensable part of friendship, for it is the virtue that makes friendship possible. So the question would be: what would a loyal person do? Surely such a person would already have acquired certain desires and dispositions that would totally rule out breaking trust, at least for this sort of reason. Now it may well be that some of us, those of us who have not cultivated these dispositions throughout our lives, do not have a present reason to act as the loyal person would. We cannot immediately acquire such a reason, since we cannot immediately acquire the requisite desires. Given our actual desires, we lack a reason to be loyal. But Aristotle

would still insist that we have reason to acquire the right dispositions and desires, because without them we cannot attain complete happiness, the human good. We do not function well as
rational beings if our desires are not moulded in the light of a
rational principle.

Is virtue theory trivial?

This, then, is the Aristotelian background to modern virtue theory,
which of course has acquired a life of its own. Whatever we say in
praise of various virtues – in particular, the cardinal virtues of
courage, justice, temperance and wisdom – there is an awkward
problem. With what, exactly, is virtue theory being contrasted?
Can it say anything true and important that other moral theories
are unable to say?

Consider the idea that there are certain praiseworthy and
blameworthy actions, and that a virtuous person (one, that is, with
well-ingrained dispositions towards certain kinds of behaviour)
would do the good things and shun the bad. Still, why shouldn't
the good and the bad themselves be understood in terms of an
action-based (non-virtue-based) theory such as utilitarianism?
Suppose that what we ought to do is promote the greatest happiness of the greatest number. Why not then say that a virtuous
person is one who has a standing disposition to promote the greatest happiness of the greatest number? Benevolence is the specific
virtue that comes closest to such a disposition, so perhaps we
should call it a utilitarian virtue. Talk of virtue, on this account,
contributes nothing distinctive. Calling people virtuous is just
shorthand for saying that they are disposed to do what is right –
and the content of what is right could be given in purely utilitarian
terms.

A similar criticism of virtue theory could, of course, be made by
a Kantian, who might say that virtuous people are those whose
characters dispose them to act on principles they can will to become universal laws. In fact, those who believe that there are
morally obligatory and forbidden actions will want to define virtue
as a disposition to do what is required and refrain from what is
forbidden (whatever these may be). In other words, perhaps virtue

theory is not a viable replacement for action-based theories of moral obligation (be they utilitarian, Kantian, or whatever). We cannot eliminate the idea of right and wrong conduct, and replace it with virtue concepts, to do with good and bad character.

This criticism of virtue theory contains an important truth. There do seem to be indispensable principles and duties, respect for which cannot be understood simply in terms of the exercise of some specific virtue. It is often pointed out that the Aristotelian idea of the virtues is incompatible with modern democratic notions (although which should be abandoned, Aristotle's ideas or the modern democratic notions is something that might still be discussed). Aristotle thought that the highest virtue could be possessed only by those of an elevated social standing; thus he is really talking about appropriate behaviour for an Athenian gentleman. However, virtue theory need not endorse all of Aristotle's ideas about the specific virtues, or those of the Greeks generally. The important criticism is that the concept of the virtues makes little sense apart from the idea that a virtuous individual is disposed to do the right things – and we seem to need some other account that can tell us what the right things are.

Virtue theory's reply

The best reply the virtue theorist can make is this. No doubt there are right and wrong actions, and perhaps some of these are so absolutely, on account of their *intrinsic nature*. But virtue theory can shed light on these moral constraints. For example, whereas an action-based theory might ask, "How is the world improved or made worse by such and such an action?", a virtue theorist might ask what the doing of this action would reveal about the one who does it. Is this the action of a just, courageous or temperate person? If we think in this way, we end up with a set of moral concerns that is more plausible than anything that can be delivered by purely action-based accounts. In particular, it can offer telling criticisms of both utilitarian and contractualist approaches.

Suppose we accept that benevolence is an important virtue, being a disposition to be moved by sympathy for others and to act for the good of others, even when there is no special relationship in place and no prior agreement to help them. We then remember that utilitarianism makes much of benevolence – indeed its governing conception of morality is that of the impartial benevolent spectator (see Chapter 3). So when we contemplate some course of action, we ask whether it would be recommended by this hypothetical figure. Now, as we saw earlier, utilitarianism allows that some individuals could be morally obliged to devote substantial effort to producing what is intrinsically evil, in order to maximize the good. The question that will be asked by one of the few people chosen to produce the evil, as small cogs in the smoothly benevolent utilitarian machinery, is: could a truly benevolent person do this? Whatever the overall net good produced (if this even makes any sense), is my production of something intrinsically bad, consistent with my possessing all the important virtues? This consideration reminds us of earlier discussions of integrity. We can now link the idea of integrity with virtue theory – for integrity purports to be a virtue, or even virtue as such.

As we saw earlier, the familiar utilitarian answer is that this is a mere rhetorical assertion. Whereas before, it seemed as though we just had a stand-off with one side saying "yea" and the other "nay" to this utilitarian implication, asking what it is to possess a virtue may get us further. If Aristotle is right, virtues are deep dispositions acquired by training and habituation. It is psychologically highly unlikely that people habituated in the ways of benevolence, with a deeply ingrained disposition to concern for others, will be able to give up this concern upon calculating that more overall good would accrue if they did so. Although, for Aristotle, virtue involves the exercise of judgement in order to see what is required by the particular situation, it is unlikely that the proper exercise of such judgement by virtuous people could ever dictate the sustained infliction of suffering on a few people, to benefit the many. That would be radically contrary to the benevolent disposition. Human nature being what it is, it is very difficult to have kind or loyal dispositions, which operate when they are needed, but which are simply abandoned when utility so requires. To demand that we become like this is to fail to take account of what we actually are. As things are, the genuinely benevolent person never, or at most very rarely, does this sort of thing. Most or all of those who have urged atrocities for the "greater good" – notably revolutionary dictators such as Hitler, Lenin and Mao Tse-tung – have actually turned out to be men of extraordinary cruelty.

The question "would a virtuous person do this?" also has implications for the adequacy of purely contractualist theories. There seem to be actions to which we reasonably take exception, but which do not appear to be forbidden by a contractualist approach. Suppose that someone goes into a cemetery one night, making sure that no one can see him, and then spits on graves. This seems to be wantonly disrespectful and offensive. But to whom? Who is hurt or harmed? If we do not believe the dead can be hurt or harmed (since they no longer exist), and if the perpetrator does his deed in secret so that others cannot be upset, it is hard to answer these questions. Yet one might object just on grounds of character. To spit on graves is a sign of a bad character, a disrespectful disposition, and a virtuous person would not dream of doing it. These considerations are perhaps not decisive, but they do present a challenge pointing to the validity of appealing to virtues and vices to explain the moral nature of acts.

Virtue and motives

In fact, this kind of case leads to more general considerations about character and motive that seem to lend credibility to virtue theory. It is sometimes said that the main deficiency of purely action-based theories is that they have nothing to say about the moral dimensions of motives. They seem, according to these critics, to be saying that you are morally all right if you simply do the right thing, whatever went on in your mind when you did it. I suggest that there is something to be said for this criticism of action-based theory.

Some qualifications must be made, however, for motives do have a kind of importance in both Kantian and some utilitarian approaches. Indeed, for Kant, motive is indispensable – actions possess moral worth only if they are (a) in accordance with the categorical imperative, and (b) performed from the motive of duty. However, Kant's view on this is absurdly restrictive: he is right that we sometimes should admire people who act well from a sense of duty, especially when they do not feel like acting well – but it is surely wrong to withhold moral praise from those who are prompted only by native kindness. In fact, when we praise dutiful people who lack natural sympathy, we are really praising them for one virtue, strength of will, which operates to counter-act a deficiency in other virtues, such as instinctive kindness. We should likewise exonerate utilitarianism of the charge of disregarding the importance of motive and character. Most utilitarians would insist that they are important – if only because a standing disposition towards benevolence, or even towards respecting certain moral rules, has a long-term utilitarian value. *Rule utilitarians* are among those who emphasize the importance of character training; it is better have a disposition to keep certain rules even when breaking them seems to bring some immediate utilitarian benefit, than not abide by these rules and risk losing the long term benefit they bring.

The real trouble with these action-based concessions to character and virtue theory is that they have latched onto the wrong reasons for valuing good character – or at least have failed to capture the most fundamental ones. Consider how we might morally assess the following things: a habit of daydreaming about others praising you; fantasies of revenge; sexual fantasies about a person you know to be unavailable; wallowing in contemptuous thoughts about someone you consider a loser; feeling happy when someone you envy suffers a setback. This sort of list could go on indefinitely. What seems common to all the items is that they may well not issue in any wrong action. Merely entertaining thoughts of revenge will not necessarily result in acting on those thoughts, and wallowing in sexual fantasies about someone else's partner need not result in any attempt to seduce that partner. In consequence, a commonly held view is that there is nothing wrong with these thoughts; provided no one else is harmed, there is no objection to entertaining them.

But is this really so obvious? There are complex questions about the relationship between fantasy and genuine desire. Many people, for example, would not opt for all their sexual fantasies to become real even if they were offered the choice. However at least some private wallowing in fantasy of various kinds expresses real desire and character. An envious person might do spiteful things, but perhaps more often he will simply have envious thoughts, nursing his unhappiness that someone else has something he has not (and perhaps does not even want). Even when he does do spiteful deeds, much of what is wrong with them is precisely that they are prompted by envy. *Motives* (e.g. envy, jealousy) are often what gives our actions their moral complexion, and motives are born from our characters, from our individual sets of virtues and vices. This goes against the common assumption that the only thing to worry about, with respect to certain private imaginings, is that they might be acted out. There is as much truth in the reverse; if they are acted out, much of what is objectionable about the actions is the motive and state of character from which they spring.

An important contribution of virtue theory, therefore, is not that it does away with moral principles, but that it helps shape them. Rather than merely telling us not to steal, lie and so on, it tells us more generally to act justly, wisely, courageously and temperately. To act justly will usually entail not lying or stealing. But, to revert to Aristotle, we display virtue in doing the right thing only if the act springs from a standing disposition of character. To have this character will exclude not only the doing of unjust or disrespectful acts when these acts have victims, but also when they do not – as in the example of spitting on graves or wallowing in envious thoughts. The job of moral philosophy is largely concerned with asking how our characters should develop and what particular dispositions we should have.

More generally, and less negatively, consideration of the virtues can help shape principles of action by bringing a certain explanatory simplicity to them. Sometimes we get a sense of the moral shape of an action if we can detect in it a general similarity to other acts whose moral complexion we already understand. The use of virtue terms is a good way to describe this similarity. Thus, we might want to say that what deception, cheating, stealing and fraud have in common is that they are dishonest and, more generally, unjust. (In fact, words like *dishonest* play a more central role in everyday moral talk than words like *wrong*). The concept of justice is the bridging idea here. If I am wondering whether I can justify a certain course of action towards another, I have a better grip on the problem if I ask whether the behaviour is just, kind, honest, and so on, than if I vaguely ask whether it is right or ethical. Again, this is not to say that we can dispense with the idea of right and wrong, or reduce it all to talk of virtue. It does say that a grasp of virtues can help us classify individual acts and make their rightness or wrongness intelligible and explicable.

The unity of the virtues

But discussion of virtue raises an important difficulty that troubled Plato and Aristotle. Is it possible to display a virtue in an action that also displays a vice? If an action manifests one virtue, can it also be contrary to another? Cases that come to mind are the apparent courage of a terrorist in planting bombs that harm innocent people, or the apparent benevolence of the Robin Hood thief who steals lawfully gained property in order to help the poor. Is the terrorist courageous? He might be thought so if he carries bombs that could go off prematurely and kill him, and if he knows that if he is caught he will be tortured, imprisoned or killed. Is the thief benevolent? His thieving certainly seems to be motivated by sympathy for the poor in their plight.

The problem is not to do with whether one individual's character can contain both virtuous and vicious traits. For surely almost everyone's character has both. The question is whether a particular benevolent act can also be unjust, or a courageous act also cruel. (If you think these are bad examples of virtues or vices, replace them with others).

Start from the plausible idea that each virtue is something everybody should cultivate to the fullest possible extent. We should try not only to be *reasonably* honest, or *moderately* benevolent, but completely so. After all, it is not as if Aristotle, in proposing the doctrine of the mean, was saying that the good life is the mean between vice and virtue, and that too much virtue could be a bad thing! Each virtue is a mean state between two opposing vices, one of excess and the other of deficiency, but there can be no such thing as an excess of virtue itself. However, if we also allow that the more heedless of human suffering the terrorist is, the more courage he shows, we are implying that if he becomes more compassionate he also becomes less courageous. If he ought to have as much courage as possible, it would be hard to avoid calling this decrease in courage a moral deficiency. Similarly, if we allow that it is better to be perfectly benevolent than only moderately so, and allow that the man who steals to help the poor shows more benevolence than one who refuses to steal, then we seem committed to saying that (at least in respect of one virtue) the one who steals or kills should be admired more.

These implications do not seem edifying. Don't we want to say that virtues like justice and benevolence never truly conflict and that a perfectly benevolent person always acts within the constraints of justice? You do not always become more benevolent in direct proportion to the amount of happiness you create, because even if it is better, *ceteris paribus*, to create more rather than less happiness, it still seems to be usually wrong (because unjust) to steal or cheat.

According to one theory, the reason the specific virtues never conflict is that all virtues are ultimately different facets of one and the same thing – perhaps some master virtue, or *virtue* itself. This notion is called the theory of the *unity of the virtues*. Thus Plato[8] discusses whether all virtue is really knowledge, that is, whether courage, temperance, justice and wisdom are all ultimately kinds of knowledge. The supposition that you can display courage on some particular occasion but show a lack of wisdom, would entail that on this occasion you both possess and lack knowledge, which seems contradictory. I shall not pursue this idea, however. For there is a more promising solution, which comes from Philippa Foot's article Virtues and vices.[9]

Foot acknowledges, as we have just done with respect to the courageous terrorist and the benevolent thief, that there is something wrong with praising people whose apparent courage leads them to ever bolder crimes, or whose seeming benevolence leads them to unjust acts like theft. However, there is still something implausible about flatly denying that the criminal is courageous or the thief benevolent. Part of the difficulty with such denial (though this is not how she puts it) is that the courage shown in the pursuit of noble ends and the courage (or "courage") shown in the pursuit of bad ones seem to be exactly the same except in respect of their ends. Although the selection of the unworthy end may spring from a deficiency of some virtue, it does not seem to come from a deficiency of courage. To deny that courage is shown in the bad act is to define the word "courage" arbitrarily; we are merely deciding to use the *word* "courage" when we happen to approve of the end, but not use it otherwise. This is what is known as a "persuasive definition".

A good example of persuasive definition is in the dispute between those who would call the terrorist a freedom-fighter and those who would call him a terrorist. Often the use of such terms is purely persuasive or emotive. If you approve of him, you use one term and if you disapprove you use another, even if there is no descriptive difference that explains the difference in the terminology. Freedom-fighters might slaughter innocent people as a means to freedom; terrorists do exactly the same. In the cases of courage and benevolence being displayed in bad pursuits, what we should say (according to Foot) is that although courage, benevolence, etc., are indeed displayed, *they do not operate as virtues* in these cases. Although courage is *by nature* a virtue, things do not always operate according to their natures. Analogously, a solvent, by nature, dissolves in water – but there can be special circumstances that prevent it from doing so. Prudence is also a virtue and normally operates as such, but not in people who are so obsessed with danger that they never take even rational risks. Such people, in fact, lack courage. Industriousness usually acts as a virtue, but not in people who neglect their families to advance their careers. These states of character are virtues because they are what a normal human needs to get through life and flourish, yet there can still be times when they do not operate as virtues.

This is a promising line of argument. However, it must be admitted that this explanation may not apply to all virtues, but only to the "executive" ones like courage and industriousness. It is harder to claim that there are occasions when justice does not operate as a virtue. But Foot's account is at least a plausible partial solution to the problem, even though it seems to leave some problems unanswered.

We have suggested that investigation of the kind of people we should be, and not just of how we should act, is an important part of moral philosophy, and that it can help us determine how we should behave. We also saw that we cannot replace action-talk with virtue-talk. We cannot get rid of the concept of right and wrong action. In fact, the more plausible virtue-based approaches do not suggest that we can – rather, they justify their views on what is right and wrong in terms of virtues. Thus, they might tell us not to cheat because it is dishonest, and not to bully others because it is cruel.

This raises another problem, however. Although there is rhetorical resonance in words like *dishonest, cruel, dishonourable* and so on, that might sometimes have an effect on behaviour when words like *wrong* and *immoral* do not, we still need some reason why we should value these virtues. What is so good about honesty? Questions like this become even more pressing when it comes to alleged virtues that do not relate to behaviour that is widely valued. The admonition to avoid casual sex because it is *unchaste* – chastity being a specifically sexual virtue – is unlikely, at least in a libertarian culture such as our own, to convince many people. What is so admirable about chastity? How can appealing to this concept, without further explanation, provide a good reason for sexual restraint?

Questions like this are perfectly legitimate, whether or not true answers to them will gain much acceptance. They become more urgent when two different virtues come into apparent conflict. Suppose loyalty impels me not to inform on my friend who is fraudulently drawing state benefit, but that a sense of justice impels me to do so. How do we adjudicate between these virtues, once we have decided that it is these virtues that are in play?

It is here that Aristotle's conception of virtue is relevant. For him, a virtue is a constitutive part of living well – of eudaimonia. Living well means living in accordance with our nature. Now, obviously enough, there is much diversity among people, for example in the way of talents, interests or occupations. Such differences indicate that, in many ways, the good life for one person is not the good life for another. But we can get the *structure* of an answer from Aristotelian virtue theory – we do not need to agree with all his claims about human nature and the content of the virtues. What we get, in essence, is plausible: that we are social beings who form plans, enjoy intimate relationships, have ambitions and pleasures – and that there are more and less fulfilling ways of going about these things. If we cultivate the virtues internal to friendship we are likely to have satisfactory and life-enhancing friendships, and if we have the virtues internal to work, our work is likely to be fulfilling. As we mentioned earlier, it is best to think of the virtues as needs. They are needed for the satisfactory fulfilment of the activities in which we characteristically engage.

This leaves many questions unanswered, of course. We cannot claim to have a blueprint for answering all moral problems or resolving dilemmas. What we do have is an idea of the sort of thing we should be looking for when we try to solve such problems.

Virtues, strange obligations and moral objectivity

There is another advantage in virtue theory, which is that even if it is vague in its prescriptions, it can rule out certain things as morally unimportant. Writers like Foot[10] and Anscombe[11] stress that anything that can be called a moral requirement must be related to human good and harm. Hence it would not merely be eccentric, but incoherent, to posit as a moral principle that you should clap your hands repeatedly, or run around trees anti-clockwise. Of course, if these activities have some meaning in a given context, then they may have a moral dimension – maybe the hand-clapping is applause that you politely offer to your neighbour's dismally untalented child at a school concert. But hand-clapping cannot in itself have any moral value. This is because it is intrinsically unrelated to human good and harm. We can make no sense of hand-clapping as a moral obligation. This is not so of all moral theories and supposed obligations that we reject. For example, although we might regard utilitarianism as substantially misguided, we can still recognize its claim to be a moral doctrine as coherent and intelligible because it aims to produce happiness, which is a good.

If the virtues are human needs relating to a flourishing life, then we can make the above point by saying that hand-clapping is entirely unrelated to any virtue or vice. We need a disposition to face danger when necessary, and we call this courage. We need a disposition to restrain our impulses at times, and we call this temperance. That we need these things is the reason why they are virtues, but we do not need a disposition to run around trees a certain way, or clap our hands. We do not think that such activities make us good people.

This brings us back to the Aristotelian conception of a good person and its relation to human function. As we saw, Aristotle thought that everything in nature had a function and that a condition of flourishing for a living being is that it should live in accordance with that function. Thinking was man's distinctive function, so he lived well if he lived in accordance with a *rational principle*. (He also believed that an even higher activity than practical reasoning was theoretical reasoning, and that consequently the best life was the purely contemplative one. The cultivation of intellectual virtues as well as moral ones contributed to the good life. For reasons of simplicity I have not discussed this aspect of his theory). Thinking well was the essence of being a good man. This idea has considerable theoretical attractions, both for answering questions about the content of morality and its objectivity. It seems to make moral truth into a kind of *naturalistic* truth; we are supposed to discern whether a man is living well simply by seeing whether he is living according to his function. Similarly, we can see whether a certain boat is a good boat by observing whether it floats, moves smoothly across water, and so on – in other words, by observing whether or not it fulfils the function of boats. If it is beautiful and expertly crafted, but cannot stay afloat, then in spite of these merits it is not a good boat.

"Good" as a descriptive term

This fact leads us to notice something quite important about the way the word "good" is used in such examples. In saying that a vessel is a good boat, we are not saying simply that it is *both* good *and* a boat. We are saying that it is good *as* a boat. Analogously, for Aristotle, to speak of a good man (feminism was not around, though women were believed to exist), is to speak of somebody who is good *as* a man, who discharges the function characteristic of man.[12]

Other examples will clarify the way "good" is used here. A good knife is not a thing which is *both* good *and* a knife. That idea is nonsense. It is just a good knife, a knife that performs the function of a knife well. Similarly, a small buffalo is not a thing which is small and a buffalo; it is small *as* a buffalo, that is, small by the standards of buffaloes. A small buffalo is bigger than a big cat. By contrast, a rectangular table is *just* something that is a table and rectangular.

The suggestion, then, is that goodness in men may be a matter of being "good men", that is, good as far as men go. This means that the term "good" is not just a term of approval: it is descriptive. Certain descriptions must be satisfied if the term "good" is to be correctly applied. The criteria for such goodness are decided according to man's function. If we can discern man's function, and discern who is living according to it, we have an objective, descriptive answer to questions about goodness in men. Correspondingly, actions performed by men are right or wrong according to whether they incline them towards, or away from, the fulfilment of their function. Furthermore (and here we return to an earlier concern) if we really can construe human goodness in this way, then certain puzzles about the objectivity of such goodness appear to have been solved, at least up to a point. There is no need to invoke mysterious action-guiding properties, or strange non-natural entities; values are instead both objective and naturalistic. We can find out whether a person is good by looking and seeing, in a wholly non-mysterious way.

Some problems

Some difficulties, however, diminish the force of this suggestion. Whereas the example of the eye's function suggests that good eyes are those that see well, and defective ones those that do not, it is unclear that people have functions so specific that we can identify the good life as the fulfilment of it. We allowed that there is something important and true in the idea that the good life is connected to the rational faculty, but there are problems in trying to identify this completely with the *moral* life. No doubt there is *some* connection between the flourishing of our most distinctive qualities, and the possession of moral virtue. However, people display many distinctively human excellences, and not all of them are moral virtues. Aristotle himself distinguishes moral from intellectual virtue, and we can mention many other kinds as well: social virtues (like being good at conversation), creativity, artistic talent, humour, physical strength, endurance, beauty. We certainly value these things in ourselves and others, and many of them are unique to humans. Activities in accordance with these have as much claim to define the function of man as the life of moral virtue. Sometimes they even conflict with moral virtue. Unusual creativity might bring with it a certain moral indifference, and a bit of malice and intolerance can contribute to the social virtues of being funny and interesting.

Aristotle does mention some of these non-moral virtues and does regard some of them as part of the good for man. He attaches value to the social virtues and treats artistic talent in his *Poetics*. He also regards endurance as meritorious. This tends to illustrate that our modern notion of virtue is different in many ways from that of Aristotle. For him, there is a far less pronounced distinction between what we call moral virtue and other excellences. This observation does not so much detract from Aristotle's theory of the good life, as from the attempt to use Aristotelian ideas to back up a narrow, modern account of the moral life. For Aristotle, flourishing as a human being is not just a matter of possessing the moral virtues. Nevertheless, if we bear this caution in mind, we are still able to derive some substantial guidance as to the moral life from Aristotle's ideas about function. Virtues like temperance really are crucial to our flourishing, and we understand the nature of temperance and our need of it if we reflect on what happens to people who lack it. There is, indeed, evidence that children who are able to defer gratification of immediate impulses become more successful and happy as adults than those who lacked this ability as children. This accords with Aristotle's advice that habituation in the virtues must begin at an early age.

A more serious objection to Aristotelian ethics is that there may be no more than a loose connection between the life that benefits us and the moral life. This brings us to a theme that occupies Plato, in his *Republic*: namely, does it pay to lead to moral life? Certainly, the virtues generally help our lives to go well – but the life that is good for us (i.e. the life that benefits us) and the morally virtuous life are not the same thing. Utilitarians, for all their faults, are right to urge that our duties of concern for strangers extend beyond what most of us like to think; that serious sacrifices to the quality of our lives may be required by morality. No doubt some self-sacrificing people, such as Christian ascetics, would urge that we *really* lead the good life if we make these sacrifices. There is some truth in this, in that, for example, too many material possessions can be a burden, but unless their fundamental religious beliefs are true, it is surely an overstatement. It is more credible to say that a certain sacrifice of genuine well-being, of the good life for us, is necessary if we are to act well.

As far as the question of the objectivity of human goodness is concerned, we can offer the following summary of virtue theory's contribution to the problem. There is considerable plausibility in the claim that actions that are morally right spring from the exercise of specific moral virtues, and that contemplation of the virtues (and indeed vices) therefore helps us determine the content of morality. It is also plausible that virtues are both a means to well-being (or human flourishing) and, in some way, a part of that flourishing. Thus morality appears at its core to be essentially connected to human good and harm, and this suggests that certain actions simply could not be accounted right or wrong in themselves, if they have no connection to human good and harm. This in turn partially breaks down the "fact-value distinction' to which we referred in Chapter 2. This distinction clearly breaks down in the case of the good knife, because not just any knife can count as a good one; only a knife that cuts well (i.e. performs the proper function of knives) can count as a good knife. Thus, certain evaluations of knives (like good, reasonable and useless) are logically tied to certain descriptive properties of them. In the same way, there is a limited sense in which not just any style of living could count as human flourishing, and not just any action could count as morally right. So far, then, there is much of importance in the Aristotelian way of looking at things.

For the reasons given above, this theory won't solve all our problems, either concerning the content of morality or its objectivity. Morality is only part of human well-being, and perhaps not the most significant part. To a great extent, a wealthy aesthete who lacks a social conscience, and who surrounds himself with fine things and refined human company, does lead the good life – he does flourish. But the demands of morality, perhaps of a Kantian or utilitarian kind, still generate objective practical reasons for him to attend to more impartial concerns. If, as is plausible, such moral concerns can override the importance of the good life he leads, then there is a way in which the objectivity of these concerns cannot be entirely captured in an Aristotelian account of moral objectivity. Virtue theory, for all its virtues, does not have the last or only word on these things.

Further reading

Anscombe, G.E.M. Modern moral philosophy. In *Philosophy* **33** (1958), pp. 1–19. A savage attempt to expose the alleged absurdity and corruption of moral philosophy as (mal)practised in Oxford in the 1950s, and a plea for a return to an Aristotelian conception of human good.

Aristotle, *Nicomachean ethics*. Transl. by W.D. Ross, revised by J.L. Ackrill and J.O. Urmson. (Oxford: Oxford University Press, 1980).

Casey, J. *Pagan virtue*. (Oxford: Clarendon Press, 1990). An attempt to revive some classical conceptions of specific virtues and contrast them with supposedly inferior modern ideas about virtue. A good read, full of literary and cultural allusions.

Foot, P. *Virtues and vices*. (Oxford: Basil Blackwell, 1978). This collection contains many seminal articles that have become classics. See in particular Virtues and vices, Goodness and choice, Moral beliefs and Moral arguments. The collection as a whole is a neo-Aristotelian challenge to "non-cognitivist" and neo-Kantian ideas about moral objectivity and moral reasons.

MacIntyre, A. *After virtue*. (London: Duckworth, 1981). For reasons of space and simplicity, I have not mentioned the works of MacIntyre in this chapter (in a way his work is a topic in itself). However, MacIntyre is a major defender of neo-Aristotelian theory, which he locates in the context of the history of ethics. If you wish to pursue these ideas, it will be necessary to read this and some later works by MacIntyre.

Chapter 8

Reasoning about ethics

It is . . . wrong to suggest that wisdom cannot be a moral virtue because virtue must be within the reach of anyone who really wants it and some people are too stupid to be anything but ignorant even about the most fundamental matters of human life. Some people are wise without being at all clever or well informed: they make good decisions and they know, as we say, "what's what".[1]

To what extent is ethical thinking an intellectual operation? How much should we reason about ethics? We all know people who, as Foot puts it, know what's what, or are sensible and wise, without having great intellectual gifts. They may become anxious and confused when challenged to argue for some moral opinion they have, yet we feel that we can trust them and their judgement when it comes to things that really matter. Just as often, we come across people of impressive intellectual accomplishments, quick and re-sourceful in argument and able to deal with highly abstract con-cepts, but who make a mess of their own lives and other people's.

They strike us as clever, but are at bottom quite silly. They might have personal weaknesses such as a susceptibility to flattery or an obsession with prestige or social status, and many of them are poor judges of character, driven by their emotional deficiencies to admire all the wrong qualities in others. In short, we might say that they value the wrong things.

This is no great revelation. But it does help us focus some important questions. What is the relation between being a good person who makes sensible moral decisions and being a good reasoner? We talk of moral reasoning, and this might lead us to think there is some connection between being a good moral reasoner and being a good reasoner in general. There seem to be good people who are not consistently good at reasoning; is it that they have a special talent for moral reasoning, but not for other kinds? Or is it rather that their moral soundness and good judgement are not really the outcome of reasoning at all?

It is useful to be clear about what we mean by reason here. What might immediately spring to mind is deductive reasoning, of the sort we see exemplified in logic textbooks (e.g. all A's are B; X is an A, so X is a B). But there is also inductive reasoning (e.g. it usually rains when black clouds gather; black clouds are gathering, so it will probably rain). In addition, there are non-linear forms of reasoning, such as might be displayed when we seek a set of moral commitments that are as coherent as possible with one another. Moral reasoning, according to some philosophers, is very like this. It aims to deliver judgements that fit into a maximally coherent set, rather than correspond with any external moral reality. Finally, and more loosely, reason could refer to any intellectual operation, including the instant recognition of a face or a building, when we are not aware of any intermediate calculations. Perhaps moral judgements exemplify a kind of intuitive discernment or recognition. In the same way as I don't know what it is about a face that tells me that it is Jane's – I just take in the whole and recognize it – so some moral judgements might be rather like this.

This last idea is important, and I shall try to suggest at the end that sound moral judgement does indeed have a central element of recognition or discernment. But for the moment, let us think about argument. In the course of arguing, we engage in such things as step-by-step inference, the framing and testing of hypotheses, the drawing of analogies and the formulation of general principles. Now our basic question is: are these sorts of process appropriate for thinking about ethics?

Reason and emotion

We are all familiar with the claim that it is bad to be over-rational in our moral judgements; that morality is about what you feel, and that no one in any case is ever persuaded to adopt some moral position by reason. (A similar claim is often made about religion; religious conviction is "a matter of faith" and no one either can or should be persuaded into it, or out of it, by reasoning). Some people think that it is somehow cold and calculating to base your moral views on rational thinking. In the same way they might think that religious belief acquired through reason lacks the personal commitment required for genuine faith. Such people are quite likely to sympathize with moral relativism, which we discussed in Chapter 1. They might add that if there are no universally applicable truths about ethics, and if reason is the process of discovering universal truths, then reason is inappropriate for genuine moral reflection.

This popular view has some (somewhat more sophisticated) background, for there is an important Humean tradition in moral thinking that holds moral judgements to be primarily a matter of the "passions". But there are a number of confusions in the popular version of the idea that need clearing up.

Reasoning about religion: an analogy

Comparison with religious belief is helpful, since many of the same confusions occur here as well. Start with the idea that it is misguided to argue about religion because it is a matter of faith and "you either believe or you don't". In discussing this, we first need to know with what sort of claim we are actually dealing. There are a number of possibilities. It might be:

(a) An empirical, psychological claim about how people actually acquire (or for that matter lose) religious commitments. The contention is that people don't ordinarily go through any process of deductive or inductive reasoning in religious matters. For example, they don't reach belief in God because they are convinced by medieval proofs of God's existence – belief is something that comes upon them; indeed, many believers would say it occurs through the direct action of God upon the convert.

(b) A stronger version of (a), which ventures that it is not just unusual but impossible to acquire or lose religious belief by reasoning.

(c) An assertion that there are no sound arguments either for or against religious doctrines, so people who think they have stumbled upon such an argument are mistaken.

(d) The more radical assertion that religion not only cannot be soundly argued for or refuted, but that there is a logical or conceptual error in the very attempt to discover such arguments. For instance, believers might say that their faith is in no way threatened by the lack of sound arguments since it does not, and logically could not, depend upon them.

Perhaps there are other interpretations as well. But these possible interpretations provide enough of a parallel with attitudes to moral reasoning to make the analogy worth pursuing. Take for instance (a). Suppose that, in both religion and morality, people do not ordinarily reach their convictions by rational processes – that they are led by their feelings, or caused by God or their cultural environment to have the views they do. I suggest that the proper response to this claim is not to deny it (surely there is much truth in it), but ask exactly what it shows. The fact that people often *do not* reach their views by reasoning, does not show that they *ought not*. Indeed, conflict between individuals and nations might be reduced if only we tried harder to listen to reasoned argument.

What about (b)? If it is impossible to reach moral or religious conclusions by reason, then clearly there can be no obligation to do so. Why should we believe it is impossible? The influence of culture, upbringing, unconscious wishes and so on is very great (and often underestimated by philosophers), but many people do think carefully about their moral assumptions and sometimes revise their views. We observe people who question what they were brought up to think and modify their views accordingly. Claim (b) therefore seems to be false.

Claim (c) was that there are no sound arguments in the areas in question. The answer to this, surely, is that although it may turn out to be true, there is no reason to assume it is true without investigating. People do give reasons for their moral convictions, even if they find such reasons persuasive only because of their culture or psychology. ("My wife ought to cook for me, *because she is a woman*" is offered as a *reason* for expecting her to fulfil a certain role, even if Mediterranean people find it more persuasive than northern Europeans). We are surely obliged to examine the reasons people give if we are to avoid mere prejudice. In fact, the outcome of finding no moral reasons persuasive might be moral nihilism, which itself would be an important conclusion.

The final claim (d) is philosophically complex, especially in religion, where it often goes with a radical approach to the meaning of religious propositions – which entails, perhaps, that religious commitments are not really factual at all. In ethics it is allied to subjectivism – which compares moral judgements to matters of taste and preference. In reply, we should point out that what is different about moral judgements is that we generally take stances concerning the moral judgements of others: we praise and condemn them. Even if moral judgements are just attitudes or preferences, they involve strong attitudes towards other people's attitudes. This is not true in simple matters of taste, such as preferring beetroot to tomatoes. This point does not prove that (d) is false, but it should provide food for further thought.

The Humean challenge and some responses

David Hume (1711–76) is the most celebrated exponent of the view that reason alone – by which he means the *faculty for judging the truth and falsehood of propositions* – can yield no moral judgements. Thus, reason might inform me that a certain remark I am about to make will cause someone pain, but knowing this will deter me from making the remark only if I already do not wish to cause pain. Reason, then, can play a *subsidiary* role in moral deliberation; it can alert me to certain facts about how I can satisfy my desires, but it cannot form those desires for me. I cannot be argued into wanting something – at least, not in a fundamental way. I can be argued into believing that a particular thing is an example of a kind of thing that I already want, and so, indirectly, I can be persuaded to want that thing. For instance, liking mild Indian food, I reject the meat korma in my local tandoori restaurant because I mistakenly think it is hot. When the waiter tells me it is actually mild, he causes me to want it after all. This is perfectly consistent with Hume's claim about reason and the passions, because my general dislike of hot foods is still something I cannot reach by reason. Morality is basically like this, according to Hume.

Hume's thesis is obviously controversial, and we have looked at two ways, the Kantian (Chapter 4) and the Aristotelian (Chapter 7), in which it may be challenged. But let us imagine he is right. It still seems that, even in a subsidiary role, reason has important work to do.

First of all, in any situation requiring a moral judgement, it will be crucial to find out what the relevant facts really are. For example, even if I cannot be reasoned out of my conviction that the guilty ought to be punished, I can be reasoned out of my belief that some accused person is guilty – and thus indirectly reasoned out of my urge to punish him. Indeed, when we accuse people of *prejudice* – for instance, against members of certain racial groups – at least part of our complaint is that they have failed to learn what these people are really like and are content to rely on stereotypes. We all have prejudices, and – up to a point – this may even have benefits. But there are many occasions when we should try to overcome them. Literally, the word refers to *prejudging* – i.e. to making judgements before, rather than after, the evidence has been properly weighed up. An important part of moral reasoning must involve trying to become aware of our own peculiar biases, perhaps originating in our personal weaknesses, that are apt to make our moral judgements unjust. Without becoming so introspective that we fail to act effectively, we should still try to become aware of our own particular tendencies to form irrational beliefs and do what we can to correct them.

Secondly, a great deal of moral reasoning relies on general logical reasoning. The ability to think clearly, relevantly and concisely cannot be underrated. An essential part of this is the avoidance of self-contradiction. This point, in fact, applies even on the assumption that morality is a matter of taste. I contradict myself if I say that I both approve, and disapprove, of lying your way out of a tight spot. If you contradict yourself – by asserting that some proposition both is, and is not the case, it is impossible that your assertion is true. So when people say they don't mind contradicting themselves, they either do not understand what they are saying, or they simply do not care about truth. For those who do care about saying true things, valuable moral debate includes exposing contradictions and inconsistencies in moral positions.

Two examples

Take a couple of topical examples. The first is the national debate about the private ownership of hand-guns. People who want this banned argue that the likelihood of people going on sudden killing sprees will be reduced if such ownership is made illegal. Critics might retort that far more people are killed in road accidents than by lone gunmen, yet no one has suggested banning cars. This argument tries to persuade someone in favour of a ban that he is applying a principle inconsistently. In effect, it urges that since he does not think it sensible to ban cars in spite of road accidents, he ought not to approve of a ban on hand-gun ownership even though there will be occasional massacres. A general principle is being tacitly attributed to him: roughly that "anything that causes the deaths of innocent people should be banned". Since he is not willing to apply this principle to cars, he should not want to apply it to hand-guns.

Another example concerns the censorship of written or visual material that causes widespread offence to a section of the population. Suppose that a woman wishes to see pornographic magazines banished by law from newsagents' shops. In support of this, she claims that many women feel offended by the presence of this material on open view. But imagine that, in reply, someone points out that if the *causing of offence* is a good reason for banning

191

pornographic material from shops, then there is a very good reason for banning Salman Rushdie's novel *The Satanic Verses* from shops. The challenger points out that all Muslims take offence at that novel – in fact, that the sense of outrage felt by Muslims is more widespread and intense than the offence taken by women about soft-core pornography in newsagents' shops. Now of course, if the opponent of pornography agrees that action should be taken against Rushdie's novel as well, then the argument might stop there. But if she does not want Rushdie's novel banned, then she is open to challenge on her grounds for wanting the pornography banned. To claim that pornography causes offence is not enough, since the novel also causes offence. In reply, she might say that only the pornography causes *reasonable* offence: Islam is a false religion and therefore it is not reasonable to take offence at criticism of it. If she can defend that view then she has made progress, though she will have a hard time explaining why, in a liberal democracy, *her* conception of what is reasonable – and not the Muslims' – should legally prevail.

This example is only meant to illustrate a point about moral argument. No doubt you will have thought of scores of reasons why the two cases might not be comparable: you might argue that Muslims don't have to read the novel, but women cannot avoid seeing pornography in shops. And so on. But this is the whole point. In coming up with these arguments, you are engaging in a form of reasoning that is essential to ethical debate. This type of reasoning can be undertaken even if a Humean view on how we acquire our basic moral commitments is correct. We haven't discussed whether it is reasonable to object to pornography, Rushdie's novel, road deaths or massacres with guns. We have basically been pointing to the importance of consistency in our moral views.

The uses and abuses of consistency

However, although we should strive for consistency in our moral views, we should be very careful not to misinterpret this requirement. One problem is that in the examples above, we have been assuming that the particular moral views in question do derive from some more general principle (such as anything that causes offence should be banned), and that this principle contradicts at least one particular view held. Maybe not all moral views are like this – perhaps some judgements are particular, deriving from no principle. A traditional conception of sexual morality seems like this: chastity, according to such a conception, is a sexual virtue disposing those possessing it to refrain from non-marital sex, but this requirement may not be derivable from anything more general. As we shall see later, moral restrictions like this one often present themselves as founded in something distinctive – perhaps even something sacred – and not derivable from any general theory. This basis for morality should not be dismissed out of hand. But apart from this, a misunderstood idea of consistency can turn moral argument into silly and pointless rhetoric.

Many examples of this come from political arguments and their moral dimensions. Suppose a right wing Member of Parliament salivates with glee over a new, stringent measure to catch social security cheats. The MP argues robustly that such fraud is dishonest and costs the tax-payer huge sums of money – much of which could go to the genuinely needy. However, left wing opponents remind us that the MP in question is markedly lacking in zeal for the pursuit of tax dodgers, even though the sums of money lost to the revenue through tax fraud far exceed what is lost through social security fraud. Now what, precisely, is the logical point the left wing critics are contributing to the question of what to do with benefit cheats? No doubt the gist is that the right wing MP is inconsistent in some way, or hypocritical, or doesn't care about fraud when committed by rich people. Let us lay out the challenge more precisely. A plausible construal is that *if* benefit fraud is wrong because it gives the fraudsters more than they are entitled to, and *if* tax evasion also gives the tax evaders more than they are entitled to, *then* tax evasion must also be wrong. This is a perfectly good suggestion to put to someone who openly denies the comparison. However, the challenge to be consistent can be used for evasive purposes. Suppose that the original debate is just about whether we should become more stringent with benefit cheats. It is irrelevant that some people who support this proposal do not support a similar proposal for tax evaders. After all, perhaps we should be more stringent *both* with tax evaders *and* with benefit cheats. The fact that the right winger is not quite so excited by the pursuit of tax evaders does not, in itself, mean he is *wrong* to support the pursuit of benefit cheats. His reasons may well be good ones: it is just that he doesn't apply them elsewhere. This may be a fault – but not one that proves that his position in the debate at hand is mistaken.

Another, more blatant, abuse of consistency involves continuing on a path we now know to be wrong, because this is how we started. Imagine that young offenders are sent on holidays abroad, where it is held that the enticements of new scenery and the challenges of a foreign environment will provide an appropriate setting for cool reflection on the errors of their ways. If, upon return, these errors persist, it would be foolish to send another batch of offenders on the same holiday simply on the grounds of consistency. It would be absurd to suggest that since this is how the first lot were treated, it is unfair or inconsistent if the second lot do not get the same treatment. On the contrary, the rational thing to do when you have made a mistake is to stop making it, not to persist in it. True, it would have been better if all the offenders had been treated in a more sensible way. But a policy that is consistently wrong is worse than one which lacks consistency but is at least partly right. The general point about moral thinking that this illustrates is that we should always be open to the possibility that our past actions or our basic principles are inadequate or mistaken, and be prepared to alter our behaviour accordingly. Without this, the virtue of being principled can degenerate into the vice of being rigid and unwilling to admit error.

Universal prescriptivism

A more formal way of laying out how moral reasoning can proceed has been defended from the 1950s onwards by the moral philosopher Richard Hare. His theory is known as universal prescriptivism, and is currently out of favour in moral philosophy. But fashion should not be our guide in these matters, and there are many virtues in this theory, such as clarity and precision, as well as an important account of moral reasoning.

Hare's first book *The language of morals* (1952) was partly an attempt to show how moral thinking could be rational, even given the general correctness of the earlier *emotivists*, whose view was caricatured as the "boo hooray" theory of ethics.[2] For A.J. Ayer, the leading British emotivist, moral utterances were really expressions of feeling or attitude. They had no factual content, and were hence neither true nor false. But in that case, what rational considerations could possibly apply to moral judgements? What was the difference between rational persuasion and mere influence or propaganda?

Hare tried to remove the scandal in various ways. He first noted that logical rules of inference could apply to practical matters as much as to factual ones. For example, there could be *imperative inference* such as the following[3] (do not be too put off by its triviality):

1. (Major premise) Take all the boxes to the station.
2. (Minor premise) This is one of the boxes.
3. (Conclusion) Take this to the station.

The imperative conclusion must follow if the premises are accepted.

The idea that moral thinking is subject to rules of reasoning is amplified in Hare's later books, in particular *Freedom and Reason* (1963). He develops the doctrine that moral judgements are prescriptive: they entail such things as commands, commendations, urgings – in short, they guide action. They are not fundamentally descriptive claims about the way the world is. To say that something is good is not like saying that it is blue, which is purely descriptive. Hare argues that the meaning of *good* cannot be given in purely descriptive terms: to say that a state of affairs is good cannot mean that it contains pleasure, desire-fulfilment, and so on. In this, Hare agrees with Moore, who (as we saw in Chapter 2) argues that there is a "naturalistic fallacy" involved in claiming such equivalence in meaning. However, it is most important to note that according to Hare, there is a secondary descriptive component to moral judgements. Again, take the simple moral term *good*. When something is called good, it must be so called in virtue of some descriptive property it has. Things cannot just be good for no reason; there cannot be states of affairs which are simply good, with no other features that make them good. A slightly technical way of putting this is as follows: goodness is a dependent or *supervenient* attribution. A person might be called good *because* – that is, in virtue of the fact that – she is altruistic. Actions might be judged wrong because they display indifference to suffering.

This has an implication that is particularly important. If moral judgements are supervenient upon other judgements, then there cannot be two situations that are exactly alike except in their moral features. If the fact that a person is helpful (under such-and-such circumstances) is what makes him good[4], then anybody else who is helpful under similar circumstances must also be good. The supervenience of the moral upon the descriptive explains one way in which moral thinking needs to be constrained by reason. If something is a reason for a moral judgement in one situation, then it must also be a reason for a similar judgement in other, descriptively similar situations.

Now this matter of supervenience is related to another central element of Hare's theory, that moral judgements are by their nature *universalizable*. (As we saw in Chapter 4, Kant had a similar idea). That is to say, "ought" judgements (to take a prominent example of prescriptive language) are more than simple imperatives, for they commit the speaker to making the same ought judgement in all circumstances that share the same universal features. If I simply say, "Do not smoke", I am uttering a mere imperative and am not logically committed to forbidding smoking on any other occasion, however similar. But if I say, "You ought not to smoke", "It is wrong to smoke", or similar, then I am rationally committed to the universal prescription "let no one smoke (at least, under such and such circumstances)". Of course, I may not realize this; I may be irrational, and make these "ought" judgements without thinking of their implications. The central idea is that moral judgements commit me, whether or not I know it, to universal prescriptions. A commonsense moral insight, namely the golden rule of doing unto others what you would have them do unto you, is easily derivable from this. If I say "I ought to (or may) behave dishonestly towards Jones", then I am implying that Jones ought to (or may) behave dishonestly towards me in similar circumstances. It is irrelevant that I don't want him to – that I would react with moral outrage if he did. This doesn't affect what I am logically committed to.

Hare's theory has been criticized on many accounts: that it seems to have no account of how we should select the universal prescriptions we make; that moral judgements are really descriptive in a far stronger sense than Hare allows; that it operates with an impoverished moral vocabulary, laying too much stress on terms like ought and good rather than on terms such as kind, honest or industrious. But its insights about universalizability and general moral rationality, even if incomplete, seem correct. The theory has valuable things to teach us about how to reason about ethics, and shows that such reasoning is not just random, subjective or emotional.[5]

So far, then, it appears that moral thinking is a rational pursuit, even if that is not all it is. Even starting from the (questionable) assumption that a limited, Humean view of the role of reason in morality is correct, we have found that there is plenty for reason to do. If Hume is wrong – which perhaps he is – then there is even more for reason. At the very least, the ability to see through sophistical rhetoric, to detect fallacies, to resist purely emotional appeals and to avoid self-contradiction are as important for moral thought as for any other kind of thought. In fact, the most plausible element in Kant's moral theory – that rational beings must be treated as ends in themselves – has obvious application here. To persuade autonomous individuals to adopt a moral stance, by appeal to irrelevant or purely irrational considerations, is manipulative, and we protect ourselves against such manipulation, and hence prevent ourselves from being treated as mere means, if we immunize ourselves against this sort of appeal.

A problem about reason: ideological conditioning

We ought now to look at other influential ways of casting doubt on the appeal to reason in morality. By acknowledging both the strengths and the weaknesses of these attacks, we shall emerge with an endorsement of moral reasoning that is more finely tuned and aware of its own assumptions.

One way of challenging the importance of reason in ethics makes use of the concept of *ideology*. This term is associated with Marxist thought about society. An ideology may be thought of as a comprehensive system of beliefs and ways of thinking, that underlies the way society is arranged and the values that hold sway in it. Ideologies are said to form the basis of social and political action in societies, and especially the power relations that hold in them. The term is often used in a derogatory fashion: much criticism of social arrangements points an accusing finger at their underlying ideology. A topical example, though not one that exercised Marx, is feminist concern at the actual or supposed injustices systematically inflicted on women in society. Feminists claim to discover an ideology of male dominance (patriarchy) as the underlying problem. This ideology is a set of beliefs about the nature of men and women, their capabilities, their desires and especially their "natural" differences. Although these beliefs – which may not even be consciously acknowledged – purport to have a basis in reason and experience, their real origin is in men's desire for power and control over women, and their real purpose is the maintenance of an unjust *status quo*. Feminists acknowledge that many women as well as men share these ideological convictions, but many say this is due to "false consciousness" on their part, making them believe that they are not oppressed and that the system is just. Thus, women who suffer from false consciousness collude with their oppressors, and their hope of liberation lies in the raising of their consciousness so that they can see the power relations for what they really are. Feminism is at present an influential social movement, and thus serves as a good illustration. Ideological accounts of class injustice and other real or alleged systems of dominance may, of course, also be given.

How might this relate to the project of reasoning in ethics? Critics of the (supposedly) dominant moral values in society like to point to the (supposed) ideological basis of those values. Their primary question concerning those values is not: are they true and justified? but rather: whose interests do they serve? Better, their negative answer to the first question derives from their answer to the second. If some system of dominance is clearly buttressed by the dominant values (for example, respect for property or individual liberty), then any arguments produced in favour of these things may be regarded as having an ideological basis that should be challenged. An early, and very simple version of the theory was articulated by Thrasymachus in Plato's *Republic*.[6] Thrasymachus defines justice as nothing but the interest of the stronger party – the party strong enough to make and enforce laws in its own favour. In this spirit, we might say that this is always what stronger parties do, and even if they bother to justify their laws by appeal to impartial reasons, such reasons are only a smokescreen; their real motive is to get what they can for themselves.

Descendants of this basic theory of ideology are to be found in a great many intellectual movements, and we can present only a brief and rough outline of the main idea. What should be said about it, in relation to the attempt to reason about our moral commitments? To begin with, we should acknowledge some of their concerns. It certainly is the case that our moral and political commitments are partly shaped by factors we tend not to acknowledge. We claim to have thought issues through and to have formed judgements that anyone could reasonably accept, whatever their circumstances. But is it an accident that high earners are more likely to be conservative voters than are low earners? Is it by chance that Arabs are more likely to accept the ethical tenets of Islam than middle Americans? Our views clearly bear some correlation both to our cultural heritage and our personal interests. It is not only our moral commitments that are thus influenced, but also the factual beliefs underlying these commitments. Notoriously, it was once widely believed that black people had smaller brains than white people, and were hence intellectually inferior to them. Similarly, traditional insistence that men and women be assigned to different spheres in life was (and is) underpinned by ill-founded convictions about universal sexual differences. To deny these things is simply naïve. However, there are still searching challenges we should put to our ideological critic.

To begin with, it is worth pointing out that a commitment may *both* have an origin in vested interest, and *also* be true. You cannot show that it is false just by pointing out the interest it serves. Even if the belief that women are generally less competitive than men is convenient for those who wish to keep business, the law and the City male-dominated, this belief may yet be true. We cannot substitute ideological criticism for honest investigation of the relevant facts.

Secondly, a commitment may spring from a vested interest and also be *rationally defensible* and not merely true by coincidence. It is no doubt sometimes right to suspect that certain beliefs people have are rationalizations of a prejudice, or a smokescreen to cover a wish to hold on to some privilege. When we have good reason to think that they have some such bias, we should scrutinize their justifications especially carefully. However, the arguments may, for all that, be sound. In fact, in a debate it is a sophistical and unfair move to call an opponent's arguments "mere" rationalizations. All that matters for establishing truth is the soundness of the rationalizations in question.

Thirdly, we should beware of polarizing the issue, insisting that our convictions are *either* wholly rational *or* wholly the product of ideology. Unacknowledged biases are indeed hard to eliminate, but we are also quite capable of good reasoning. Indeed, if the force of ideology were so strong that genuine rational justifications for moral beliefs could never be found, one would have to ask how ideological critiques ever got going. Entrenched and ideological beliefs take time to disappear, if they ever do – but they are not completely resistant to argument. If they were, there would be no point in mounting ideological criticism of them.

Fourthly, it is worth pointing out that supporters of the *status quo* can turn the tables on ideological critiques, pointing to an ideological basis for mounting those very critiques. If conventional moral beliefs must be looked upon with suspicion because of their origin in vested interest, what of those who mount such critiques? Why should they alone be able to see reality for what it is? Might they not have an interest in subverting the *status quo*? If so, they are susceptible to the very criticism they make of others.

There are also other cautionary points to make. When traditional institutions (e.g. marriage, the family, private property) come under scrutiny, we should beware of assuming that just because they reinforce some power relations, they are therefore bad. There may be such a thing as legitimate power or authority; whether such power is legitimate or not will need to be discussed case by case. Furthermore, whatever the merits of some ideological criticism, we should be sceptical that we can ever achieve a view of human flourishing or justice that is free from ideology. Even the visions of justice or human flourishing held by critics of accepted moral values are bound to be shaped by something. We do not make judgements about these matters in a void.

Another problem about reason: the idea of objective truth

There is another way in which we might criticize the enterprise of trying to found our moral commitments on reason. This criticism is more radical and perhaps more popular than the first. We have already seen how a critique deriving from Marxist thought about class relations regards many moral commitments as distorted by vested interest. A more radical kind of criticism challenges the very enterprise of reasoning. The difference is that whereas the first critic just says we often come up with unsound reasons due to our ideological conditioning, the second critic is suspicious of reason *per se*. He or she might regard reason itself as an ideology, whose real purpose is oppressive and may be suspicious of concepts like objectivity and truth, perhaps even thinking of them as tools of domination. There is something inescapably exclusive about these notions. They imply the existence of an external standard against which our beliefs and moral commitments must be measured and perhaps found wanting. Striving for objectivity carries the risk of getting things wrong.

I shall not go into the historical details of the emergence of this kind of challenge to reason. Many readers will have encountered this sort of view in any case. It is associated with the cluster of theories about philosophy, literature and culture known collectively as *postmodernism*. This loose movement is in rebellion against many aspects of the "modern" period (actually from the seventeenth and eighteenth centuries), which encompassed the European "enlightenment" and the "age of reason".[7] The emergence of science is one of the key features of this period. Postmodernism sees connections between the period of European colonization of much of the world, and the objectivist approach to knowledge, truth and value that characterized modern European thought at the time. Colonialism was intellectually justified by a belief in the objective superiority of modern European values and institutions to indigenous ones. These things, it is said, were imposed upon subject peoples. Such reflections led, in some schools of thought from about the 1960s onwards, to the idea that Eurocentric notions of objective truth, reason and value are inherently linked to colonial oppression. As a recent commentator, Ernest Gellner, puts it, this outlook held that

> ... independent facts were the tool and expression of colonial domination; by contrast, subjectivism signifies intercultural equality and respect. The world as it truly is (if indeed it may ever truly be said to be anything) is made up of tremulous subjectivities; objective facts and generalisations are the expression and tools of domination![8]

The same sort of allegation is made in some (though not all) feminist critiques of the way moral philosophy has usually been conceived. Few would doubt that in many cultures and periods, women have been regarded as less rational and principled than men, and more childish, volatile and unreliable. In moral philosophy, say some feminists, there is still an excessive stress on *principles* and *theories* (reflecting masculine ways of thinking), and practical examples are too often taken from male domains, such as sport, business or warfare.[9] Traditional feminists in a liberal tradition strongly object to the characterization of women as less rational and logical than men. A more recent feminist critique has emphasized that the stress on reason, principles and objectivity is indeed masculine and boosts male power, and that the liberation of women requires the overthrow or downgrading of these notions. What has become known as *standpoint feminism* emphasizes the inherently female perspective on things, which according to some thinkers stresses intuition, care, compassion and sensitivity to the particular rather than universal features of situations.

The discerning reader will have detected echoes of relativism in these proposals, and some of our earlier discussion (Chapter 1) is relevant to it. What should we say about attempts to downgrade reason? Our guiding question, we should remember, is about the role of reason in moral thinking. There may be peculiar features of moral thinking that make exclusively rational methods inappropriate to it, but we shall not need to discuss this possibility if we can show that reason generally is malign or oppressive in some way. So we should look at this general claim first.

Let us take on board the critique of masculine ethics, part of which is that it unduly emphasizes theory and principle, to the exclusion of such things as the virtues, sensitivity to particularities, human relationships, and so on. There is something to be said for this kind of critique. It is plausible that the values that typically guide the public sphere (which feminists say is male-dominated) are not the only values that are important. If contracts, justice, competition and legalistic reasoning predominate in the public sphere where men have great influence, and if theoretical philosophy has throughout most of history been the preserve of men, then perhaps these public values have been overrated in this philosophy. None of this, however, shows that reason itself is oppressive or male-dominated – unless we can assume, without much warrant, that it restricts itself to contracts, theories, general principles, and the like. We should really take reason to be something much more general – something like, in Hume's words, the discovery of truth and falsehood. Indeed, when feminists try to raise the profile of the private virtues, they use their reason: they *argue* (or should do) that moral thinking should be balanced by these considerations. Whether they do so soundly is not the point here – the point is that argument and reason can be used to support feminist conclusions. In other words, feminist reasoning at the normative level is still reasoning; it involves the giving of reasons. If it didn't, then feminists would not be able to argue in favour of feminism.

There is still a related attitude to reason, objectivity and truth that is quite common in moral debate, and it is expressed by saying that there is something arrogant, narrow-minded or unduly exclusive about appealing to these notions. Suppose you assert that some moral outlook is rationally defensible and true. You should not be surprised if you get the impatient riposte: "Whose reason? Whose truth?" If you answer that you are referring to your reason and your truth, you will sound arrogant; while if you say that it is "*our* reason" to which you are appealing, you again risk seeming arrogant in assuming that your reason is bound to be shared by all.

We are dealing here with a relativist attack on absolute reason and absolute truth, but it is surely confused. Of course, there are different *kinds* of reasoning – for example, deductive and inductive reasoning – and these different kinds are appropriate in different enquiries. There are also different sorts of truth, in the banal sense that there is historical truth, mathematical truth, and so on. Furthermore, as some feminists claim, there may be styles of reasoning that predominate among males and different styles among females. None of this supports the idea that there is literally more than one reason or more than one truth. Compare: there are competing theories in physics, but there is only one physics. So in morality and elsewhere, critics who challenge your convictions because they derive only from "your reason" are setting up a meaningless contrast between your reason and their reason, and insinuating that there can be no fruitful dialogue between you and them. At its most extreme, this entails that all the rules of good and bad reasoning are entirely up to each individual, which itself entails that there can be no such thing as getting things wrong. If it is impossible to get things wrong, then it is meaningless to say that you have got things right. What we should be saying is that reason is something available to all of us, that it is not irremediably relative and that it aims at objectivity – at least in the sense that in reasoning, we are trying to follow norms that are valid independently of our subjective preferences.

Conservative critiques of reason

So far, then, it seems that attacks on reasoning *per se*, are unfounded. It is incoherent to talk of male or female reason except in the sense that certain sorts of reasoning (e.g. logical deduction) might appeal more to one sex than the other. It is also wrong to claim that objectivity and reason are inherently oppressive, even if, throughout history, certain beliefs held by the powerful to be objectively true have been imposed upon others. Finally, the total rejection of reason cannot be defended by reason. Similarly, someone who says "there is no such thing as truth" is inconsistent if he believes that that very statement is true. He cannot, of course, be argued out of his position, since there is no arguing with people who reject argument. But that doesn't mean his position is logically unassailable; all it means is that he won't listen.

There are other grounds for questioning the role of reason in ethics. When philosophers talk about reaching a "rational morality", they are often implicitly attacking *prejudice*, *superstition* or appeals to *mere authority*. They are suspicious of appeals to *intuition* and will not accept anything unless it can be rigorously argued for. However, those of a morally conservative disposition have reservations about this sort of attitude. They might claim that insistence on abstract reason has had catastrophic results, as Edmund Burke did when attacking the moral consequences of the French Revolution.[10] They might also deny that all moral truths must be understood if they are to be accepted, and think that one bad result of philosophy is its cavalier treatment of sacred things.

Two practical examples will illustrate their concerns. One concerns the value of human life. The other concerns sexual morality. It is significant that the difference between religious and secular ethics is particularly noticeable in these matters. Notably in matters of life and death, recent secular moral philosophy has produced many theories on which to base practical decisions. In this domain, there is much discussion of such things as abortion, euthanasia, the allocation of scarce medical resources and genetic research. Most of these discussions seem to reject the belief in the sanctity of human life, and offer other accounts of what makes human life valuable – for example, by referring to its quality, which is cashed out (for instance) in terms of the degree of autonomy it displays. It is also widely held that a person has a right to die – that he does nothing inherently wrong if he consents to euthanasia (though it may be ill-judged on grounds of self-interest).

Conservatives tend to reject this way of thinking. Take the idea of consent. Liberal thinkers will often say that what is fundamentally wrong with murder is that it violates an individual's right to life, but that since you cannot violate your own right to life (any more than you can steal from yourself), it is not intrinsically immoral to commit suicide or perform requested euthanasia. Thus the *right to life* turns out just to be the right *not to be killed without your consent*. Now a moral conservative would object that the order of priority has been reversed here. Actions, he says, do not become permissible just *because* they are consented to: rather, things should be consented to *only if* they are already permissible. To ignore this risks making the giving of consent into an arbitrary and whimsical matter, based on no morally weighty reasons. There may be some things to which we ought never consent. Sexual morality is an excellent example. A familiar liberal view of sexual morality is that any sexual act is permissible if, and only if, all those taking part in it, or at least directly affected by it, give their informed consent. For a conservative, this ignores the possibility that there are some sexual acts, for instance those he or she would class as perversions, that we should never consent to, even if we feel the urge to engage in them.

According to the conservative, one thing that is wrong with these approaches is that they succumb to the temptation to find a *theory* to explain moral commitments, and then try to apply the theory as widely as possible. In science, theories are often chosen for their simplicity and their ability to explain the widest possible range of phenomena. Moral theories also aim at these goals. Thus the notions of contract, utility and autonomy are the favoured concepts in such theories, and we have looked at some length at contractualism and consequentialism. But the trouble, according to our conservative, is that simplicity is being bought at the cost of depth. We need to pay attention to the richness and profundity of the moral dimensions of human life. We also need to investigate the concepts mentioned in the more popular moral theories. Do we really know what happiness is? If not, we had better find out before becoming Benthamite utilitarians. Do we know what gives a life its quality? We had better enrich that idea before we start making life and death decisions based upon it. And what about the concept of the sacred, which is hardly ever mentioned in secular moral theory, but which actually inspires a great deal of ordinary thinking? The concept of the *sanctity* of human life has a resonance that is simply lacking in the idea of its *value*. (Value for what or whom, anyway?)

Conservatives try to do justice to morality as they think it presents itself to most ordinary people. Both moral and political conservatives tend to be suspicious of theory, preferring to rely on the old adage "if it ain't broke, don't fix it". Moral conservatives might well insist that morality starts where calculation ceases. They accept that calculation has some role to play, as when we need to know the consequences of our decisions. But they suspect that the most fundamental moral principles are not reached in this way. Morality reveals itself as containing absolute interdictions and a certain sense of awe for sacred things.[11] Religion is an obvious ally of morality in this respect, but it is possible to be a moral conservative without being a religious believer. In fact, something of this attitude sometimes finds expression in concern for the environment – in the idea that nature has an intrinsic value independent of its benefit for humans. These feelings are bound up with a sense of the proper place of humans in the total scheme of things, and warn against grand and far-reaching attempts to alter our destinies.

There are further, more familiar considerations that moral conservatives advance against the constant attempt to reason about ethics. One is that instinct, custom and convention have survived in the forms they have because they are mostly beneficial. We do better if we live most of the time following these instincts fairly unreflectively than to question them all the time. Another consideration is that the very attempt to think about what you are doing can actually frustrate thought. This kind of thing can happen when you are doing something ordinary, like reading or driving. You can grasp the general gist of what you read without obsessively going over every word to check that you have taken it in. In fact, constant checking can diminish your grasp of the overall sense. Similarly, good drivers have certain instincts that enable them to take right decisions without always thinking about why they made them. According to conservatives, something similar happens in moral decision-making. There can be good reasons for what we do unreflectively, even though we are not always aware of them. It is enough to know that such reasons are likely to be found if we ever need to investigate closely.

Conclusion

To reach a reasonable answer to our questions, we need to accept both the value and the limitations of reason. Our sympathetic consideration (Chapter 4) of some Kantian themes led us to uphold the idea that rational beings should be treated as ends in themselves, and thus that their autonomy – their ability to act for reasons they have formulated for themselves – is something supremely valuable. We also have considered the important role of logical reasoning in moral matters, ranging from the importance of acting by principles that can be accepted as universal, to the need to cultivate a capacity to see through shallow rhetoric, appeals to irrelevant considerations and general shoddy thinking. (It is indeed remarkable how much shoddy morality comes down to lazy, shoddy thinking). At the same time, conservatives warn us, with some justification, that we should not expect all traditional moral views to be instantly defensible by reason, and that if they are not, we may not be justified in abandoning them. As we saw when discussing contractualism (Chapter 5), when theories are formulated they must be tested against the pre-theoretical moral judgements we already hold. It is wrong to think that every such judgement needs the prior backing of theory; rather, to use Rawls' term, theory and pre-theoretical judgements should exist in a state of "reflective equilibrium", that is, of mutual balancing and adjustment. Similarly, one important function of reason (including, but not limited to moral theorizing) is to clarify our intuitions and draw out their implications.

Clearly, some such intuitions are prejudices, in a pejorative sense, and their resistance to rational scrutiny suggests that they arise for reasons we may be unwilling to acknowledge. A good example is the attitude of most respectable people towards charitable giving; they think that it is very nice of well-off people to give to charity, but not in any way an obligation. It is hard to defend this view, although very comfortable to hold it. However, it is a mistake to assume that all our intuitions are (bad) prejudices. Awareness of certain obligations and prohibitions may spring from deeply ingrained states of character that it is good for us to have, even if people without the appropriate character can be given no reason to observe the obligations or prohibitions in question. Or as

Scruton puts it, ". . . while it is supremely rational to possess them [i.e. many moral attitudes and feelings], they are not themselves amenable to reason, and the attempt to make them so produces the kind of ludicrous caricature of morality that we witness in utilitarianism".[12] This is an Aristotelian thought, which I have discussed in Chapter 7.

Mention of Aristotle brings us back to virtue theory, and what it may be able to tell us about the proper role of reason in ethics. As the extract from Foot at the beginning of this chapter suggested, good moral reasoning is not the same thing as logical acumen or cleverness. Impeccable logical reasoning will lead to false conclusions if the premises it starts from are false. But if you already know the correct conclusion, it need not matter much if you cannot follow the reasoning from the premises. It is this knowing the conclusion to which Foot seems to be referring when she mentions good, though intellectually unremarkable, people who know "what's what". What they have is a rational capacity, but one best expressed in words like imagination, discernment, or judgement. This, as we saw in Chapter 7, is close to Aristotle's account of practical wisdom. Such people are good judges of the quality of actions, and especially of character. Judgement is something broader than deduction or calculation, but is rational none the less. It does not involve random feelings, or sudden flashes of insight. It has a cognitive basis, whether or not it is easy to articulate that basis. When this basis is articulated, it is best expressed in terms of virtue concepts, rather than primarily in terms of theories of right action. The discernment of kindness, self-deception, vanity, selfishness, hypocrisy, loyalty, justice and tolerance – among the other virtues and vices – is, I suspect, the main function of this rational faculty.

If we understand the project of reasoning about ethics in this way, at least in part, then we can accommodate some of the insights of the moral conservative. For his ultimate enemy is the radical who seeks to reject principles that he cannot see an immediate reason to preserve. The imagination and discernment needed to be a good moral judge take time and experience to acquire. It is perhaps this fact that will incline good judges to be cautious before revising their moral judgements in the light of philosophical theories.

Further reading

Ayer, A.J. *Language, truth and logic* (London: Gollancz, 1936). (Reprinted many times). See Chapter 6. It may be worth asking whether Ayer's emotivism reduces all moral persuasion to mere propaganda.

Gellner, E. *Postmodernism, Reason and Religion* (London: Routledge, 1992). An entertaining account of postmodernist subterfuges concerning reason and objectivity. The book contrasts postmodernism with both the Enlightenment, and Islam.

Gilligan, C. *In a different voice: psychological theory and women's development* (Cambridge, MA: Harvard University Press, 1982). A feminist attempt to show that a feminine ethic of *care* is at least as important for ethics as a masculine ethic of *justice.*

Hare, R.M. *Freedom and reason* (Oxford: Oxford University Press, 1963). Sets out very lucidly the prescriptivist account of how moral reasoning is possible and develops an intriguing argument for utilitarianism on the basis of universal prescriptivism.

Hare, R.M. *Moral thinking* (Oxford: Clarendon Press, 1981). This book develops the theory defended earlier, but adds an explanation and defence of "two-level utilitarianism", which allows us to stand by conventional moral principles at the intuitive level, while being able if necessary to switch to the critical level if basic principles conflict, or if we encounter hard cases. As I have not developed a discussion of this in my Chapter 3, it is useful to read it and see whether utilitarianism is made any more plausible by it.

Scruton, R. Man's second disobedience, in *The philosopher on Dover Beach*, R. Scruton (Manchester: Carcanet Press Limited, 1990). A suggestive piece which helps clarify what conservatives, like the author, find wrong with a certain kind of rationalism in ethics and politics.

Scruton, R. *Animal rights and wrongs* (London: Demos, 1996).

Williams, B. *Ethics and the limits of philosophy* (Cambridge, MA: Harvard University Press, 1985). Among other things, an attack on moral theory.

Notes

Chapter 1

1 This theory is the emotivist theory, defended in the 1930s and 1940s by the American philosopher C.L. Stevenson and the British philosopher A.J. Ayer, among others. It regarded moral judgements as neither true nor false, but just expressions of attitude.

2 Immanuel Kant (1724–1804) is one of the most important philosophers of the modern period, and he wrote seminal works on ethics, among many other things. We shall examine Kant's moral theory in detail in Chapter 4.

3 It should, however, be noted that many philosophers, whether relativists or not, deny that the concept of truth can be applied to moral judgements at all. More will be said about this in Chapter 2.

4 I shall return to this approach to morality and moral reasoning in Chapter 8.

5 I leave on one side the disputed supposition that different people who make exactly the same discriminations between colour

patches might still privately experience different colour sensations. But it is clear that this idea could also form an analogy for moral relativism: for could there be such a thing as the way red "really" looks, as opposed to "looks to me or you"?

6 The debate about the relationship of law and morality came to prominence in the late 1950s, with the publication (in Britain) of the Wolfenden committee's recommendation that consensual homosexual activity should be decriminalized. At that time, most of those who advocated a change in the law thought that such activity was morally wrong, but they thought the law should not always enforce morality.

7 See G. Harman, "Moral relativism defended", *Philosophical Review*, **84** (1975), and *The nature of morality*, (Oxford: Oxford University Press, 1977)

8 Aristotle was a Greek philosopher who lived from 384–322 BC. His moral theory and the theory of virtue it inspires are discussed in more detail in Chapter 7.

9 The Greek philosopher Plato (429–347 BC) invented an ideal state (the Republic), run on strictly hierarchical lines, and argued that justice in such a state would consist in rulers, auxiliaries and producers performing only their own proper role.

Chapter 2

1 See G.E. Moore, *Principia ethica* (New York: Cambridge University Press, 1959). First published 1903.

2 The best known moral theories that take the view that moral judgements do not state facts are emotivism and prescriptivism – though there may be some disagreement about what is meant by "facts". The emotivist A.J. Ayer argued that moral utterances were just expressions (not even statements) of attitude, and could not be true or false. He could not see what could be meant by a moral property, since there would be no way of verifying its existence. (At least, that was his view in his first book *Language, truth and logic* (London: Gollancz, 1936), Chapter 6.)

3 See for example, S. Blackburn, *Spreading the word*, (Oxford: Oxford University Press, 1984) Chapter 6.

4 Hume is the inspirational figure lurking behind much discussion of "non-realist" approaches to moral reality. See his *Treatise of*

human nature, Book III (ed. L.A. Selby-Bigge, Oxford: Clarendon Press, 1978).

5   See J.L. Mackie, *Ethics: inventing right and wrong* (Harmondsworth: Penguin books, 1977), Chapter 1. Although hardly anyone seems to agree with Mackie's view that moral judgements contain an inbuilt error, and although there have been mountains of literature on the subject since his book, his argument is still discussed.

6   In the *Republic*, Plato elaborates his notorious theory that ultimate reality consists of forms or abstract universals (such as beauty and goodness) and that this reality is inaccessible to sensory experience. For Plato, the Form of the Good is, in a way, the most real thing there is – in contrast to Mackie, who thinks there is no objective goodness. See Plato, *Republic*, translated by H.D.P. Lee (Harmondsworth: Penguin, 1955).

7   Strictly speaking, a moral objectivist could also be a relativist. If moral truths are truths about what is accepted in particular societies, then a statement like "infanticide is morally acceptable" could be objectively true for those societies that actually accept infanticide. This way of rescuing objectivity, however, will not appeal to those objectivists who reject relativism – i.e. the majority.

8   See Plato, *Euthyphro*, in *The last days of Socrates*, translated by H. Tredennick (Harmondsworth: Penguin, 1955).

9   B. Russell, *Human society in ethics and politics*, in *The central questions of philosophy*, A.J. Ayer (Harmondsworth: Pelican Books, 1976), p. 226.

10 Aristotle's ethical theory can be found in his *Nicomachean ethics*, translated by D. Ross (Oxford: Oxford University Press, 1935, reprinted in paperback 1980).

11 Blackburn's position is explained in *Spreading the word*, Chapter 6 (see Note 3). He coins the term *quasi-realism* to refer to his own view, which is that although moral realism is false, there is no error built into ordinary moral talk, as Mackie thought there was. We are still able to judge individual moral utterances as true or false, in the light of our best (projected) moral sensibilities. Blackburn's view is open to the charge that it is an unstable compromise between moral realism and moral nihilism.

12 See in particular T. Nagel, *The view from nowhere*, (Oxford and New York: Oxford University Press, 1986), Chapter VIII.

Chapter 3

1 See J.S. Mill, *Utilitarianism*, (London: 1863) in A. Ryan (ed.), J.S. Mill and J. Bentham, *Utilitarianism and other essays* (Harmondsworth: Penguin, 1987).

2 See Aristotle, *Nicomachean ethics*, translated by D. Ross (Oxford: Oxford University Press, 1935, reprinted 1980), Book 1.

3 This is an important issue, which I do not treat in detail in this chapter. We may distinguish between direct and indirect consequentialism. Both theories agree that only consequences ultimately matter, but indirect consequentialists say that better consequences accrue in the long run if we do not always think about consequences when we act, but are guided by other considerations such as our projects and special relationships. Compare pleasure: we might get more pleasure from an activity if we concentrate on something other than the pleasure it brings. For a good discussion of this, see P. Railton, Consequentialism, alienation and the demands of morality, in *Consequentialism and its critics* S. Scheffler (ed.) (Oxford: Clarendon Press, 1988).

4 You might ask what the difference is between motives and intentions. Motives spring from character, and include loyalty, compassion and envy, whereas intentions concern the objectives that a person with a certain motive tries to bring about. For example, jealousy (a motive) might be behind the causing of a rival's death (an intentional action).

5 See B. Williams, A critique of utilitarianism, in *Utilitarianism: For and against*, J.J.C. Smart and B. Williams (Cambridge: Cambridge University Press, 1973).

6 See T. Nagel, *The view from nowhere*, (Oxford and New York: Oxford University Press, 1986), Chapter IX.

7 See J. Rawls, *A theory of justice*, (Cambridge, MA: Harvard University Press, 1971) pp. 22–7. It is in his brief section on classical utilitarianism that he makes his criticisms.

Chapter 4

1 I. Kant, *Groundwork of the metaphysic of morals*, trans. H.J. Paton (London: Harper and Row, 1964), Chapter II, Section 421.

2 Kant, *ibid.*, Chapter I, section 402–3.

3 Kant, *ibid.*, Chapter II, section 428.

4 Kant, *ibid.*, Chapter I, section 394.
5 To make the point clearer, we should distinguish between (i) a
  foolish course of action that just happens to turn out well, and (ii)
  a rationally calculated risk. Clearly there can be rationally calculated risks that turn out badly, and in such cases it seems unrea-
  sonable to blame the agent. But it seems reasonable to blame the
  agent in the former case. Both these things, however, may be
  denied by the advocate of moral luck.

Chapter 5

1 T. Hobbes, *Leviathan* (1651) J.C.A. Gaskin (ed.) (Oxford: Oxford
  University Press, 1996).
2 See J-J. Rousseau, *The social contract* (originally published 1762),
  transl. C. Betts (Oxford: Oxford University Press, 1994).
3 In the Protagoras, 320D–328D, the sophist Protagoras outlines a
  mythical account of the origins of human society, stressing
  that justice and respect for others is essential for society to survive. See W.K. Guthrie, trans., Plato, *Protagoras and Meno*
  (Harmondsworth: Penguin, 1956).
4 D. Gauthier, *Morals by agreement* (Oxford: Oxford University
  Press, 1986). For a useful summary of his theory, see D. Gauthier,
  Why contractarianism?, in *Contractarianism and rational choice*,
  P. Vallentyne (ed.) (Cambridge: Cambridge University Press,
  1991).
5 See J.L. Mackie, *Ethics*, (Harmondsworth: Penguin, 1977), p. 115.
6 To forestall an objection many of you are now making – namely,
  that some animals may be rational – it should be noted that
  even if this is true (which I doubt), it isn't an objection to
  contractualism as such. For despite appearances, contractualism
  is not "speciesist": it is quite prepared to admit any type of
  creature able to make agreements into the moral realm. It is just
  that most contractualists think that only humans can make
  agreements.
7 See, for example, the lucid defence of a contractualist view of
  animals offered by P. Carruthers, *The animals issue*, (Cambridge:
  Cambridge University Press, 1992). Better still, see R. Scruton,
  Animal rights and wrongs, (London: Demos, 1996) for a comprehensive and, I think, largely persuasive account of the issues
  which sidesteps some of the more repellent aspects of
  contractualism while retaining its core insights.

Chapter 6

1 See P.F. Strawson, Freedom and resentment, *Proceedings of the British Academy*, **xlviii**, 1962, pp. 1–25. Reprinted in G. Watson (ed.), *Free will* (Oxford: Oxford University Press, 1982). This article is the basis for all my references to Strawson in this chapter.

2 D. Hume, *An enquiry concerning human understanding*, L.A. Selby-Bigge (ed.) 3rd edn (Oxford: Clarendon Press, 1975), Section VIII.

3 One of the most thorough defences of incompatibilism is by P. van Inwagen, in *An essay on free will*, (Oxford: Clarendon Press, 1983). See also his article, The incompatibility of free will and determinism, in Watson (ed.), *Free will*.

4 The matter is a bit more complicated than this, since there are arguably plenty of beliefs, such as the belief that the future will resemble the past, that are induced in us by non-rational causes and which are not overturned by our recognition of this fact. These tend to be very general beliefs which must be presupposed by the more specific beliefs we have.

5 It could be said that there are different issues here. One is that of whether freedom is compatible with determinism, the other is that of whether moral responsibility is compatible with determinism. Someone could believe in free will but doubt that this is strong enough to sustain moral responsibility. However, I am treating these two questions as substantially the same for the purpose of this discussion.

6 Strawson, Freedom and resentment, in Watson (ed.), *Free will*, p. 70.

Chapter 7

1 Modern Aristotelians would accept that most or all of what Aristotle says about the good life for "men" applies to women as well. However, Aristotle himself is referring to a life that he thinks is appropriate mainly for males of high standing. I therefore shall often use the masculine pronoun in my discussion of Aristotelian ethics.

2 See Aristotle, *Nicomachean ethics*, trans. W.D. Ross (Oxford: Oxford University Press, 1980).

3 Aristotle, *ibid.*, I.7, p. 12.

4 Aristotle, *ibid.*, I.7, p. 14.

5 Aristotle, *ibid.*, I.7, p. 13.

6 Aristotle, *ibid.*, II.7, p. 41.

7 Aristotle, *ibid.*, II.5, p. 35.

8 Plato, Meno, in W.K. Guthrie, trans., Plato, *Protagoras and Meno* (Harmondsworth: Penguin, 1956).

9 See P. Foot, Virtues and vices, in P. Foot, *Virtues and vices* (Oxford: Blackwell, 1978). This succinct and seminal article should be studied carefully by anyone wishing to pursue virtue theory.

10 See for example P. Foot, Goodness and choice, in P. Foot, *Virtues and Vices* (Oxford: Blackwell 1978). See many other articles in that book as well.

11 See a landmark article of G.E.M. Anscombe, Modern moral philosophy, *Philosophy* **33** (1958), pp. 1–19.

12 Aristotle did in fact think there was such a thing as being a good woman, that is, good *as* a woman but it was not his concern to elaborate this in his *Nicomachean ethics*.

Chapter 8

1 P. Foot, *Virtues and vices* (Oxford: Basil Blackwell, 1978), p. 6.

2 See A.J. Ayer, *Language, truth and logic* (London: Gollancz, 1936, reprinted many times), Chapter 6. Emotivism was an influential metaethical theory, which held that moral judgements stated nothing, but only gave vent to the attitudes of the speaker and could not be true or false. Although not mentioned specifically in my Chapter 2, it is clearly an approach that denies the objectivity of moral value, and fits well with a "projectivist" account of morality.

3 See R.M. Hare, *The language of morals* (Oxford: Clarendon Press, 1952), Part I, section 2, paragraph 5.

4 The phrase "makes him good" should not be understood in a causal sense: it is not the man's helpfulness that *causes* him to be good. The point is that it is in virtue of his helpfulness that the judgement that he is good is true. In explaining supervenience, it is unfortunately quite difficult to avoid language that can be misconstrued as referring to causes.

5 Hare has developed his theory in many books and articles since *Freedom and reason*, and I have not had space to go into them.

Readers should pay particular attention to *Moral thinking* (Oxford: Oxford University Press, 1981). This develops his universal prescriptivism, and also – importantly for his normative ethics – his "two-level" utilitarianism (see under Further reading).

6   See Plato, *Republic*, trans. and ed. H.D.P. Lee (Harmondsworth: Penguin, 1955), Book 1, 338c.

7   The quotation marks around the phrases "enlightenment" and "age of reason" should not be interpreted as expressing scepticism as to whether modern thinking about science, religion and so on really was enlightened – they are only to acknowledge that such claims are controversial.

8   E. Gellner, *Postmodernism, reason and religion* (London: Routledge, 1992), p. 26.

9   An influential approach of this kind is adopted by C. Gilligan, *In a different voice: psychological theory and women's development*, (Cambridge, MA: Harvard University Press, 1982).

10   See E. Burke, *Reflections on the revolution in France*, (1790) C.C. O'Brien, (ed.) (Harmondsworth: Penguin, 1968).

11   A clear exposition and defence of the importance of piety in moral thinking is presented by R. Scruton, *Animal rights and wrongs*. (London: Demos, 1996), pp. 55–8.

12   Roger Scruton, *ibid.*, p. 56.

Index